Lend Me Your Ears

All you need to know about making speeches and presentations

Professor Max Atkinson

Vermilion
LONDON

16

First published in the United Kingdom in 2004 by Vermilion, an imprint of Ebury Publishing

A Random House Group company

Random House UK Limited Reg. No. 954009
www.randomhouse.co.uk

A CIP catalogue record is available for this book from the British Library.

ISBN 9780091894795

Designed and typeset by seagulls

Penguin Random House is committed to a sustainable future for
our business, our readers and our planet. This book is made from
Forest Stewardship Council® certified paper.

MIX
Paper from
responsible sources
FSC® C018179

Printed and bound in Great Britain by Clays Ltd, St Ives plc

The author and publisher would like to thank the following:

Methuen Publishing Ltd. for permission to reproduce copyright material from
The Complete Beyond the Fringe, London, 1987: Copyright © 1963, 1987, 2003
by Alan Bennett, Peter Cook, Jonathan Miller and Dudley Moore.

The Royal Institution of Great Britain for permission to reproduce copyright material
from Sir George Porter and James Friday (eds.), *Advice to Lecturers: An Anthology
Taken from the Writings of Michael Faraday and Lawrence Bragg*, London, 1974.

'For all those who are serious about the art of making speeches, Max Atkinson's previous book, *Our Masters' Voices*, was a bible. There was scarcely a single major speech in my eleven years as leader of the Liberal Democrats that I made without benefiting either from it or from his personal advice and help. *Lend Me Your Ears* includes many new insights into the art of effective speaking, and will be invaluable to all those interested in making words count and using verbal communication to influence people.'

Paddy Ashdown
Leader of the Liberal Democrats, 1988–99

'As a speechwriter for Ronald Reagan, I relied for rhetorical direction on the great speakers from Demosthenes to Churchill, on the great guides from Aristotle to the President himself, and on Max Atkinson. No one surpasses Atkinson in the rigor and clarity with which he spells out how to move audiences to applause, get quoted in the media and become known as the most brilliant presence on any podium.'

Clark Judge
Managing Director, White House Writers Group

'Over the last 30 years I have spoken in 28 countries, launching cars, opening buildings and guest speaking at conferences. Throughout I have read any book on oratory that I can lay my hands on and Max Atkinson's *Lend Me Your Ears* is by far the best. I had planned, in my retirement, to write the perfect book on public speaking. I will now have to find something else to do!'

Peter Hancock
Managing Director, Peter Hancock International, Ltd.

For Joey

Contents

Preface

When academic research delivers findings that attract interest beyond a narrow field of specialisation, it is an added bonus for the author. If the results turn out to have practical applications that directly benefit other people, it's an even bigger bonus. So I count myself fortunate that my previous book* apparently hit the mark on both these counts. The analysis of political speeches on which it was based was originally motivated by a purely technical interest in the workings of speaker–audience interaction, and its practical potential only started to become apparent after publication. In the original preface, I had written:

> The question of how far this study could be exploited in training politicians to become more effective speakers is one to which no definite answer can be given at present: as far as I know, it has not yet been tried.

Twenty years on, it has been tried and tested on countless occasions, not only in the training of politicians, but also in coaching

---

* Max Atkinson. *Our Masters' Voices: The Language and Body Language of Politics*. London: Methuen, 1984 (reprinted by Routledge, 1988 onwards).

business presenters and speakers from almost every possible industry and walk of life.

The approach was first put to the test in full view of a mass television audience, an opportunity for which I have to thank former editor of Granada Television's *World in Action* series, Gus Macdonald (now Lord Macdonald of Tradeston). It was his idea to make a programme in which I was challenged to coach a novice to make a speech at the SDP Conference in 1984. Armed with a script, bristling with all the most powerful rhetorical devices that trigger applause in speeches (see Chapters 6–7), Ann Brennan became the only non-platform speaker at that year's conference to win a standing ovation, and some previously unpublished background to this is included in Chapter 8. Her success was to change my life. The day after the programme was transmitted, I was inundated with phone calls from people asking if I could do the same for them. After completing only one experiment, I suppose I should have told them that I really did not know. But my interest had been aroused enough to want to find out whether the techniques would work for other people making other kinds of speeches in other situations.

Without realising it at the time, I had embarked on an irreversible metamorphosis from Oxford researcher to freelance training consultant. I found myself working for more and more companies, running courses, writing speeches, coaching individuals and advising on special events like stock market flotations, reports to shareholder meetings, new product launches and pitches for new business.

These experiences did more than merely confirm that the approach first tried in the televised experiment could be adapted to work just as well for other speakers, regardless of subject matter, audience or particular aims of the speaker. By giving me the chance to observe different types of presentation, they also enabled me to extend my studies and to test out the results in practice in a wide variety of settings. Even more important than watching so many speakers in action has been the experience of listening to thousands of them discussing video recordings of their own and each other's performances. This has provided a rich source of data about what members of audiences actually like and dislike about different styles of speaking, steadily adding new material that has been fed back and incorporated into training programmes over the years.

According to many who have attended these courses, the approach differs from others on the market in a number of ways. Delegates seem to appreciate the fact that the practical advice is grounded in empirical research, rather than one person's subjective opinions about what constitutes good or bad practice. The emphasis on rhetoric and how to make more effective use of language is also often mentioned as something that is not widely taught elsewhere. The focus on understanding and responding to audience needs seems to strike chords with people's own experience of having been on the receiving end of so many uninspiring speeches, lectures and presentations, and helps to build their confidence in trying to do things differently.

On the practical front, the main finding to report is that the more a speaker uses the approach and techniques described here, the better their impact on audiences and the more their confidence improves. So anyone who masters all the principles will be equipped with, in the words of the subtitle of the book, 'all you need to know about making speeches and presentations'. This is, of course, not the same as 'everything anyone could ever possibly know' about the subject, which is unlikely to be available in my lifetime, if ever. The crucial words are 'all you *need* to know', which is intended to make the point that any speech or presentation composed and delivered in accordance with the principles outlined in the following pages is more or less guaranteed to go down well with an audience. The primary purpose of the book is therefore to encapsulate as much as possible of what I have learnt about the impact of speeches on audiences, and to make it available for anyone to use for themselves.

More people than it's possible to mention have played a part in this journey of discovery. Without the pioneering research into conversation by Harvey Sacks, Emanuel Schegloff and Gail Jefferson* at the University of California, I would never have thought of studying talk in the first place. My original research into political speeches benefited greatly from being replicated and developed in a major statistical follow-up study by John Heritage and David Greatbatch.** I owe a great debt to Paddy Ashdown for being a model pupil and giving me the chance to test the principles out on the national political stage for more than a decade. I am also grateful for his permission to use background material on work we did together to illustrate some of the points in Chapter 8.

Teaching presentation skills on various executive and MBA programmes at the Henley Management College continues to give

---

* H. Sacks, E. A. Schegloff and G. Jefferson. 1974. 'A Simplest Systematics for the Organization of Turn-Taking in Conversation.' *Language* 50: 696–735.

** J. C. Heritage and D. Greatbatch. 1986. 'Generating Applause: A Study of Rhetoric and Response at Party Political Conferences.' *American Journal of Sociology* 92: 110–157.

me access to business speakers from a very wide range of companies, organisations and nationalities. For this and the chance to work with and learn from the late David Ellis-Jones, I shall always be grateful to Professor Keith Macmillan, also sadly no longer with us. David Woodward joined me as a co-tutor for a few years, and did a good job in educating me about the virtues and vices of computers. More recently, courses run both at Henley and by Atkinson Communications have benefited greatly from the arrival of Anne Danks, whose many helpful comments on earlier drafts of this book have been greatly appreciated.

The people from whom I have learnt most are the countless pupils whose contributions to workshops have been a continuing source of insight into the minds of audiences. But the greatest support and encouragement in writing this book, as in everything else in my life, has come from my family – Simon, Anne, Holly, Isobel, Joe, James, Edward, William and Bridget – and especially from my wife Joey, who insisted that it be written, and without whom it would not have been.

Max Atkinson
Westbury-sub-Mendip, Somerset
www.speaking.co.uk
February 2004

Introduction
Audiences Are Always Right

Lecturing has been defined as 'the transmission of the lecturer's notes to the students' notebooks, passing through the minds of neither'. It would be nice to think that this is just a witty quote, far removed from any reality that members of an audience ever have to experience. But there was a history teacher at my school who followed the definition more or less to the letter. For him, teaching meant dictating notes, complete with headings, subheadings and sub-subheadings, from a thick hard-backed notebook. The job of those of us on the receiving end was to copy out his dictation into identical hard-backed notebooks. There was a good reason why our notebooks were exactly the same as his, because years of dictation took their toll on his master copy. So, every two or three years, when our books were full and the exams were over, he would tour the classroom to find out which one of us had the neatest handwriting. The winner's reward was to have his pristine notebook exchanged for the teacher's dog-eared copy, so that the dictation could continue, uninterrupted by torn pages or fading ink, for the benefit of later generations of victims. The teacher's nickname, not surprisingly, was 'Dry Jack'.

Later on, at university, we had a philosophy lecturer whose discourses on Plato and Aristotle were punctuated by a minimum of four cigarettes per hour. And there was the economics professor, for whom lecturing was such a chore that he would lean on a radiator doing *The Times* crossword, while droning on about the supply and demand for oranges.

It would be unfair and inaccurate to say that a flagrant disregard for the needs of audiences is only to be found in the world of academia, where there are, of course, some highly accomplished communicators. In fact, there can be few people who have never had to sit through wedding speeches that convey more bad taste than good cheer, or eulogies at funerals that demonstrate little more than the speaker's total ignorance about the life and character of the deceased. Countless times a day, audiences the world over are being subjected to speeches, presentations, sermons, briefings and lectures that are inaudible, incomprehensible or uninspiring. And, when it comes to inflicting maximum pain on listeners, there are few styles of speaking more stultifying than the modern slide-driven presentation. I deal with this in more detail in Chapters 4 and 5, but the following preview highlights some of the general problems audiences are up against, and the central premise of this book, namely that the key to effective speaking is an objective understanding of the needs of your listeners.

1. Death from 1,000 slides: the industry standard model of presentation

The past few decades have seen the emergence of an industry standard model of presentation, currently in a stage of transition as overhead slides give way to the projection of computerised graphics

> All too often, the commonly heard line 'I'm going to talk to some slides' means exactly that, with speakers spending more time looking back at their slides than at the audience.

driven by programs like PowerPoint®.* In the earlier form of this ritual, speakers would stand next to an overhead projector, putting on one slide after another. Some presenters would position themselves between a section of the audience and the screen, depriving them of access to the gems of wisdom emanating from the screen. All too often, the commonly heard line 'I'm going to talk to some slides' meant exactly that, with speakers spending more time looking back at their slides than at the audience. Many seemed to have little or no idea what to say next until another slide was safely in place, not that getting slides in place was always a simple or straightforward matter. Frequently it involved a frantic shuffling through piles of acetates, as slides fell to the floor or floated gently across the illuminated area of the overhead projector on the cushion of warm air generated by the bulb below. Few speakers bothered to remove the backing paper from the acetates in advance, so yet another source of irritation became institutionalised as part of the ritual: every slide change would be prefaced by the sight and sound of paper and acetate being ripped apart – the dread signal of yet another awful slide to come.

The audience's agony of having to endure regular 10- to 15-second gaps between slides would sometimes be aggravated further

---

* PowerPoint is a registered trademark of Microsoft Corporation.

by speakers who insisted on repeatedly turning the projector off and on as part of the slide-changing routine. On one occasion I saw a professional training consultant criticising one of his class for failing to do this. The hapless pupil complained that, when he was in an audience, he found it extremely annoying when speakers kept turning the projector on and off. He even dared to ask *why* it was deemed to be good practice. After some initial hesitation, the consultant quickly recovered his capacity to sound authoritative in the face of mindless ignorance with the memorable line: 'because it's correct'.

2. Technological progress and technical hitches

Then came computer graphics, and Microsoft's inevitable domination of the marketplace with PowerPoint. The ability to change slides at the push of a button has eliminated some of the fumbling routines of the overhead era, but new nightmares have arrived in its wake. Now audiences are obliged to watch speakers trying to find plugs, leads and sockets, or to see them getting more and more flustered in their attempts to persuade the local resident projector to marry up with a visiting laptop. With luck a volunteer from the audience will come to the rescue. Otherwise, there may have to be an unscheduled comfort break, while a technician is summoned to the rescue from the furthest corner of the building.

When something finally does materialise on the screen, it usually turns out to be a message telling us to wait. More time goes by before the familiar icons of the Windows®* desktop display finally appear. Then we are treated to the exciting spectacle of an arrow whizzing around the screen in search of the

---

* Windows is a registered trademark of Microsoft Corporation.

PowerPoint folder. A double click later, and we get the opportunity to inspect a long list of files, as the arrow moves up and down in search of the particular delights in store for us today. It comes to rest on the chosen file, we get a glimpse of the first 20 slides and are left wondering just how many more lie in wait after that. Finally, the presenter clicks triumphantly on the slide show icon, and up comes the opening slide with the first two breathtaking pieces of news: the title of the presentation and the name of the speaker, both of which had been widely advertised in advance, and were perfectly well known to everyone in the audience long before they arrived anywhere near the meeting room.

Apart from the size and legibility of fonts, few changes for the better, and some for the worse, have accompanied the replacement of overhead slides by computerised projection. In spite of the tremendous scope for using pictorial and graphical material provided by programs like PowerPoint, and the ease with which lists of bullet points can be built up one by one, positive assets such as these are not yet being exploited to the full. The vast majority of slides are still much the same as they always were, consisting of written words, phrases or sentences, usually given a semblance of order by being arrayed as lists of blobs and bullet points. This prompted one recent observer to suggest that, if a Martian were beamed down into the middle of a PowerPoint presentation, he would think it was either an adult literacy class or a mass eyesight test.

In short, the industry standard model of presentation not only survives, but, as will be seen in Chapter 5, some of its most dubious assumptions are actually built into the templates that come with PowerPoint and similar programs. They encourage presenters to produce headings, subheadings and sub-subheadings, with the result that the typical presentation amounts to little more than a series of lists. These are invariably far longer than anyone in an audience could ever possibly remember, and serve little useful purpose other than to remind the speaker what to say next.

3. The silent majority

Yet the extraordinary fact is that anyone who takes the trouble to ask audiences what they really think of the typical slide-driven presentation quickly discovers a deep groundswell of dissatisfaction. The depth of this feeling first came to my notice on the only occasion in more than 30 years of teaching that an audience suddenly started clapping in the middle of a lecture. In response to a question, I heard myself saying something that even I thought might be overstating the case: 'the more I work in this area, the more I'm coming to the view that the slides are the biggest single obstacle to spoken communication ever invented.' I had apparently touched a nerve, and the applause it prompted turned out to be only the first hint of mass audience discontent. Other evidence began to accumulate. One example was a visit by the president of a major American multi-national corporation to one of his UK offices. The night before his local managers were due to give presentations to him, he had all the overhead projectors in the building locked away in cupboards and pocketed the key. When they pleaded their inability to speak without them, he told them that he was 'sick and tired of travelling the world looking at slides. I just want you to tell me what you're up to, and how things are going.'

To these admittedly isolated examples must be added the much more extensive evidence that has come from running hundreds of group workshops, in which speakers are invited to comment on positive and negative aspects of each other's presentations. One of the main findings from these is that the vast majority of comments about visual aids are negative ones. This highlights an intriguing contrast in people's attitudes, depending on whether they are speakers or members of an audience: the same people who use slides in their own presentations are often highly critical of exactly the same kinds of slide when it comes to listening to similar presentations by others. They also tend to be just as critical of their own slides when they see themselves on videotape, often becoming confessional in tone, with comments to the effect that the slides are more of a crutch for their own benefit than for the enlightenment of the audience. As if to underline just how entrenched and universal the industry standard model has become, another common refrain is that colleagues, superiors or clients *expect* them to use slides, and would not otherwise consider it to be 'a proper presentation'.

4. Time to face facts

The fact that attitudes towards this model of presentation differ so dramatically, according to whether a person is speaking or listening, raises a number of intriguing questions. Why is it that so many people continue to aspire to a style of speaking that fails to impress or inspire them when they are on the receiving end? Why has the modern business presentation become such a bore? Why do so many companies pay out so much money per hour for so many of their staff to prepare and deliver slide shows, and yet more money per hour for others to endure the tedium of having to listen to the resulting presentation. And if there are tens of thousands of people a day attending presentations from which they get

> 'The customer is always right' may have become a standard motto in the world of business, but the idea that 'the audience is always right' has yet to make much of an impression on the world of presentation, even though, for the duration of the presentation at least, the audience is the speaker's only customer.

little or no benefit, how many millions or billions of pounds, dollars and euros are being wasted each year by the world's leading economies?

The starting point of this book is that it is high time we began to face up to these questions. This will include an argument to the effect that the modern business presentation has lost its way, and should certainly not be used as a model for making other kinds of speeches. The problem of public speaking, in all its various manifestations, lies in a profound and widespread misunderstanding of how spoken communication works. At the heart of this is a failure to appreciate that there are important differences between speaking to an audience and other much more familiar forms of communication, notably everyday conversation and the language of the written word. Somewhere along the line, speakers seem to have stopped thinking about the needs and preferences of their audiences. 'The customer is always right' may have become a standard motto in the world of business, but the idea that 'the audience is always right' has yet to make much of an impression on the world of presentation, even though, for the duration of the presentation at least, the audience is the speaker's only customer.

If the battle against boredom is to be won, a crucial first step is to be clear about the precise nature of the problems that audiences face. Only then does it become possible to come up with practical solutions that will give their listeners a more rewarding, stimulating and inspiring experience. Once speakers begin to understand the techniques that impress audiences, they are well on the way to mastering them. They will discover how to liberate themselves from the all-too-familiar feelings of nervousness and fear that come with the prospect of having to make a speech or presentation. And the more they are able to do this, the sooner they will realise that effective public speaking does not have to be the monopoly of the gifted few, but is the product of a set of techniques that anyone can learn to use.

PART I
THE LANGUAGE OF PUBLIC SPEAKING

The Battle for Audience Attention

Keeping Listeners Awake and Engaged

Most of us find it easy enough to discuss aspects of our life or work with one or two colleagues, friends, or even with complete strangers. But it's a very different story when it comes to standing up and talking about the same subjects to an audience. Confident communicators suddenly find themselves crippled by nerves, the normally articulate sound muddled and confused, and enthusiasts for their subjects come across as dull, boring and monotonous. You will almost certainly have seen this happen. It may even have happened to you – but you may not be quite sure exactly why it happens.

This difference in our level of confidence and effectiveness, depending on whether we're speaking in a conversation or to an audience, is so great and so debilitating for so many people that it demands an explanation. The chapters in Part I set out to provide an answer by showing that there is what amounts to a 'language of public speaking'. Less complicated and much easier to learn

> Speaking to an audience requires different skills from those that serve us so well during the rest of our talking lives. The trouble is that it is not immediately obvious what these are, let alone why our normal resources are failing us.

than a foreign language, it involves subtle deviations from every-day speech that can make life difficult for anyone who isn't fully aware of them. Knowing what these deviations are is an essential first step towards understanding and mastering the techniques of effective speech making.

1. Different ways of speaking

Speaking in public is obviously different from just about any other form of communication we ever get involved in. The sense of unease experienced when making a speech or presentation tends to be accompanied by a vague realisation that our normal, every-day style of speaking doesn't seem to be working in quite the way we expect. Speaking to an audience seems to require skills other than those that serve us so well during the rest of our talking lives. The trouble is that it's not always immediately obvious what these are, or why our normal resources are failing us. This is why we can find ourselves, often good communicators in every other way, struggling and bewildered against the tide of polite indifference washing over us from an audience who would clearly rather be somewhere else.

One reason for this is that our ability to speak is something that we have taken for granted since infancy. Apart from a few academic researchers who specialise in the study of talk, hardly anyone ever gives much thought to the detailed mechanics of how speech works. Most people's technical understanding of conversation is similar to their technical understanding of what's involved in riding a bicycle. Both are things we can do, without so much as a second thought, but the basic principles of how to do them are far from easy to put into words.

An ability to use language is often cited as the crucial factor distinguishing humans from other animals. But it is probably more accurate to say that the crucial factor is an ability to *converse* – and it's more than mere ability. As conversationalists we are absolute experts. We listen, we understand, we contribute, all within fractions of a second. And we're able to do this because we start learning to converse from the moment we make our first sounds. The type of speech we first learn as infants is conversation. As we grow older, it is the speaking skills of conversation that we spend most time practising and developing. In effect, we become specialists in conversational techniques, and it's as conversationalists that we spend the vast majority of our talking lives. Only very occasionally do we have to speak in ways that are clearly different from conversation, such as in classrooms, courtrooms, places of worship, interviews, meetings, debates, speeches or presentations. As narrow specialists in conversation, it's hardly surprising that we feel so uneasy when we have to speak in these less familiar situations. Nor is it surprising that the few who do develop these more specialised speaking skills – such as teachers, lawyers, politicians or clerics – come to be viewed as (and paid as) professionals.

2. Why conversation keeps us awake

Our starting point, then, is that becoming an effective public speaker depends on having as clear a picture as possible of the key differences between conversation on the one hand, and speeches and presentations on the other. The most important of all of these is the dramatic change in our motives for paying attention that occurs as soon as we stop conversing with other members of the audience, and settle down to listen to the speaker of the day. When I ask audiences if any of them ever find it difficult to stay awake during speeches, presentations, lectures or sermons, a typical result is that 100 per cent of them put up their hands. When asked how many have trouble staying awake listening to what someone is saying during conversations, the typical result is zero per cent.

The first statistic is proof that everyone knows that speeches and presentations have a tremendous capacity for boring audiences out of their minds, and that holding the attention of an audience is a major challenge for speakers. The second statistic points to something that people know when they think about it, but probably never give much thought to most of the time: most of us have little or no trouble in staying awake while engaged in conversation with a small number of others. This is because there are powerful incentives to pay attention built into the way conversation works. And these incentives are underpinned by implicit rules that are not written down and formally taught, but are understood by everyone capable of having a conversation.

One at a time

The most obvious feature of conversation is that we take it in turns to talk: one speaker says something and, when that one's turn comes to an end, a next speaker starts, and so on until the end of the conversation:

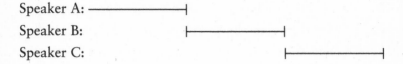

Speaker A:
Speaker B:
Speaker C:

If someone else suddenly starts speaking when you are still in the middle of your turn, it's natural to feel annoyed. In fact, you're likely to regard anyone who trespasses on your space as 'rude' or 'impolite'. You are not only within your rights to complain, but are equipped with the necessary vocabulary for referring to the misdemeanour: the words 'interrupt' and 'interruption'. When you complain of being 'interrupted', you are actually drawing attention to the fact that a basic, though implicit, rule of conversation has been broken: *only one speaker should speak at a time, and others in the conversation should wait until the end of any current turn before starting the next one.*

Occasional failures to observe this rule may be tolerated, but anyone who makes a regular habit of starting to speak in the middle of other people's turns soon finds that there's a heavy price to pay. Your reputation will go into a nosedive. At best, you'll be regarded as impolite or inconsiderate; at worst as a pushy, domineering control freak who'd rather 'hog the conversation' than listen to what anyone else has to say. If you'd rather not be seen like this, you have a strong incentive to pay attention at least closely enough to know when the previous speaker has finished, and when you can launch into a turn of your own without being accused of interrupting.

🔊 Coming in on cue

The incentive to listen during conversations isn't just a matter of paying close enough attention to notice when a speaker gets to the end of a turn, as there is another rule about when you can start the next turn. Fail to get this right, and people will have another reason for wondering about your manners and motives. You only have to think of how you react if, after greeting someone with the turn 'Good morning', the other person doesn't reply at all. Charitable explanations are that they must be half asleep, or perhaps a little deaf. But you're much more likely to start worrying about why they aren't speaking to you, what you've done to offend them or what's gone wrong with the relationship. So the only way to stop other people from thinking such negative thoughts about you is to make sure that you start speaking *before* the silence has lasted long enough to be deemed 'awkward' or 'embarrassing'.

This raises the question of just how long you've got before the silence starts to make things difficult? The answer is that you can't afford to let the silence last for more than a split second. Research into conversation shows that silences of less than half a second are not only long enough to be noticed, but are enough to start us thinking that some kind of trouble is on its way. Studies of how people respond to invitations, for example, have found that an immediate reply usually means that the speaker is about to accept, whereas a delay of even a fraction of a second means that a refusal is on its way. The same is true of the way people reply to offers of various kinds: positive replies start straight away, and negative ones are delayed. So the safest way of preventing people from getting the wrong impression is to pay close enough attention to

> The main incentive to pay attention in conversation is the ever-present threat that you might have to speak next. As audiences know that they won't have to speak until a speech is over, their incentive to listen is massively reduced, sometimes even to the point where they fall asleep.

be able to start speaking as soon as possible, and certainly before the silence starts to get embarrassing.

💬 Showing you were listening

Another extremely important reason for listening in conversation is that you have to be continually at the ready to say something that relates directly to what was said in the previous turn. Even a small lapse in concentration can cause you to say something that leads the previous speaker to conclude that you had not been paying attention, are not in the least bit interested in what they were saying, or that you are just plain rude. It often prompts accusations, arguments and conflict – so much so that it may well be at the heart of large numbers of domestic rows. If these could be traced back to their original source, many of them would surely be found to have started just at that moment in a conversation when one speaker says something – or perhaps says nothing – that gives their spouse or partner the impression that he or she had not been listening.

💬 The threat of having to say something

Conversational success and failure obviously depend on our continually maintaining a very high level of attentiveness to what others are saying. We have to keep listening closely enough not to interrupt, closely enough to come in on time and closely enough to be ready to say something that relates to the previous turn. In short, the ever-present threat that we might have to speak next amounts to an extremely powerful incentive for us to stay alert and wide-awake during a conversation. It also points to a fundamental reason why audiences will be in a very much lower state of attentiveness when listening to a speech or presentation.

3. Why audiences fall asleep

🔈 *Speeches and presentations are long*

Compared with the talk we're used to listening to in conversations, the most unusual thing about a speech or presentation is its sheer length. In essence, all forms of public speaking involve the production of exceptionally long turns at talk, in which one person is given the floor for far longer than anyone ever gets to speak during a conversation. Rather than having to pay attention to short conversational turns lasting an average of seven or eight seconds, members of an audience are faced with the daunting prospect of having to listen to one person speaking continuously for 10, 20 or 30 minutes – and often for even longer than that.

🔈 *Audiences know they won't have to speak for a while*

This may seem a grim enough prospect in itself, but it's only part of the attentiveness problem we face when sitting in an audience. What makes life really difficult is that our only job is to listen. We can therefore relax in the knowledge that we're not going to have to speak for however long the speech or presentation lasts. The absence of any immediate threat of having to say something at a moment's notice amounts to a massive reduction in the incentives to pay attention that work so efficiently in everyday conversation. This goes a long way towards explaining why we are so much more likely to fall asleep when in an audience than when participating in a conversation.

If audiences get confused, they stop listening

Another extremely important and taken-for-granted feature of conversation that also changes dramatically in speeches and presentations is the relative ease with which we're able to deal with any difficulties we may have in understanding what someone just said. If, at some point in a conversation, we're unclear about something, we can use our next turn to ask for clarification, and get an immediate solution to the problem. But, when sitting in an audience, most of us are much more inhibited. For one thing, it involves interrupting, and therefore runs the risk of offending the speaker. Not only that, but a request for clarification can all too easily sound like a public complaint about the speaker's incompetence at explaining things clearly enough. Our reluctance to intervene may also be fuelled by a fear of exposing our own ignorance in public – because, for all we know, everyone else in the audience may be finding it perfectly easy to follow the argument. So the safest and commonest option is not to ask for clarification. Instead, we start reflecting on what the speaker has been saying in a bid to disentangle what it was all about for ourselves. The trouble is that trying to make some kind of retrospective sense of what we've just heard takes priority over concentrating on whatever comes next. And if we miss some or all of that, we become even more muddled and confused, sometimes to a point where we simply give up on making any further effort to understand, listen or stay awake.

🔊 Presentations are not always designed so that audiences can follow them

Our reluctance to ask for clarification from a speaker is only one deviation from routine conversational practice that poses problems of understanding for audiences. Another is the way the subject matter is selected and managed. In conversation, there are no restrictions on the topics we can talk about, and everyone involved can play an active part in influencing the direction it takes. As a result, the subjects covered in conversations are constantly changing, and can suddenly take off in completely unexpected and unplanned directions.

Compared with the more or less infinite range of topics we can talk about in conversation, the subject matter of speeches and presentations is much narrower and more restricted. As members of an audience, we may not even be particularly interested in the topic to begin with. Worse still, and unlike in conversation where we can do something about our lack of interest by changing the subject, we have no control over how the subject of a presentation or speech will be developed. It's the speaker who has sole responsibility both for selecting the material and organising it into an orderly sequence. Nor do we have much idea about exactly what's going to be included, or how the subject matter is going to be divided up – until or unless the speaker gives us advance notice of what's to come, and the order in which the points will be covered. In other words, having a sense of sequence and structure plays a crucially important part in helping us to make sense of what we're hearing. All too often, speakers either fail to do this or, having done it, make no further reference to how any particular item under discussion fits in with the overall structure announced at the start. And if we're confused about where things have got to in relation to where they were supposed to be going, our ability to understand and keep on paying attention will go into a progressive decline.

The problems of understanding faced by audiences and the difficulty of doing something about them are therefore very different from the way they arise and are dealt with in conversation. This means that the speaker's main challenge is to make sure that the subject matter is presented in a way that the audience can follow. If our problem as members of an audience is trying to pay attention to a continuous stream of talk many hundreds of times longer than anything we ever have to listen to in a conversation, the parallel problem for speakers is producing such an abnormally long turn. To make matters worse, they are deprived of a very efficient means of checking on understanding that we use continuously during conversations. This is the way in which we routinely inspect other speakers' responses to gauge whether or not our previous turn was understood in the way we intended. If it was, we can safely carry on; if it wasn't, we can elaborate, revise or otherwise expand on the point we were trying to get across.

Ideally, of course, a speech or presentation should be designed so that anyone in the audience will be able to follow it. This is why the selection and structuring of the subjects to be covered is (or should be) at the heart of the preparation process, and why it is an important enough topic to have the whole of Chapter 9 devoted to it.

4. The battle against boredom

The greatly reduced pressure on audiences to listen means that winning and holding their attention can never be taken for granted. It poses a far greater challenge than many speakers realise, and is a battle that has to be fought relentlessly for the entire duration of a speech or presentation. This is why it's so important to be aware of the nature of the beast we are up against, and the weapons available to keep audiences awake and defeat the ever-present threat of boredom. Later chapters deal with the importance of delivery, language and the use of visual aids in holding the attention of audiences, but it's also sometimes possible to win minor victories by interacting more directly with the audience.

🔍 *Conversing with a crowd*

If being released from the pressures of conversational turn-taking erodes our motivation to listen, it follows that our level of attentiveness will increase if we have an opportunity to respond to what a speaker says. This is borne out by situations where audiences do become involved, which tend to generate a good deal more liveliness and interest than the average speech or presentation.

One example of a speaker and audience taking it in turns that has a long and successful history is the pantomime ritual of 'Oh yes it is!' – 'Oh no it isn't!' and 'It's behind you!', in which a character on stage interacts directly with everyone else in the theatre. It is, of course, more difficult for audiences to take it in turns with a speaker than it might seem at first sight, because of the probability that several individuals will drown each other out by saying different things at the same time. However, as the pantomime example shows, this problem can be avoided if everyone chants the same thing in unison.

A similar form of collective response also enables a smooth flow of interaction to take place between priests and congregations during church services, a form of turn-taking that has occasionally been extended into the political arena. The most notable exponent of this was Martin Luther King, who adapted the preaching style he had developed as a Baptist minister to create some of the greatest speeches of the twentieth century. In many of them, the responses were so frequent that his speeches sounded like a conversation between him and his audience, as in the concluding moments of the speech he made on the night before he was assassinated in 1968:

King:	And He's allowed me to go up to the mountain,
Audience:	Go ahead.
King:	... and I've looked over,
Audience:	Yeah.
King:	... and I've seen the promised land.
Audience:	Holy – Holy – Holy.
King:	I may not get there with you.
Audience:	Yah-ha yah – Holy.
King:	But I want you to know tonight
Audience:	Yeah.
King:	... that we as a people
Audience:	Yeahhhh.
King:	... will get to the promised land.
Audience:	Yeahhh (applause).

Coming in together and at the same time like this is, of course, only possible if everyone in the audience is paying very close attention to each and every phrase of the speech.

🗨 *Clapping and booing as incentives to pay attention*

The speaking tradition exemplified by Martin Luther King is fairly localised to the southern Baptist Church in the USA, but other forms of collective response are much more widely found. Audiences will clap, cheer or laugh to show their approval, and boo or jeer to show their disapproval. What all these have in common is that they involve making a noise, rather than producing words or sentences. This avoids the kind of disorderly hullabaloo that would inevitably occur if a lot of people were saying different things at the same time. In effect, responses like clapping and booing are collective turns that are easy for members of an audience to produce in unison – and, like turns in a conversation, they can significantly increase people's motivation to listen. As will be seen in Chapter 6, responses like applause do not occur randomly, but are found at specific points during a speech. For members of an audience to be able to come in at the same time, they have to be continually on the lookout for things to applaud or boo at, which means that they have to pay very close attention to what is being said.

Seen in this light, the apparently rowdy behaviour of British Members of Parliament during debates in the House of Commons may have some rather more positive benefits than its negative public image would suggest. After all, if the odds of being called upon to speak are as poor as one in several hundred, there's so little chance of getting the next turn that you might as well go to sleep. But the tradition of cheering, booing and heckling not only provides an alternative way of expressing a view, it also gives members more of a reason to listen. To be effective, booing and cheering require a degree of precision timing that can only be achieved by paying attention closely enough to be able to identify statements worth responding to.

Negative responses like booing and heckling are thankfully extremely rare in the context of the vast majority of speeches and presentations that most of us have to give. Nor are audiences very likely to interrupt us with applause, usually saving this until we get to the end. But there are two other forms of response that can help to keep an audience attentive: laughter and audience participation.

◖ Laughter

In the absence of interruptive bursts of applause, laughter is the only immediate positive response that most of us can ever expect from an audience, which is why humour is such a powerful weapon in the armoury of the public speaker. Audiences obviously enjoy laughing – otherwise, professional after dinner speakers, most of whom rely heavily on humorous anecdotes, would not be so much in demand or able to command such high fees. Nor would lecturers who make their audiences laugh enjoy such high ratings from their students.

Laughter is not only evidence of audience enjoyment or approval, but is also a powerful spur to continued attentiveness. This is because, as soon as members of an audience have laughed for a first time, they will start looking out for more fun and the chance to laugh again. Even if none comes immediately, they will at least be listening closely to whatever the speaker says next. This is no doubt why so many speakers like to start with a joke, or some other form of humour. When it works, it breaks the ice with the audience, and at the same time gives them more of an incentive to pay attention to what follows than more serious and earnestly worded openings.

More generally, if you illustrate a key point with an example or anecdote that makes an audience laugh, the laughter not only implies agreement with the point, but also increases the chances of it being remembered in the longer term. This point was made some years ago in a television talk show, in which John Mortimer, the well-known barrister and author, was asked if he could ever tell whether he'd won a case before the jury returned with their verdict. He replied that the one situation where he could be almost 90 per cent certain that they would find in his client's favour was if, during his final address to the jury, he had managed to make them laugh.

✆ Audience participation

Another way to establish some of the pressure to pay attention associated with conversational turn-taking is by getting the audience to do or to say something. This might simply involve asking for a show of hands, inviting suggestions or embarking on a question–answer session. As every teacher knows, getting pupils to answer questions can be a very effective way of keeping them on their toes. Once we realise that the speaker is no longer treating us as passive listeners, but might fire a question at us at any moment, we know that it's time to start listening closely enough to be able to speak if and when we are spoken to.

Although inviting audience participation may increase their incentives to listen, it is not without its risks. First of all, you need

to be clear about how long you are going to allow audience inter-
ventions to continue, as well as how you plan to relate their
contributions to whatever comes next. If you ignore some or all of
their suggestions, they are likely to feel aggrieved, and may even
start to suspect that you have no real interest in their contributions
and are merely using this as a ploy to keep their attention.

Audience participation can also fail if you overdo it, as this
can sometimes prompt them to start wondering whether you have
anything original to offer at all. This is an all-too-common problem in the world of management training, where the ethos of
participant involvement is often carried to extremes. For example, at a recent course on dealing with difficult children, the
trainer began the first session by asking a group of classroom
assistants what kinds of problems caused children to become
difficult. As trainees, they could have legitimately replied with
'we wouldn't be here if we knew that', or 'I thought it was your
job to tell us'. But no one did, and they all spent the best part of
half an hour diligently dictating suggestions for the trainer to
write up on a flip chart. Each point was greeted with comments
like 'very good', 'yes, that's another important one' and 'I'm glad
someone's mentioned that'. At the end of the session, the trainer
congratulated the group on having produced such a comprehen-
sive list, but made no attempt to add any points of his own, or to
discuss the relative importance of the various items in the list. At
least one of the trainees was so disgruntled by his lack of input
that she walked out of the course at the earliest possible coffee
break. Her complaint was that she had had enough of going on
courses where trainers used this kind of audience participation as
a smokescreen to conceal their ignorance. As she saw it, placing

so much emphasis on what the audience had to say was a way of 'copping out' from teaching them something new, something they didn't already know.

Encouraging questions

Another type of audience participation that people often ask about is the wisdom, or otherwise, of extending a generalised invitation to members of an audience to intervene with questions whenever they feel like it. Except in cases where your main objective is to stimulate a discussion on issues raised by the audience, it is safest to avoid such open-ended invitations. This is because unsolicited contributions can easily knock you off course, and may even take up so much time that you have to rush through the later sections of the presentation, or perhaps even miss them out altogether. Audience questions quite often raise issues that you are planning to deal with later on, forcing you to choose between making an unplanned change to the structure or fobbing them off with an assurance that the matter will be covered shortly. A much safer option is to make it clear at the outset that there will be plenty of time for questions at the end.

5. Eye contact and attentiveness

In the battle for attention and understanding, one conversational resource that retains much of its power when addressing audiences is eye contact between speaker and hearers. If the threat of having to speak next is the most powerful incentive to pay attention in conversation, another important source of pressure comes from the fact that our reactions are visible to the other person or persons involved. This enables them to keep a continual check on our level of attentiveness, not to mention any other reactions that may show up in our eyes, faces or posture. If we want to prevent others from getting the wrong impression, we therefore have to be constantly alert to how we are reacting to what they say, as well as to how they seem to be reacting to what we say.

Using gaze to increase attention

Similar pressures are at work in the relationship between speakers and audiences. Knowing that they are not going to have to speak for the next 30 or 40 minutes may release people from the most intense conversational incentive to pay attention, but their behaviour and responses are still visible to the speaker. As a result, the more you can keep everyone under surveillance, the more likely it is that they will at least try to look as though they are paying attention. Indeed, if you focus on any one individual in the audience for more than a second or two, the chances are that you'll elicit a slight nod, a smile or some other non-verbal response. It's as if they feel obliged to confirm that they're awake, listening and on track with what you're saying.

As a means of encouraging audience attention, the importance of speakers and audiences being able to see each other becomes very clear from looking at situations where the listeners think that the speaker can't see them. We all know from our school days about the opportunities for flicking paper pellets and other mischief that came our way whenever teachers turned their backs to write on the blackboard. An almost identical form of deviant audience behaviour came to light in a study I did of a series of video-conferences that involved transmitting presentations given in one location to an audience located overseas. The videotapes showed that the audience in the same room as the presenter behaved in much the same way as any other audience, whereas those watching via the video link had no inhibitions whatsoever about wandering around the conference room, making cups of coffee or chatting to colleagues. The few in the remote location who showed any sign at all of paying attention did so with the kinds of negative responses (loud sighs, groans and critical asides) that were completely absent among members of the audience who were in the same room as the speaker.

Quite apart from the implications these observations have for managing video-conferences more effectively, they show that, once audiences are freed from surveillance, they can opt out from what is, in effect, a contract with the speaker to behave like 'a proper audience'. This means that maintaining very low rates of eye contact with your audience releases them from some of the pressure they might otherwise feel, and will reduce their level of attentiveness accordingly. The trouble is that a lot of people say that one of the things about public speaking that makes them so nervous is that they feel uncomfortable and exposed by being looked at by so many people all at once – and by having to look at so many people looking at them. But the ostrich solution of averting your eyes from the audience altogether has little to commend it. The important thing is to be aware that audiences are not made up of people who are all wired together to consti-tute some kind of collective and intimidating super-viewer, but of separate, unique individuals, not much different from yourself (see also Chapter 11).

🗨 *Gaze to check audience reactions*

Gaze avoidance not only reduces the pressure on the audience to look attentive, but also makes it far more difficult to monitor positive and negative reactions. Nods, smiles and other non-verbal responses, such as writing notes, usually mean that things are going well, and that there's no need (so far) to think about changing course. On the other side of the coin, we ignore yawns, head scratching and other signs of puzzlement or confusion at our peril, as they are obvious signs that something is going badly wrong. The most usual problem is that the audience is losing the thread, to which the solution may lie in a recap of the argument so far, or further simplification, clarification or exemplification.

🗨 *Gaze to engage the audience*

Eye contact is not only important from a speaker's point of view, but is also valued by audiences. They are unlikely to be impressed if your eyes spend most of their time focused on a script or notes, as it gives the impression that getting through the text is more important than taking any notice of those in front of you, let alone how they might be reacting. Eye contact may put audiences under a degree of pressure to look attentive but, for most people, this is a small price to pay for feeling that they are being spoken to and included, rather than spoken at and ignored.

🗨 *Gazing at the screen*

As eye contact plays such a vital part in the relationship between you and your audience, it's important to be aware of just how easily things can go wrong without you even realising it. A problem referred to in the Introduction is that of spending more time looking back at the screen than towards the audience. The trouble is that many speakers who do this are completely unaware of it. When they see videotapes of themselves in action, they are often amazed to discover just how long they spent gazing at their slides. It's as if the screen is working like a powerful magnet that draws speakers' eyes towards it, holding them there for long periods and preventing them from tearing themselves away to look back at the audience. Being aware of just how common and easy a trap this is to fall into is a good start to solving the problem. It can also help if you model your stance in front of a screen on that of television weather forecasters, who stand facing the camera (i.e. the audience), pointing at the maps with the backs of their hands. There is also a mnemonic – *touch, turn and talk* – which provides a useful reminder that glances at the screen should be short, and quickly followed by a resumption of more extended eye contact with the audience.

Phoney eye contact

Another practice to which speakers can seem completely oblivious is a form of 'phoney' or 'simulated' eye contact. As members of audiences, most of us will occasionally have seen speakers who spend most of their time scanning their eyes along the line where the ceiling joins the wall at the back of the room, or along the top of the tables in front of the audience or even perhaps along the feet of the people sitting on the front row. These are speakers who know perfectly well that eye contact is a good thing, but can't quite bring themselves to look directly into the eyes of the audience. Discussions with people who have seen themselves on videotape doing this suggest that they are afraid of what they might see if they actually look at members of the audience. They assume that what lies in wait are signs of dissatisfaction, whether of boredom, puzzlement or downright hostility. Yet, as we've already seen, fixing our gaze on particular individuals is much more likely to prompt a positive and reassuring response than a negative one: once people learn this important fact, they discover that abandoning simulated eye contact in favour of the real thing is far less painful than they feared.

● *Skewed eye contact*

More common, and rather more difficult to identify, is something that can be characterised as 'skewed' or 'biased' eye contact. This is when a speaker spends much more time looking at one part of the audience than another. In feedback sessions the problem usually comes to the surface when the people sitting on one side of the room congratulate a speaker for having maintained such good eye contact with them – only to be contradicted by complaints from those on the other side that eye contact was poor and they had felt left out. This tendency to look one way more than another is quite common. Even Margaret Thatcher, with all her experience as an orator, would look up to her left much more often than to her right when reading speeches from a lectern.

One form of this syndrome involves speakers concentrating most of their attention on the one or two individuals in the audience whom they consider to be the most important people in the room. The danger here is that it will look as though you are discriminating between senior and junior members, trying to ingratiate yourself with the powers that be.

The main obstacle to correcting skewed eye contact is finding out that you suffer from it in the first place. The only sure ways of knowing are to see yourself in action on videotape, or to be alerted by people who have seen you speaking. Otherwise, the safest solution is to *assume* that you do have a problem, and make a conscious effort to move your head and eyes towards every part of the audience at regular intervals, so that no one feels left out.

🔲 *Looking down and looking up*

The above reference to the way Margaret Thatcher looked up and down while reading her speeches brings us to another source of concern that many speakers have. They often worry about the potential loss of eye contact when referring to notes or a script. While it is certainly the case that looking down more or less continuously has a negative impact on the audience, regular glances up and down are not really a problem, as is demonstrated by the fact that some politicians are able to deliver inspiring speeches when reading a script from a lectern.

The reason why eye contact doesn't have to be continuous probably has to do with the way gaze works in everyday interaction. Although avoiding eye contact during a conversation usually creates a negative impression, people also find it uncomfortable if someone looks at them continuously. An easy way to check this out is to look straight into another person's eyes while speaking to them, without glancing away for so much as a split second. This usually results in signs of discomfort, and may even prompt them to ask why you are 'staring' at them. From a very early age, of course, we have been taught that staring is something to be avoided, which prepares us for the fact that normal patterns of eye contact in everyday conversation are not continuous. What actually happens is that we alternate between looking at the other person and glancing away, looking at them again, and then glancing away again. Transferred to the public arena, this pattern of 'look–look away–look–look away' can be mapped on to the pattern of looking up at the audience and down at the notes or script. So long as the timing is similar to what we're used to in conversation, the chances are that the audience will hardly notice the regular glances away – unless, of course, the speaker hardly ever looks up.

6. Conclusion

I started this chapter by suggesting that much of the anxiety associated with public speaking comes from the way it differs from the commonest type of speaking we engage in most of the time, namely everyday conversation. The most general and important differences concern the basic mechanisms that ensure attentiveness and understanding in everyday speech. Taking it in turns to talk not only provides a powerful incentive to listen, but also enables conversationalists to make continual checks on how well they are making themselves understood. But the suspension of turn-taking, which is effectively what happens when we become members of an audience, involves a massive reduction both in our motivation to pay attention and in our capacity to monitor and check on understanding. Meanwhile, our everyday familiarity with using eye contact to gauge other people's reactions gives us a powerful weapon in the battle for attention that benefits both speakers and audiences.

Although the maintenance of attentiveness and understanding may be the most fundamental difference between speaking in conversation and speaking in public, there are other, taken-for-granted features of everyday speech that cause problems if used unchanged when addressing an audience. The trouble is that a great many speakers perform under the false assumption that there is no need to change their usual conversational style of speaking when making a speech. Unfortunately, the more conversational the talk, the more likely it is to come across as flat, uninspiring, rambling and difficult to follow. So the next chapter looks at what these features of conversation are, why they cause problems for audiences and how you can overcome them.

1. Paying attention is much more of a problem for audiences than for participants in a conversation because:

❏ Speeches and presentations go on for a very long time compared with the average length of the turns we are used to experiencing in a conversation.

❏ If we know that we're not going to have to be ready to say something within the next few seconds, we have much less of an incentive to listen.

❏ It's more difficult for speakers to know whether they're being understood and for audiences to ask for clarification when they need it.

❏ If we find the talk difficult to follow, we're likely to stop making the effort to listen.

2. Audiences have more of an incentive to listen when:

❏ They have a chance to join in.

❏ They are on the lookout for a chance to clap, cheer, boo or heckle.

❏ The speaker makes them laugh.

❏ The speaker keeps good eye contact with them.

3. Making the most of eye contact:

❑ The more you look at the audience, the easier it is to monitor their reactions, so you should always be on the lookout for positive and negative signs.

❑ The more you look at the audience, the greater the pressure on them to pay attention.

❑ Some audience members are more responsive than others, so keeping an eye on them is a useful barometer of how things are going.

❑ Make sure you include everyone – spending time looking only at one section of the audience may please them, but will make others feel excluded.

❑ Look people in the eye – looking above or below their heads will not do.

❑ Spend as little time as possible looking back towards the screen, blackboard or flip chart – *touch, turn and talk*.

Speaking in Private and Speaking in Public

Conversation and Public Speaking

When going through videotapes of people's presentations with them, one of the things I find myself saying most often is that they are speaking in 'conversational mode', and need to work at making the transition to 'presentational mode'. By 'conversational mode', I mean that they sound much the same as they do when speaking in a conversation. Things like hesitations, pace, volume and intonation combine in a style of delivery that makes such speakers come across as though they are merely 'chatting' their way through the presentation. As most of our talking is done in conversation, it's hardly surprising that we should prefer the style of speaking that makes us feel most comfortable. But when you're in front of an audience, speaking in conversational mode is unlikely to do much to help them with the problems of attentiveness and understanding discussed in the previous chapter. It's therefore important to be clear about what these components of conversation are, and why they need to be modified when it comes to speaking in public.

1. Sounds of silence: *ums* and *ers*

🗨 *Needless noises?*

A normal feature of conversational speech is the way we punctuate much of what we say with *ums* and *ers*. But this can become a major source of irritation for audiences trying to listen to a speech. If you *um* and *er* from the platform at the same rate as you normally do in conversation, audiences will notice. In extreme cases, it becomes so distracting that they even start counting them – at which point, the speaker is in serious danger of losing it altogether. The trouble with *umming* and *erring* during a speech is that it makes you sound hesitant, lacking in confidence, uncertain of your material and badly prepared. This raises the intriguing question of why *ums* and *ers* are acceptable, and often hardly even noticed, in conversation, but stand out as irritating distractions in speeches and presentations.

Experts in linguistics sometimes refer to *ums* and *ers* as 'voiced pauses', or breaks between words that we fill with sound. On the face of it, they might seem to be more or less random noises that come out of speakers' mouths in no particular place and for no apparent reason; but research has shown that there is actually a good deal of regularity in where they are most likely to occur and what we use them for.

🗨 *Don't worry – I've started*

One of the commonest places for *ums* and *ers* is right at the start of a new conversational turn. The previous speaker has just finished, and it's now time for someone to come up with an immediate response. But you're not always quite ready, and need a moment or two to think what to say. If you delay, you might create an embarrassing silence and give the wrong impression. So the obvious solution is to start immediately, even if it's only to say 'er' or 'um'. The noise kills off the silence at a stroke, shows that you've started to reply, and reassures the other(s) that you're not being difficult or impolite.

The fact that we start so many of our turns in conversation in this way probably explains why some presenters and public speakers make a habit of starting almost every new sentence with an *um* or an *er*. It's as if they implicitly regard each next sentence as being like another turn, to be started in the same way as they would if they were speaking in a conversation. As such, it's an example of something else that people tend to be completely unaware of until they hear themselves on tape – at which point they are usually appalled at the thought of the negative impact they must have had on their audience.

Hold on – I haven't finished yet

Another place where we often *um* or *er* in conversations is the middle of a turn: as we all know, we can suddenly find ourselves at a loss for the word or name we need to be able to carry on. We also know, though perhaps at a less conscious level, that if we simply pause while searching for the right word, the chances are that someone else will seize upon the silence as an opportunity to start speaking, so preventing us from finishing the point we were trying to make. A simple and widely used technique for warding off such unwelcome intrusions on our space is to produce an *um* or an *er*, and to stretch it out for however long it takes to recover our fluency. This lets everyone else know that you haven't finished yet and that it's still *your* turn. And the fact that you're still making a sound, even if it is only an extended *um* or *er*, means that you can accuse anyone who dares to start speaking of interrupting you. As such, it's a neat and effective way of asserting your right to carry on with the turn until you've got to the end of whatever it was you were in the process of saying.

🔊 *Pause avoidance syndrome*

All of this points to the fact that the primary function of *ums* and *ers* in conversation, whether to mark the beginning of a turn or to hold the floor until the end of a turn, is to avoid silence and its potentially negative connotations at all costs. It partly explains why pauses in conversation are quite rare, and why, when they do occur, they tend to be short – so short, in fact, that a second of silence can sound like an eternity. In effect, speakers collaborate with each other during conversations to make sure that the flow of sound remains more or less continuous, both during and between turns. Speakers in conversational mode will therefore do anything they can to avoid silences, which shows up in the two main symptoms of 'pause avoidance syndrome': the production of regular *ums* and *ers* at a similar rate as is normal (and hardly noticeable) in conversation, and speaking so quickly that the audience doesn't have enough time to take things in.

The reason why *ums* and *ers* are likely to irritate members of an audience is that the problems they solve in a conversation are no longer problems when it comes to making a speech or presentation, which means that killing off silences ceases to serve any useful purpose. After all, once a speech is under way, there isn't any need for speakers to keep on signalling that they have started their turn. Nor, on the whole, do they have to worry that someone else will hijack their turn by speaking during a pause, or indeed that a silence will embarrass members of the audience. In fact, far from being regarded as an indicator of embarrassment, awkwardness or impending trouble, regular pausing when addressing an audience has positive advantages, both for members of the audience and for the speaker.

2. Pausing with purpose
ℛ *Pausing and pace*
Punctuating talk with much more frequent and longer silences than is normal in conversation helps audiences by breaking up the flow of ideas into short, digestible units. Pauses as short as a second or half a second can give us quite enough time to grasp one point before the speaker moves on to the next, and so take things in, one chunk at a time. Without regular breaks, the material is likely to come at us so quickly that we hardly have time to digest it before having to listen to whatever comes next. At worst, we start to lose the thread, and may even give up completely on making any further efforts to pay attention.

Just as regular pauses are helpful to audiences, they also have a number of advantages for speakers. The first is that they make it easier to control breathing. If you avoid pausing, and speak at your normal conversational rate of about 170–180 words per minute, you risk becoming breathless or hoarse long before you get to the end. By pausing regularly and speaking more slowly than in conversation, you can reduce the pace to somewhere

Punctuating talk with much more frequent and longer silences than is normal in conversation helps audiences by breaking up the flow of ideas into short, digestible units. It also helps speakers to slow down, keep their breathing under control and to change the meaning and dramatic impact of what they are saying.

between 120 and 140 words per minute, which is a more suitable speed for a speech or presentation. As for how long and how often you should pause, there are no hard and fast rules. Some professional speechwriters operate on the principle that an average of one pause every seven words is about right, adding that, with a highly educated audience, this average can be safely extended to once every nine words. It should be stressed, however, that these are only *averages*, and should not be taken as meaning that speeches should be delivered in staccato bursts of exactly the same duration – the effect of which would be to come across as too regular and robotic. The key to effective delivery lies in variation, both in the number of words between pauses, and in the overall pace at which different segments are delivered.

The fact that we are so used to associating pauses in conversation with negative implications means that inexperienced speakers often feel very uneasy about pausing while speaking to an audience. One reason for this is that the way we perceive silences differs according to which kind of talk we are listening to. A pause that would sound long and potentially troublesome to someone involved in a conversation will sound like little more than a split second when that same person is in an audience, a fact that can readily be checked out by listening to a speech by anyone with a reputation as an effective orator. Indeed, if you notice the pauses at all, the chances are that you'll regard them as a positive virtue, because they help to make the pace of delivery easy on the ear and comfortable to follow.

🗨 Pausing and meaning

Regular pausing not only helps you to control your breathing and pace, but also enables you to change the meaning and dramatic impact or mood of a particular statement. In extreme cases, changing where you pause can give a sentence a completely opposite meaning, as in this example:

> The government said the opposition has completely lost its way.

If you read it aloud, pausing at the end of each of the three lines below, the sentence means that the opposition is attacking the government:

> The government
> said the opposition
> has completely lost its way.

Change where you pause, and it sounds like a government attack on the opposition:

> The government said
> the opposition has completely
> lost its way.

🐾 *Pausing for effect*

As well as having the capacity to change meaning, pausing in different places can alter the dramatic impact of sentences. Here, for example, is the text of the final part of Churchill's radio address to the nation after the fall of France in 1940:

> Let us therefore brace ourselves to our duty, and so bear ourselves that, if the British Empire and its Commonwealth lasts for a thousand years, men will still say 'This was their finest hour.'

In delivering it, he actually paused six times, at the end of each of the following lines:

> Let us therefore brace ourselves to our duty,
> and so bear ourselves
> that, if the British Empire and its Commonwealth
> lasts for a thousand years,
> men will still say
> 'This
> was their finest hour.'

Like many other politicians, Churchill marked pauses into his text beforehand laying them out in the same way as is done here, with the end of each line indicating a pause (this and other ways of producing scripts that help speakers to improve their delivery are discussed further in Chapter 9).

In a speech to the Canadian parliament in 1941, Churchill produced what was to become a famous line by using pauses to increase the impact of two humorous punch lines:

When I warned them [the French government] that Britain would fight on alone whatever they did, their generals told their prime minister and his divided cabinet, 'In three weeks, England will have her neck wrung like a chicken.' (PAUSE) Some chicken. (PAUSE) Some neck.

As for when to pause, there are no hard and fast rules, and it is certainly not the case that the only appropriate places are at punctuation marks in a text. Sometimes, pausing at counter-intuitive places like between an adjective and a noun or between an adverb and a verb can be very effective. In the first of the above two examples from Churchill, two of the pauses came between the subject and verb in a sentence:

... if the British Empire and its Commonwealth (PAUSE) lasts for a thousand years ... 'This (PAUSE) was their finest hour.'

One way to get used to the different meanings and the range of effects that can be achieved by pausing is to listen closely to effective speakers in action, paying particular attention to where the pauses occur. Another is to take the text of a speech or a newspaper article and read it aloud several times, pausing at different places and reflecting on how the meaning and emphasis change.

● *Pausing to plan what to say next*
The advantages of pausing dealt with so far have all been ones that benefit audiences in various ways. But pauses can also be a considerable help to speakers. Even a moment's silence is enough

to give you time to glance at your notes, plan what to say next, or make a slight change in direction. You might, for example, have seen signs of puzzlement or boredom emanating from the audience, in which case you may decide to add some previously unplanned words of clarification, an illustrative example, or perhaps a summary of the argument so far. On the face of it, a short pause of a second or so might not seem nearly long enough to take stock, let alone to change course if that appears to be necessary. But our years of experience as conversationalists have already made us old hands when it comes to interpreting and producing talk in the split seconds that separate the turns in everyday conversation. In fact, thinking so quickly is second nature to us, which means that we don't need very long at all to be able to make instant adjustments while speaking to an audience.

⬤ Pausing for how long?

As for how long pauses should be, the short answer is that they can be much longer than feels comfortable in a conversation, where half a second, one second or a second and a half can seem interminable. But pauses of similar length during a speech or presentation don't sound nearly as long to an audience. Again, this is something that you can easily check on, either by listening to effective speakers in action, or by trying out pauses of different duration for yourself. The main challenge here is to discard your normal conversational perceptions and inhibitions about silences, and to realise that, from an audience point of view, the talk will sound more natural and easier to follow if you pause at frequent intervals.

🗨 *Pausing to recover*

Being aware that pauses sound normal to audiences is a useful resource for people who worry about what to do if words suddenly fail them and they find themselves drying up in the middle of a presentation. Silence at such a point may be a cause of major panic for the speaker, but the audience is unlikely to notice that anything is amiss. They obviously have no idea of what's going on inside your head, and will assume that this particular pause is no different from any of the others that have punctuated the speech so far. Meanwhile, your best strategy is to use the pause to do something, whether it's to rearrange or inspect your notes, or to take a drink of water. Simple movements of this kind may well work in a similar way to a method that can help stroke victims when they find themselves stammering to find a word. A nudge or pinch of a hand sends new signals to the brain that interfere with whatever it was that was blocking their speech, and is often enough to enable them to regain their fluency. In a similar way, movements and activity not directly related to speaking also seem to help presenters regain their composure enough to be able to continue as if nothing had happened. Meanwhile, the sight of speakers pausing to have a drink or to check their notes is so familiar to audiences that they are unlikely to notice that anything is wrong.

🗨 *Pausing to avoid 'ums' and 'ers'*

As we have seen, *umming* and *erring* to avoid silences are thoroughly normal features of everyday conversation, yet distracting to audiences during speeches. Therefore one of the biggest challenges in making the transition from conversational to presentational mode is to get used to the idea of doing the exact opposite of what we do in conversation. It means eliminating something that is common and normal in conversation (*umming* and *erring*), and doing something that is rare and potentially troublesome (pausing). Not surprisingly, this requires effort and practice, and some suggestions as to how to go about it are included in the exercises at the end of Part I.

3. Intonation and stress

Our conversational assumptions about silences and *ums* and *ers* are not the only taken-for-granted features of everyday speech that can't be relied on to work in exactly the same way when speaking to audiences. Another is the way we use intonation and stress. A commonly heard complaint from audiences is that a speaker just droned on and on. The word 'drone', of course, refers to a continuous and unchanging stream of sound, and highlights the fact that speaking in a monotone is widely regarded as a bad thing. It is therefore important to be clear about how tonal variation plays a positive part in the communication process. In general, intonation and stress work in a similar way to pausing, in that they provide a way of conveying different meanings and different moods.

Intonation and meaning

Putting the stress on different words can result in quite dramatic changes in the meaning of a sentence. Sometimes, as in the following example, there can be as many different meanings as there are words in the sentence. Try saying it aloud eight times, putting the stress on the words in italics, and you'll find that the meaning changes to that in the right hand column.

The way the most famous sequence from Abraham Lincoln's

Sentence with stress on a different word	Different implied meanings
I didn't say you stole my red hat.	But someone else might have said it.
I *didn't* say you stole my red hat.	I deny that I said it.
I didn't *say* you stole my red hat.	I may have thought or implied it.
I didn't say *you* stole my red hat.	I said someone else stole it.
I didn't say you *stole* my red hat.	I said you did something else with it.
I didn't say you stole *my* red hat.	I said you stole someone else's red hat.
I didn't say you stole my *red* hat.	I said you stole my green hat.
I didn't say you stole my red *hat*.	I said you stole my red scarf.

Gettysburg address is usually quoted tends to assume that he stressed the words 'of', 'by' and 'for':

> ... government *of* the people, *by* the people and *for* the people.

Given that stressing particular words plays an important part in clarifying precisely what you mean, anyone whose delivery is flat and regular is losing out on one of the most basic techniques for ruling out ambiguity and communicating meaning. As a general guide, there will be at least one word in every sentence that needs some extra stress. That is why, when using a script, it's a good idea to go through it and underline or highlight words that are to be delivered with extra emphasis.

Putting the stress on particular words is only part of the way in which intonation can affect meaning. Upwards and downwards variations in tone can also make a big difference to how we interpret what we hear. Depending on how we say it, a sentence like 'he spoke for well over an hour' can sound like a statement of fact, a compliment or a complaint. Add a question mark to it, and anyone reading it will produce the rising intonation at the end that will turn it into a question, even though it is not grammatically constructed as a question.

🗨 Intonation and mood

Changes in intonation are at the heart of the way we communicate different moods and emotional feelings like passion, conviction and enthusiasm, all of which play a critically important part in holding the interest and attention of an audience. Intonation is so crucial that, if you listen to someone speaking in a language you don't understand, you can often get a rough idea of whether a conversation is serious or light-hearted, and whether the participants are relaxed or tense, friendly or hostile, interested or bored, and so on. You can also listen to speeches in foreign languages and get an impression of how passionate or otherwise the speaker sounds, and even sometimes anticipate when applause is about to start.

In the battle for the hearts and minds of an audience, intonation is a two-edged sword that can either reduce or increase a speaker's impact. This was clearly illustrated on an occasion when a large multi-national corporation was launching some new products. The main event was taking place in a West End theatre, and being broadcast to theatres in other parts of the UK. Just before one of the breaks, a videotape of a short statement by the company's marketing director was played on a large screen. He concluded with the words, 'I hope you're all as excited by these new products as I am' – only to be greeted by loud and raucous laughter from the audience of about 300 people in one of the remote locations. The reason was that his flat intonation was in such stark contrast with the sentiment of the message he was trying to get across. He had succeeded in sounding bored, uninterested and unenthusiastic while saying words that were intended to communicate the exact opposite.

If you sound bored with your own subject matter, the audience can hardly be expected to feel any differently about it. This is why, of all the emotions that can be conveyed through intonation, enthusiasm must surely be the most important one of all. When people think back to their school days, the teachers they are most likely to remember with affection are the ones who were the most passionate and enthusiastic about the subjects they were teaching. And this is a lesson that we ignore at our peril in the vast majority of public-speaking situations. Only very occasionally will speaking in a flat, disinterested tone strike exactly the right note.

When flat intonation works

When talking robots appear in science-fiction films and television series, they typically speak in a flat, highly regular and monotonous tone of voice. Stripping out normal patterns of intonational variation provides film-makers with a way of making robotic speech sound dehumanised and mechanical.

Another situation where there is a case for adopting a flat style of delivery is when speakers specifically want to avoid showing how they feel about what they are saying. This is often the case with official statements that are explicitly intended to come across as being on behalf of someone else, rather than as the committed personal view of the speaker. During the Falklands War, for example, there was a British foreign office spokesman called Mr McGregor, who appeared regularly on television reading out progress reports in a flat, deadpan monotone – presumably because it was his job to give nothing away that might encourage or discourage viewers about the way things were going. Another example is the annual State Opening of Parliament, where the Queen's Speech is written by the government of the day, but read out by her. The way she typically does this seems designed to make it clear that she is not the author of it, but is merely reading someone else's words. Given that a constitutional monarchy depends on the monarch remaining neutral about the policies of whichever political party happens to be in power, it could obviously cause considerable disquiet if her intonation showed enthusiasm (or lack of it) about the government's legislative proposals for the coming year.

One obvious lesson to be taken from this is that, if you want to sound objective and neutral about something, or perhaps don't want the audience to know what you really think about a particular subject, your best bet is to speak in a flatter tone than usual.

Sounding less enthusiastic than we think

Situations where a lack of intonational variation strikes exactly the right note are, of course, fairly rare, and most audiences will expect you to show at least some interest and enthusiasm for your subject. Unfortunately, there is a hidden obstacle that often prevents us from sounding as enthusiastic as we feel. During training workshops, criticisms about flat intonation and stress are extremely common. Such complaints not only come from members of the audience, but are also frequently made by speakers about themselves as soon as they listen to their performance on tape. What surprises them most is the realisation that they are coming across to the audience as far more monotonous and boring than they sounded to themselves while they were actually delivering the presentation.

This is another example of something that is very likely to happen if you stay in conversational mode while addressing an audience. The point is not that flat tone is normal or desirable in conversations, but that conversationalists are in a much better position to hear small variations in tone, and pick up even the slightest inflection. This is because conversation is a form of communication that typically takes place across very short distances, with participants seldom being more than two or three metres apart. At such close range, it is easy enough to hear and interpret slight changes in tone and emphasis. It's much the same with telephone conversations, where the voice at the other end of the line is amplified directly into one of your ears. But the problem for audiences is that, as the distance between a speaker and hearer extends beyond a few metres, a level of tonal variation that works well enough to express meaning and mood in a conversation flattens out by the time it reaches them. The inevitable result is that speakers who make no adjustment to their normal conversational style of speaking will actually sound more monotonous to their audience even than they do to themselves.

If conversational variations in tone and emphasis are too slight to carry across a distance and register with an audience, the solution is to make it easier for them to hear the shifts and nuances more clearly and recognise the changes of meaning and mood we are trying to convey. The way to do this is by exaggerating our normal

> Changes in intonation and stress are extremely important for conveying irony, humour, passion, conviction and enthusiasm. The danger of speaking in a normal conversational tone is that the speech will flatten out to a monotone by the time it reaches the audience.

conversational patterns of intonation. The sound will still flatten out across a distance. However, unlike the slight peaks and troughs of conversational intonation that flatten to the point of sounding monotonous, more exaggerated variations will flatten to a point where they sound normal by the time they reach the audience.

Learning to do this successfully is, of course, easier said than done. Most people will initially find it rather embarrassing, and worry that they will sound stupid if they 'ham it up' too much. Not everyone is a born actor, and it's only natural to feel uneasy at the prospect of speaking in a way that departs, however slightly, from the conversational mode with which we are so much more comfortable. But this is not quite the same thing as acting, which would mean trying to come across as someone different from our normal self. In public speaking, it is only our own familiar characteristic patterns of intonation that should be exaggerated. Such changes may make us sound a little bit larger than life inside our own heads, but will come across as our normal selves to those sitting some distance away (see exercises at the end of Part I).

The fact that public speaking requires us to exaggerate our usual conversational pattern of speaking probably explains why so many people find it more difficult and inhibiting to speak to an audience that includes people they know well. As we are conscious of not speaking in quite the same way as we do in conversation, we worry that friends and relations will spot the difference. We become anxious about what they must be thinking and how they will react: do they understand why it's necessary for us to speak like this, or are they going to criticise us for showing off? The answer is that they probably won't even notice. If you get it right, the chances are that you will sound just as normal to the people you know well as you do to those who have never heard you speak before.

Stress, emphasis and varied intonation are important weapons in the battle for audience attention, partly because they help to clarify meaning, and partly because of their role in communicating passion, enthusiasm and conviction. It follows that the price of making no effort to modulate our tone is a very high one. At best, it's likely to confuse audiences and leave them wondering about where you really stand on the particular issues you are discussing, and uncertain about how strongly you feel about them. At worst, monotony will result in a progressive, and perhaps even complete, loss of audience attention.

4. Delivery style and audience size

🔊 Learning from television

When it comes to addressing audiences of different sizes, you have to be ready to modify the way you speak according to how many of them there are, and the distance between you and them. The issue is reflected by the different styles of delivery that work on television as compared with the live theatre or large conference auditorium.

In contrast with acting in a theatre, television performances are characterised by a more low-key, conversational style of delivery. Unlike speakers in conversation, a speaker on the stage of a theatre or conference hall has to communicate across a very much larger distance. Without some degree of exaggeration of intonation, emphasis, pausing, movement and gesture, they will come across as static, flat and monotonous. This creates a real dilemma for politicians and others, whose speeches to large rallies are broadcast on television. The problem is that the zoom lens produces a close-up, head-and-shoulders image of verbal and non-verbal behaviours that are designed for long-distance communication, and transmits this into millions of living rooms. A style of speaking appropriate for a large audience in a formal setting is therefore seen and heard by small audiences of two or three viewers in the very informal setting of their living room. To viewers sitting a conversational distance away from their television screens, often chatting with other people in the room, traditional theatrical styles of delivery are likely to come across at close range as too fanatical and over-dramatic.

If a politician wants to avoid coming across on television as too manic, the safest solution is to cultivate a lower-key style of speaking that is closer to the way we speak in conversation. Early examples of this were the fireside chats to American radio listeners given by President Roosevelt in the 1940s, a style that was later adapted for television by Presidents Reagan and Clinton. A background in radio and Hollywood films made Ronald Reagan so conscious of the issue that he briefed his speechwriters never to forget that 'we're guests in the nation's living rooms'. As a former film actor, he was also very experienced at performing in front of a camera, though he is reported to have attributed his skill as a communicator to his earlier career as a radio commentator, which had required him to learn how to get messages across to a mass audience with the voice alone.

Viewed in these terms, Hitler's histrionic style of delivery would probably have been much less effective on the small screen in people's living rooms than it was at the mass rallies, where he was able to inspire audiences across very long distances indeed. Similar considerations probably go some way towards explaining why former Labour leader Neil Kinnock, one of the finest live orators of his generation, never managed to achieve high personal ratings with the mass audience beyond the conference hall. His theatrical style of delivery ensured that his passion and conviction came across even to those sitting on the back row of a large auditorium. But seen in close-up via the zoom lens, it probably came across as too melodramatic to the viewers at home. During his last few years as leader of the Liberal Democrats, Paddy Ashdown actually stopped reading his big set-piece speeches from teleprompter screens, and reverted to the use of typed scripts on a lectern. This was because he felt it was so easy to read from teleprompter screens that he looked and sounded as though he was ranting at the audience. But having to look up and down at a traditional script worked as a constraint against going over the top, and ensured a lower-key style of delivery that was likely to be more acceptable to the mass audience of television viewers in their homes.

Presenting in conversational mode

Although the vast majority of presentations that most of us have to make will never appear on national television, the way in which presentational style is affected by the size of an audience, whether sitting at home or in a small office or meeting room, has much more general implications. One is that there are some occasions when a low-key, chatty style of delivery will be appropriate. I first became aware of this when, as a young and inexperienced lecturer, I was speaking at an academic conference. At the start of the session, there were only three or four people in the audience, and it seemed right to stay in my seat and chat informally to them about my research. The room then began to fill up, and I remember feeling progressively more uncomfortable as the numbers increased. What had started out, to all intents and purposes, as an informal gathering was changing by the minute into a more and more formal one. At some stage, I took the decision to stand up, stop chatting and, in effect, to start 'lecturing'. It was so long ago that I can't remember how many people had joined the audience at the point when I felt a change of style was needed. However, what I have learnt since would lead me to guess that I began to feel uneasy when the number in the audience started to rise beyond six.

Before explaining why that might be so, the important point to note is that, with small audiences of around six or less, especially when they are sitting a short distance away from you, a conversational style of delivery is likely to work perfectly well. It should be easy enough for them to pick up the nuances of intonation and stress without your having to depart very much from the way you normally speak in conversation. It is, however, still worth making the effort to eliminate as many *ums* and *ers* as possible, as members of a small audience are likely to be just as irritated by these as those in a large one.

What happens when six people come to dinner?

As for why something critical seems to take place when the size of a group reaches six, the answer is that the dynamics of conversation undergo subtle changes as the number of people involved increases. These have the effect of making it progressively more difficult to sustain a single conversation in which everyone takes it in turns to speak, and only one person speaks at a time.

For example, when there are only two people involved, conversation is likely to be at its most intense and intimate: there is no doubt whose turn it will be to speak next, so you had better pay attention as closely as possible. In a three-person conversation, the intensity is somewhat relaxed, as the two who are waiting for a turn have the choice of either competing to speak next, or of opting out and letting the other two get on with it for a while. When there are four people present, it becomes possible for two conversations to take place at the same time. However, if dinner parties involving four people are anything to go by, it seems to be fairly easy to sustain a single conversation; after all, a one-in-three chance of speaking next gives you a reasonable chance of getting a turn from time to time, and to participate on equal terms with everyone else.

This is very different from dinner parties at which there are seven or eight people present, and where hardly anyone will be willing to sit around waiting for a one-in-six or -seven chance of speaking next. As a result, there will be several conversations taking place at the same time, with diners switching from one to another, depending on which sounds the most interesting or amusing. The fact that different people are speaking all at once means that there will be a lot more noise than in a single conversation, and this 'buzz' creates an impression of liveliness and a good time had by all. But this tends not to happen when there are only five or six of you sitting around a table, because no one is quite sure which rules apply. Is this supposed to be a single conversation, and do I have to wait for a one-in-five chance of getting to speak next? Am I really going to have to sit here listening to this crashing bore droning on and on, or can I safely start up a separate conversation with someone else without appearing rude or impolite for opting out? The fact that this dilemma tends to set in when the number reaches six suggests that this is the point of maximum tension, where the group size starts to threaten the survival of a single conversation, and makes a split into more than one increasingly likely.

🔎 *Why small audiences may be a speaker's biggest challenge*

Although dinner parties and other social occasions may improve for the better when one conversation divides up into several, business meetings certainly do not. This is why they have to be regulated in ways that involve significant changes from those with which we operate in everyday conversation. If we don't hand over control of turn-taking to the chair, meetings either become free-for-alls dominated by the most talkative few, or end up with different sub-groups talking to each other at the same time. Things can degenerate even more if the person in the chair fails to keep a close check on whether or not speakers are sticking to subjects on the agenda, as the natural conversational tendency to go off at tangents will take over – and divert the discussion towards topics far removed from what the meeting was supposed to be about.

The fact that special rules apply at meetings makes them feel more formal than conversation, but the trouble is that meetings involving fewer than six participants have a less formal and more conversational feel to them. With so few present, it would be perfectly possible for everyone to take turns and behave as if it were an ordinary, informal conversation. Anyone who has to make a presentation to such a small group comes up against an awkward ambiguity that pulls in opposite directions. On the one hand, you are expected to do something very different and much more formal than conversation, namely to talk on a narrowly defined topic for 20 or 30 minutes. On the other, you find yourself in a situation where it would be much more comfortable for everyone to chat informally with each other about the matters at hand. In short, the challenge is to speak formally in a context that feels informal and conversational.

This is probably why so many people tell me that they feel more uncertain and ill at ease when speaking to very small groups than when addressing larger gatherings. With audiences above a certain size (probably six), a single conversation isn't even on the cards. The tension between the air of informality and the need to be formal fades away, and removes any doubt about what rules of the game apply: it is unequivocally a presentation, a speech or a lecture, and as such it should be delivered in presentational rather than conversational mode.

This feeling that we are in an informal conversational context is not, of course, confined to those who have to speak to very small audiences. Members of your audience will feel exactly the same about it, so much so that they often start to behave as if they were involved in a conversation rather than listening to a presentation. This makes them much more likely to interrupt with questions, comments or suggestions than if they were members of a larger audience. If they persist, or feel encouraged by your responses, the presentation can all too easily disintegrate into a conversation between you and them, with the result that you may never get to develop your argument in full, or in the way you had originally intended. Assuming you want to avoid this, there is an even stronger case than usual for making it clear from the outset that you'd prefer to take questions at the end.

5. Conclusion

This chapter has concentrated on how various features of our everyday conversational style of speaking can't be relied on to help us in the battle for audience attention and understanding. Some, like *umming* and *erring,* should be eliminated as far as possible, while others, like intonation and stress, need to be modified. The transition from conversational to presentational mode also involves learning to become comfortable with something we're used to avoiding in conversation, namely pausing.

But conversation is not the only familiar form of communication that you can't rely on if you want to impress an audience. Becoming an effective speaker also depends on understanding some important differences between the spoken language and the language of the written word. What these are is the subject of the next chapter.

Summary

1. *Ums* and *ers* are normal in conversation, but distract and irritate audiences.

2. Silences may be embarrassing and troublesome in conversation, but pausing at regular intervals is good practice when making a speech or presentation because:

- ❑ It slows down the pace of delivery, and breaks material into short, digestible chunks that are easier for audiences to understand.
- ❑ It helps to clarify and convey different meanings.
- ❑ It can increase dramatic impact.
- ❑ It gives you a chance to recover when things go wrong.

3. Changes in intonation, stress and emphasis convey different meanings and moods.

4. Of all the emotions it is possible to convey through intonation, enthusiasm is the most important one of all.

5. Everyday conversational intonation flattens out across a distance, so you need to exaggerate your everyday conversational patterns to avoid sounding monotonous (see also Chapter 9 and exercises at the end of Part I).

6. When using a script, underline or highlight words to be delivered with extra emphasis (see also Chapter 9 and exercises at the end of Part I).

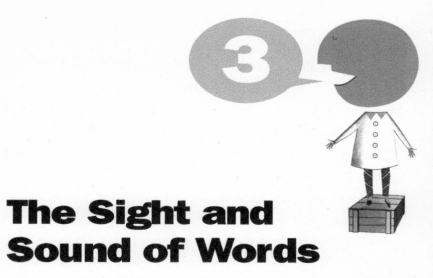

The Sight and Sound of Words

Differences between Writing and Speaking

The first thing that most people do when preparing a speech or presentation is to pick up a pen, or sit with fingers poised over the keyboard of a computer. Whichever you do, your brain effectively locks into written mode, so that the kind of language that goes down on the page, or up on the screen, will be very similar to the kind of language you would use when writing a letter, report, proposal or some other written document. This wouldn't matter if the way we write for readers were exactly the same as the way we speak to listeners. Unfortunately, it is not, and there are various subtle differences, most of which mean that you can't rely on the written word to see you through a speech or presentation. This will be familiar enough to anyone who has ever tried reading out to an audience something that they have written out in full. In the course of actually reading it, we often discover that it doesn't sound quite right, and sometimes even manage to insert a few improvised changes and corrections as we go along.

The other side of the coin is that much of what we say may sound fine, but looks odd when transcribed verbatim on to the page, a point neatly summed up by a Nobel Prize-winning scientist who was also well known as a brilliant lecturer:

> It is my experience that when I have to read a literal transcript of one of my lectures I am quite appalled, even when I have felt that the actual talk was rather a good one. The account taken from the tape-recording is ungrammatical, with jerky, unfinished sentences and repetitions, and one blushes to read it. **Professor Sir Lawrence Bragg**

When it comes to understanding why the written word can make life difficult for audiences, there are two general issues to be taken into account. The first part of this chapter deals with the way our approach to grammar, word selection and sentence construction differs according to whether we're writing or speaking. The second part looks at how the written and spoken language compare when it comes to communicating large volumes of detailed information.

I. THE CLOAK OF FORMALITY

1. Hyper-correctness

One of the main differences between the written and spoken language is that we make much less effort to observe the rules of grammar when we're speaking than when we're writing. If a properly formed sentence requires a subject, verb and object, then much of what we say, in both conversations and speeches, fails the

> If you speak in a 'hyper-correct' way you risk coming across as unduly stilted, wooden or pompous. At worst, it will seem as though you have left your personality in the chair, and put on an invisible cloak of formality as you got up to speak.

test. But when we're writing, we put much more effort into sentence construction, if only because grammatical errors might give the impression that we're ignorant or uneducated. To help protect our reputations, the designers of word processing programs have supplied us with spelling and grammar checkers. And, though we may not always agree with their automated suggestions, their very existence underlines the fact that grammatical correctness is seen as an essential part of the writing process. The fact that the written word conforms more closely to the rules of grammar than the spoken word is not really surprising, as grammar was originally developed as a set of rules to handle the translation of biblical texts. Its origins were therefore very much rooted in the written, rather than the spoken, word.

This is not to suggest that you should make a deliberate effort to flout the rules of grammar when making a speech, but to warn that making a special effort to speak more grammatically than usual can have a negative impact on audiences. If you speak, as some people do, in a 'hyper-correct' way, you risk coming across as unduly stilted, wooden or pompous. At worst, it will seem as though you have left your personality in the chair, and put on an invisible cloak of formality as you got up to speak. People in the audience who don't know you may simply conclude that you're rather affected or pompous; those who do know you may be puzzled by the curious difference in style between the speaker they are listening to, and the person they know on a day-to-day basis.

One of the most obvious symptoms of the cloak of formality syndrome is the production of grammatically faultless sentences of a kind that are hardly ever heard in everyday speech. For example, the following extract from a political speech at a party conference might pass unnoticed in an essay on social philosophy. But try reading it aloud, and you'll find just how stilted and formal it sounds.

> A theme that emerges from several papers is that equality cannot and should not be measured purely by a financial index. An acceptance of some inherent inequality is coupled with an approval of variety and diversity, but income maintenance for the low waged and the unwaged in a rapidly changing industrial climate is just as strongly seen as an obligation on us all.

There was also nothing wrong with the grammar in a sentence produced by former Prime Minister John Major in a radio interview, in which he described what he sometimes did on his way home from watching a game of cricket:

> I have been known on occasions to call in at a local hostelry with whomsoever I happen to be.

Although 'with whomsoever I happen to be' is grammatically correct, the sentence sounds stilted and formal. This is because words like 'whomsoever' are more likely to be found in written documents like insurance policies and legal agreements than in everyday speech. His use of the word 'hostelry', rather than the more usual 'pub', also gives the sentence something of an old-fashioned ring to it. This may, of course, have been exactly what he intended. But its formal tone stood out in marked contrast with the main theme of the interview, in which he seemed to be using his interest in sport to demonstrate that he was 'a man of the people', with the same tastes and passions as ordinary voters.

2. Words

The simpler the better

The above examples illustrate the fact that there are various words and usages that are more likely to be found in written documents than in speech. When writing, we tend to use words that are longer, more unusual, or more technical than the words we habitually use in everyday conversation. And if you rely on this written style when addressing an audience, as some speakers do, it will strengthen the impression that you are hiding behind a cloak of formality. Using words that are hardly ever heard in everyday speech will also make it more difficult for an audience to understand the point you're trying to get across. For example, the two columns in the example on the next page contain sentences that convey the same message, but the lines on the left and right use different words. Just how much difference the alternative wording makes to the degree of formality and comprehensibility becomes very apparent as soon as you try reading the two versions aloud.

As this example shows, the English language gives us a tremendous choice of different words for referring to the same thing. This

Formal/written	Informal/spoken
We shall endeavour to commence	We shall try to begin
the enhancement programme forthwith	the repairs immediately
in order to ensure that	so that
there is sufficient time	there's enough time
to facilitate the dissemination of	to send
the relevant contractual documentation	the contracts
to purchasers ahead of the renovations	to buyers before the work
being brought to completion.	is finished.

is because its vocabulary comes from a mixture of different languages of Latin, Nordic and Anglo-Saxon origins. In general, words originating from Latin tend to be longer, more abstract and more obscure than those of Nordic and Anglo-Saxon origin. You obviously don't need to know where any particular word originally came from, but you do need to bear in mind that the words you do select can help or hinder an audience in following what you are saying. During a presentation on one of my courses, for example, one speaker kept talking about 'increasing revenue generation'. When pressed as to what exactly this meant, he said 'making more money', adding 'which is, I suppose, what I should have said in the first place'.

🔊 Jargon and acronyms
The huge choice of words our language gives us means that, wherever possible, it is always worth making an effort to use simple

words that are in common spoken usage. This includes avoiding any specialised, technical or analytic terms that may be second nature to you, but are unfamiliar to the audience – and especially the mass of jargon and acronyms that are continually forcing their way into our vocabulary. Sometimes, of course, it may be impossible to exclude them altogether, as when discussing abstract concepts or theoretical ideas. But the key point is to make sure that you clarify the meaning of any technical terms, using illustrative examples where necessary, before talking about them in any detail. With jargon and acronyms your best bet is to keep them to an absolute minimum. They may be a useful form of shorthand for specialists who know what a 'securitised transaction' is, or what the acronym BBKA stands for, but unexplained concepts and obscure initials are likely to be a source of confusion and irritation to most members of most audiences.

🗨 Shortened forms

Just as some usages are more common in written texts than in the spoken language, the opposite is also the case. For example, when speaking, we make frequent use of shortened or contracted forms for various tense constructions, such as 'I'll' rather than 'I shall', 'you'd' instead of 'you had', and so on. We do the same with negatives, as when we say 'don't' rather than 'do not', or 'wasn't' rather than 'was not'. In the spoken language, the full forms are mainly used on occasions where we want to give extra emphasis or clarity, as when we say 'I did not ...' or 'I shall ...'. When we learn to write, however, we are taught to use the full forms, a habit that tends to stay with us for the rest of our writing lives. If, as is sometimes the case, speakers make an effort always to use the full, rather than contracted forms, they are likely to sound rather stilted or pedantic, adding further to the impression that the speaker has put on a cloak of formality. As the shortened forms are an essential part of the way English is spoken, continuing to use them when addressing an audience is likely to sound more natural and less formal.

Colloquialisms and slang

Another set of words that we use frequently in everyday speech, but tend to avoid when writing, comes under the heading of colloquialisms and slang. When speaking to an audience, it's as well to approach the use of such language with caution. If you're reporting what someone else actually said, then there's usually no problem in including slang. If certain colloquialisms are part of your normal everyday vocabulary, it may also sound perfectly natural to use them in a speech or presentation, and can sometimes be exploited to introduce a degree of lightness or humour. The problems arise if you rely so heavily on colloquialism and slang that it comes across as offensive or patronising.

If you sound patronising, or as though you are talking down to the audience, you obviously risk alienating your listeners. So too do attempts to convey an impression of being a rather different type of person than the one we know the speaker to be. For example, some of Tony Blair's appearances on television chat shows attracted criticism because he seemed to be adopting the language of so-called 'Estuary English', or the tendency of people brought up further and further away from the east end of London to take on characteristics associated with a Cockney accent. Coming out of Tony Blair's mouth, it contrasts sharply with the language of the Oxford-educated lawyer speaking at a press conference or political rally. If something is so blatantly out of character, it will prompt people to start wondering about his motives, and whether this is someone who is perhaps working rather too hard at coming across as an 'ordinary bloke'. The lesson to be drawn from this is that, if a colloquial style is not part of our normal way of speaking, we shouldn't suddenly start adopting it when speaking in public. After all, a cloak of contrived informality can be as noticeable and counter-productive as a cloak of formality.

Words that give offence

The biggest risk in using slang is that some members of an audience may find it offensive. On the whole, it is safest to avoid the use of swear words, however mild they may seem to us. We also need to remember that there may be someone in the audience who will regard some of our words or phrases as racist, sexist or as evidence of any other '-ism' in the ever-changing lexicon of political correctness.

For example, something as apparently harmless as saying 'my God' and 'good God' during a lecture once led to a formal complaint being made against a colleague of mine for blasphemy. On another occasion, the audience at an after-dinner speech by a television personality started to hiss and boo after he was about five minutes into the speech, because his vocabulary and subject matter were almost entirely sexist, racist or homophobic. Regardless of what proportion of the audience happened to be female, gay or from an ethnic minority, there are many who fall into none of these categories who find the use of such words equally offensive.

3. Sentences

🔊 *The shorter and simpler the better*

Just as long and complex words tend to feature more in written documents than in spoken communication, so too do longer and more complex sentences (not that this is necessarily an indicator of good writing style). Here the problem for audiences is that the more extended and complicated the structure of a sentence, the more difficult it will be for them to make sense of it. One reason for this is that longer sentences usually include more than one key point or idea. As a result, audiences may find too much information coming at them too quickly to be able to take it all in before the speaker goes on to the next sentence. Another source of difficulty is that, unlike a reader, who can either read a long sentence more slowly, or read it through it again if necessary, audiences only have one chance to make sense of it.

Sometimes, of course, a sentence can remain incomprehensible even after several readings, as with the following example, taken from the script of a real presentation. In this instance the sentence also appeared on a slide projected on the screen – though it's doubtful whether the opportunity to read and reread it did much to improve the audience's comprehension.

Rather than investing in the security issued by a corporation or institution which carries the usual credit risk of that corporation or institution, by reference to its overall financial standing, the risk to the investor in a securitised transaction is isolated to the performance of the specific underlying asset pool.

In the same way as pausing helps to break things up into more digestible chunks, using short, simple sentences when speaking makes it easier for audiences to take things in one point at a time. This improves their chances of being able to understand how the various parts of an unfolding argument fit together.

Separating sentences

One reason why we tend to use longer sentences when writing than when we are speaking is that we often join more than one sentence together with a conjunction, the commonest of which is 'and'. An interesting exercise is to take a written text and eliminate as many of the 'ands' between sentences as possible, replacing each one with a full stop and a new sentence. This usually has the effect of making it sound more like a speech than a written document. For example, the following three sentences, unlinked by any conjunctions, are taken from a speech made by Neil Kinnock, former leader of the British Labour Party:

> You learn that they have no children in local schools.
> You learn that they have no relatives on YTS.
> You learn that they don't have a loved one waiting in pain
> on a National Health Service list.

If this had been written in a text aimed at readers rather than hearers, it would almost certainly have been written as a single sentence, with no repetition of the first few words, and with 'and' at the start of the final item in the list:

You learn that they have no children in local schools, no relatives on YTS and no loved ones waiting in pain on a National Health Service list.

When reading the sentence, it is easy enough to see how the first few words 'You learn that they have' relate to each of the points. But if you had to listen to this version, you would have no way of knowing from the first few words that the speaker is launching into a list of things that 'you learn' – a fact that only becomes apparent to listeners after the second part of the sentence has got under way. At that point, you might suddenly realise that you hadn't been listening closely enough at the start of the sentence to be able to retrieve exactly what it was that links the points in the list together.

A simple and effective solution to this potential difficulty is to divide it all up into three separate sentences and, as in this case, to repeat the opening few words at the start of each one. By doing this, Mr Kinnock not only gave his audience plenty of time to take in each point before moving on to the next, but also provided repeated reminders that the points are all linked by things that 'you learn' about *them* (i.e. the then Conservative government). In a sense, this form of repetition can be thought of as the spoken equivalent of bullet points on a page, implicitly reminding the audience that a list of similar items is in the process of being delivered.

4. Repetition

The above example illustrates another interesting and important difference between the spoken and written word: the spoken version uses extensive repetition, whereas the written one does not.

As such, the written version follows the rule against the repetition of words, phrases and clauses that most of us work very hard to observe when we're writing. If, while composing a sentence, we notice that we have just repeated something that appeared in the previous one, we start looking for an alternative. This rule against repetition is so entrenched in the way we write that the designers of word-processing programs have been thoughtful enough to build in a thesaurus that enables us to summon up alternative words at the push of a button. When it comes to speaking, however, the rule against repetition no longer applies in the same way.

◖ Repetition to connect sentences

As the example from a speech by Neil Kinnock showed, certain forms of repetition are not just acceptable when speaking, but can be a positive asset from the point of view of a listening audience. In that particular case, it was used to establish a connection between a series of sentences. This form of repetition really comes into its own when you want to group together messages that take more than a few words to deliver. If they can be expressed in single words, you don't need to repeat them in order to make sure that the audience grasps the connection between them.

For example, if a speaker said, 'I have a dream about equality, fraternity and justice,' we would have no trouble getting the point. Repetition would not have added very much, and even comes across as unduly long-winded, as in:

I have a dream about equality,
I have a dream about fraternity,
I have a dream about justice.

But the six dreams described towards the end of Martin Luther King's famous speech in Washington D.C. in 1963 were each made up of at least a full sentence. If he had not repeated 'I have a dream' at the start of each one, it would have been much less clear to the audience that each successive point was a component of the same overall dream:

> *I have a dream* that one day this nation will rise up and live out the true meaning of its creed: 'We hold these truths to be self-evident: that all men are created equal.'
> *I have a dream* that one day on the red hills of Georgia the sons of former slaves and the sons of former slave owners will be able to sit down together at a table of brotherhood.
> *I have a dream* that one day even the state of Mississippi, a desert state, sweltering with the heat of injustice and oppression, will be transformed into an oasis of freedom and justice. **Martin Luther King**

🗩 *Repetition to increase impact*

Repetition is not only a useful way of making things clearer for audiences, but can also greatly increase the impact of the message you want to get across. For example, written in accordance with the repetition-avoidance rule, a famous excerpt from one of Winston Churchill's wartime speeches would have looked like this:

> We shall fight on the seas and oceans, in the air, on the beaches, on the landing grounds, in the fields, streets and hills.

Read it aloud, and then compare it with the actual version, in which he repeated the words 'we shall fight' no less than six times, the effect of which is to shift the emphasis from a list of places where fighting will take place to an unequivocal determination to *fight*.

> We shall fight on the seas and oceans,
> we shall fight ... in the air ...
> we shall fight on the beaches,
> we shall fight on the landing grounds,
> we shall fight in the fields and in the streets,
> we shall fight in the hills;
> we shall never surrender. **Winston Churchill**

Churchill used repetition in a similar way when describing the objective of the war:

> Victory!
> Victory at all costs,
> victory in spite of all terror,
> victory however long and hard the road may be.
> **Winston Churchill**

If he had not repeated the key word, the aim would have come across as much less emphatic, and even sounds rather lame: 'Victory at all costs, in spite of all terror, however long and hard the road may be.'

As will be seen in the discussion of rhetoric in Chapter 6, there are various other forms of repetition that are effective when speaking. For the moment, however, the important point is that it can be a positive disadvantage for speakers to follow the no-repetition rule that applies when writing, as they will miss out on using a technique that can greatly increase clarity and impact. I have sometimes seen speakers running into difficulties as a result of trying to avoid repetition: they start 'umming' and 'erring' in a desperate bid to find words that are different from those used in a previous sentence, when it would actually have been much more effective to have used them again.

Repetitive bogey words

Not all forms of repetition are helpful to an audience, and something that can easily become a distraction is the excessive repetition of a particular word or phrase, a habit that most of us have suffered from at one time or another. The commonest bogey words of this kind are *actually* and *basically*. Some speakers repeat one or other of these with such regularity that it becomes just as noticeable and irritating as repetitive *erring* and *umming*. The main difficulty is in discovering that we have a problem in the first place, as most members of audiences are far too polite to draw our attention to it. Here again, the use of audio or video recordings comes into its own as an aid to diagnosis. Once people have heard themselves repeating *actually*, *basically*, or some other word or phrase, they react with a combination of shock and a strong determination to eliminate the bogey words from their repertoire. Once we become aware of the problem, the cure lies in careful monitoring of what we are saying, and in making a conscious effort to avoid the particular word or words.

5. Active and passive

If you use a word-processing program, you'll almost certainly have noticed that, whenever you write something like *'it has been decided'*, the grammar checker springs into action to point out that this is the passive voice, and advises you to change it to the active 'we have decided'. Somewhere along the line, software designers seem to have got the idea that use of the passive is *always* a bad thing. Nor are they alone, as the passive gets a bad press in much of the literature on good writing style. The odd thing about this is that, if it really is something that should always be avoided, it's difficult to see why or how the linguistic tools for generating sentences with the passive voice would have ever evolved in the first place.

One situation in which the passive voice comes into its own is where we are in no position to specify who did the thing that is being referred to, as in 'my lawnmower has been stolen'. Nor does there seem to be anything particularly reprehensible about saying something like 'I'm delighted to have been invited to speak to you today', which, in spite of using the passive once, sounds a good deal more natural than the active alternative, 'Your invitation to me to speak to you today has delighted me.'

But the use of the passive can sometimes make life difficult for audiences by obscuring the precise meaning of a sentence. The following sentence implies that managers may have played a part in causing the malfunctions in the process. It is also not clear whether the aim is to change and eliminate the malfunctions or the managers (or both):

Identification and evaluation of malfunctions in the process by managers is required so that they can be changed and eliminated.

But use of the active makes it easy enough to get rid of the ambiguities and make the point easier to understand:

Managers must identify and evaluate malfunctions in the process so that we can change the processes and eliminate the problems.

◖ *The passive and neutrality*

As well as causing problems of understanding for an audience, use of the passive can add another thread to the cloak of formality. In the above example, the first version sounds more 'official' than the second. As such, it shows how the passive voice really comes into its own when you specifically want to convey neutrality and objectivity, or where you have good reasons for wanting to leave out any references to particular individuals. This is why it features so prominently in legal and bureaucratic documents, and is such a well-established convention in scientific and technical writings – all of which are areas where there is a premium on generality, objectivity and detachment.

The following alternative introductions to a research report show how the passive works to create an impression of detachment:

The study is based on a random sample of the population, and respondents were interviewed over a period of four weeks.

By leaving out details of the people involved, this concentrates on what was done, and describes it in a way that almost suggests that the study carried itself out without any human intervention at all. This has the advantage of implying that the same methodology would have produced the same results, regardless of who actually did the day-to-day work involved in completing the research. By contrast, using the active voice makes it necessary to include references to persons in the sentence, the effect of which is to remove some of the detachment:

> My research assistant selected a random sample from the population, and a part-time team of students interviewed the respondents over a period of four weeks.

The second version even implies that the researchers were amateurs, and that the project might not have been carried out quite so professionally or scientifically as is implied by the first one.

This example shows that there are occasions when a speaker will specifically want the material to come across as neutral and detached, and where the use of the passive is therefore perfectly appropriate. If this is not the case, however, we need to be wary about sounding as though we are speaking pedantic 'officialese', and coming across as more formal than intended.

✎ *The passive and responsibility*

One final point about the use of the passive is that the removal of references to particular individuals makes it very easy to compose sentences that exempt people from taking personal or collective responsibility for their actions. For example, a sentence like 'We have decided to fire 20 per cent of the workforce' may sound blunt and to the point, but at least the speaker is openly admitting to a share in the responsibility for the decision. But using the passive makes it all too easy to distance yourself from direct responsibility, as when this example is rewritten as: 'It has been decided that 20 per cent of the workforce is to be made redundant.'

There will, of course, be occasions when speakers deliberately want to distance themselves from particular decisions or actions, and the passive provides a simple and effective tool for doing this. On other occasions, however, you will create a better impression with audiences if you avoid obscuring the issue by unnecessary or excessive use of the passive.

6. Simplicity

The negative impact on audiences that can come from ignoring differences between the written and spoken word have so far had to do with grammar, word selection and sentence construction. The general message is that the interests of audiences are best served by keeping things as simple as possible on all fronts, and to be aware that there is much about the written word that will draw us in the opposite direction. But there is a second and even more important difference between written and spoken language that has nothing to do with syntax or grammar, but which can inflict just as much damage on an audience's ability to stay awake and follow what the speaker is saying. This is the way the two forms of communication compare when it comes to getting across large amounts of information, or information that is detailed, complex or technical.

II. INFORMATION OVERLOAD

When asked about the biggest single problem I have come across since starting to study speeches and presentations, I always give the same answer. Without any doubt at all, it is that far too many speakers spend far too much time trying to get far more detailed information across than it's possible to convey within the limitations of the spoken word. All too often, audiences are subjected to massive and painful information overload that serves little or no useful purpose. At best, they will retain no more than a fraction of what was said; at worst they will give up making the effort to pay attention altogether, fall asleep and end up no wiser than they were at the start.

1. Taking literacy for granted

The tendency of speakers to pack in as much as possible seems to reflect a widespread misunderstanding of how the spoken and written word compare in their capacity to handle detail and large volumes of information. This in turn may be a natural consequence of the high levels of literacy that have become a taken-for-granted part of our culture in recent generations. Reading and writing are the number one priority at the very beginning of our school days, enshrined by government as a compulsory 'literacy hour' in the daily timetable of English primary schools. As we go through the educational system, reading and writing remain at the heart of learning, grading and examination success or failure. In adult life, we start the day reading newspapers over breakfast or on the train to work. On arrival at the office, there are letters to be read and replied to, memos, reports and proposals to be read, not to mention the ever-increasing tidal wave of written words that has come in the wake of the e-mail revolution. In an environment so dominated by writing, it's hardly surprising that most people respond to any requests to give a presentation without giving so much as a second thought to any differences there might be between the spoken and the written word as alternative vehicles for communicating large amounts of information.

Since writing became such a taken-for-granted fixture of the modern world, there seems to have been a decline in our understanding of just how limited and restricted the spoken word is when it comes to dealing with detailed information. Indeed, it seems likely that the further we have left our pre-literate heritage behind, the poorer has our understanding of oral communication become. The starting point for that journey was the invention of writing, which, by most definitions of what counts as writing, was little more than 4,000 years ago, a mere fraction of a moment in the tens of thousands of years it took for *homo sapiens* to evolve. Yet although writing may be fairly new to our species, the technological and social changes that came in its wake would seem incredible to our pre-literate ancestors. Without writing, they lacked an ability to store knowledge in detail, to spread it across distances and to pass it on from one generation to another. However, once writing had been invented, philosophy, science and technology quickly followed. So too did the capacity to develop the bureaucratic and administrative systems on which larger-scale social and political entities could be founded. In essence, writing was the first really effective form of information technology, providing a means of storing and transmitting detailed knowledge that was far in excess of anything that could ever be achieved solely on the basis of the spoken word. The enormity of this gap may be a matter of no consequence to us for most of the time, but, when it comes to making speeches and presentations, we ignore it at our peril.

2. Writing in more detail than we can ever say

The nature of the difference is dramatically illustrated by the fact that a single page of a broadsheet newspaper, such as *The Times* or *The Guardian*, contains more words than a 20-minute news programme on radio or television. With another 20 or 30 pages to go, not to mention review sections, business pages, sports and other supplements, newspaper coverage of the news is clearly much fuller and far more detailed than anything that can be achieved even by news broadcasts lasting 30 or 60 minutes. The obvious point is that if there is a lot to say about a particular subject, there is nothing to stop us writing hundreds of pages about it. However, at a speaking rate of about 130 words per minute, it is equally obvious that half an hour will restrict us to about 4,000 words. Like editors of broadcast news programmes, then, speakers face the challenge of having to select, simplify, edit, summarise and shorten the mass of material that is potentially eligible for inclusion.

3. Resistance to simplification

Slides

Unfortunately for audiences, there are various obstacles that prevent speakers from getting down to the task of simplification with the diligence it deserves. The first, which is discussed in more detail in Chapters 4 and 5, comes from the development of slide projection technologies, and the widespread adoption of a slide-dependent style of presentation that has followed in its wake. This has made it possible for speakers to project huge amounts of detail on to a screen. The net effect of this has been to create the illusion that there is no problem in transmitting large volumes of complex and detailed information directly from a screen to the brains of the audience. And if you can put as much detail as you like up on a slide, why bother to simplify?

🔊 *Fear of sounding ignorant*

Some speakers resist simplification because they fear it will create a negative impression with the audience if they demonstrate anything less than the full extent of their knowledge of a subject. Indeed, it sometimes seems as though the main aim of some speakers is to parade every last detail, however tangential or irrelevant it may be to the main thrust of their argument, in front of the audience. In most situations, however, you don't need to work as hard as this to convince the audience that you know what you're talking about – for the simple reason that, without at least some advance recognition of your specialist knowledge or experience, you wouldn't have been given the chance to speak in the first place.

If you fall into the trap of including masses of information, in the hope of impressing an audience with your expertise, you may well end up achieving exactly the opposite of what you intended. Speakers who insist on wading through endless amounts of detail can easily give an audience the impression that they are insecure and lack the confidence to cut through the details to arrive at a clearly presented summary of the main points they want to get across. By contrast, if you use details sparingly to develop your argument, you stand a better chance of coming across as confident and authoritative, and are much less likely to leave your audience

> The biggest problem facing audiences is that too many speakers spend too much time trying to get far more detailed information across than it is possible to convey within the limitations of the spoken word.
> Effectiveness depends on being willing to simplify your subject matter beyond the point at which you feel comfortable.

in a battered state of bewildered incomprehension. The trouble is, of course, that people have often had to work long and hard to achieve the expertise needed to get to the point of giving a presentation on a particular subject, which means that leaving details on one side can be quite a painful and uncomfortable experience. But the cost of not doing this is so high that the motto I recommend people to follow is to *simplify your subject matter beyond the point at which you, as a specialist, feel comfortable.*

Fear of being caught out

Some of the surplus detail often featured in presentations and lectures consists of precautionary padding that seems to be motivated by a mistaken belief that we are just as accountable for what we say as for what we write. But speakers can achieve greater brevity and succinctness by exploiting the fact that the spoken word evaporates the moment it comes out of our mouths, whereas the written word has a permanence that enables it to be read by anyone who happens to stumble across it. This is no doubt why the law treats written defamation (libel) as a more serious offence than spoken defamation (slander), which highlights the need to be more careful about what we put down in writing than what we say.

This more cautious approach to writing extends way beyond the fear of falling foul of libel law. For example, authors of research reports in learned journals sometimes include sentences along the lines of 'On the basis of present evidence, it would appear that, all other things being equal, X is the case.' When speaking, however, whether in a radio interview or to some other non-specialist audience, we can afford to be much more definite, and can perfectly well get away with saying simply that 'X is the case'. The only purpose of the extra 15 words in the written version is to cover the author against the possibility that someone might know something that he or she does not. To an audience, however, the shorter version will obviously sound less cagey, less pompous and a good deal clearer than the longer one. In the unlikely event of there being someone in the audience who knows about some research that contradicts our claim, we can deal with the problem at question time. And, even if someone starts raising questions after hearing about it at a later date, we have the option, as a last resort, to claim that we were 'quoted out of context'.

Other manifestations of the hyper-cautious approach are exhibited by speakers who pepper their presentations with words like 'hopefully', 'perhaps' and 'maybe', or who open with lines like 'I'm going to try to explain why we need to ...' rather than 'I'm going to explain ...'. Speakers who opt for the balder versions not only come across as confident, but also spare their audiences having to cut through redundant verbiage for themselves. The only caveat is that there are obvious dangers in taking blunt speaking to extremes, as was dramatically illustrated in the case of Gerald Ratner, the jewellery boss whose business empire collapsed after a speech in which he described his company's products as 'crap'.

💬 *Introducing detailed documents*

Finally, resistance to simplification often arises because the aim of many presentations is to introduce detailed written documents, such as reports and proposals. A common mistake here is for speakers to try to go over as much as possible of what is already included in the accompanying written material. If people in the audience have read the report or proposal beforehand, they are likely to be much less impressed by an attempt to cover all the same ground than by a lively summary of the key points. It will be the same for any members of the audience who have not read the document in advance, because an interesting summary of the material is more likely to motivate them to go away and read up on the details for themselves. In other words, it is important to face up to the fact that the written and spoken word have different advantages and disadvantages. As speakers, our job is to summarise and give life to the main points – otherwise, we serve little useful purpose as far as the audience is concerned. The job of the written document is to give them as much detail and complexity as the subject deserves, and any attempt by a speaker to reproduce it in its entirety is doomed to end in failure.

The ideal relationship between a written report or proposal and a spoken presentation can be likened to the relationship between a 300-page novel and an adaptation of it for the stage, film or television that only lasts for an hour or two. The dramatised version is obviously the product of massive editing and abbreviation. However, if it goes down well with the audience, many of them will be motivated to read the unabridged novel, in all its constituent detail, for themselves. The equivalent challenge for anyone who has to give a presentation about a detailed report or proposal is to make the audience interested enough to want to read it.

4. Conclusion

The starting point of this chapter was that writing, like conversation, is not only a more familiar form of communication than speeches and presentations, but also involves important differences that need to be taken into account by speakers who want to avoid inflicting boredom and confusion on their audiences. One type of difference has to do with grammar, word selection, and sentence construction, and another with the way written and spoken language compare as vehicles for communicating information in quantity and in detail. In the quest to resolve both types of problem, the watchwords are the same: simplicity, brevity and clarity.

Summary

The written word differs from the spoken word in various subtle ways that need to be taken into account if you are to avoid inflicting boredom and confusion on your audience.

I. The cloak of formality

☐ If you speak in a 'hyper-correct' way, you risk sounding unduly stilted, wooden or pompous, and are unlikely to get your own personality across.

☐ Using words that are hardly ever heard in everyday conversation will make it more difficult for an audience to understand what you are talking about.

☐ Jargon and acronyms should be kept to an absolute minimum. If you must use them, make sure that the audience knows what they mean.

☐ If you always use the full forms of words that are usually shortened in conversation, ('will not' rather than 'won't', 'it is' rather than 'it's', etc.) you are likely to sound formal and stilted.

☐ As using slang and swearing may offend some members of an audience, the safest option is to avoid doing either.

☐ The longer and more complicated the structure of a sentence is, the more difficult it will be for audiences to make sense of it. So keep your sentences as short and simple as possible.

❏ Repeating the first few words at the start of each sentence in a sequence works like bullet points on a page, as it reminds the audience that a list of similar items is in the process of being delivered.

❏ Repetition is not only a useful way of making things clearer for audiences, but can also greatly increase the impact of the message you want to get across.

❏ Not all forms of repetition are helpful: the repeated use of a particular word like 'actually' or 'basically' is likely to distract the audience.

❏ Using the passive can sometimes obscure the precise meaning of a sentence.

❏ The passive tends to convey neutrality, objectivity, detachment or distance from direct responsibility for something – impressions that you may not always want to give.

❏ When it comes to word selection and sentence construction, the interests of audiences are best served by keeping things as simple as possible on all fronts.

II. Information overload

❏ Writing provides a means of storing and transmitting detailed knowledge far in excess of anything that can ever be achieved solely by the spoken word.

❏ One of the commonest mistakes of all is to try to get far more detailed information across to an audience than is possible within the limitations of the spoken word.

❏ The slide-driven style of presentation has enabled speakers to project huge amounts of detail on to screens, acting as a deterrent against simplifying the subject matter (see also Chapter 4).

❑ If you go through endless amounts of detail, you risk coming across as insecure and lacking in confidence.

❑ Simplifying the content (beyond the point at which you feel comfortable) not only makes it easier for the audience to follow, but also gives the impression that you are authoritative and in full command of your subject matter.

❑ In presentations associated with written documents like reports and proposals, it is almost always a mistake to include as much detail as possible. The aim should be to make your summary so interesting that your audience will want to go away and read it for themselves.

Part I
Exercises

The following exercises are designed to develop familiarity with the experience of reading aloud, and in organising texts in a way that will help to improve delivery. It is important to stay conscious at all times of how you are sounding. Even better is to record (audio or video) and review your work, and/or to get a friend, colleague or family member to give you feedback.

Sample texts can be drawn from almost anywhere, but best of all are scripts of well-known speeches, which are widely available in books and on websites. Speeches are best because they were originally written to be spoken, and only become famous because they had a greater than average impact on an audience. One of the easiest ways of obtaining such material is from the website www.americanrhetoric.com, which includes a section on the top 100 American speeches. This enables you to download the scripts, as well as audio recordings of some of the speeches. To be able to listen to how the original speaker delivered a speech at the same time as reading the text is an extremely useful way of getting a feel for the structures, style and rhythms involved in the language of public speaking.

For convenience, however, you may prefer to use the following closing sequence from a speech at a management conference:

🔊 *Specimen script for use in exercises 2–7*

To sum up, then, there's much to be done to meet the demands of the changing market.

We know we have to become better at what we do.

And we know what needs to be done.

All this will mean a change of attitude.

The old 'them and us' approach will have to go.

We need a new basis for our relationship with suppliers.

We've got to be much more proactive in the marketplace.

And we've got to streamline the way we make our purchases.

Because the brute fact is that there are only three alternative routes to increased profits: higher sales, higher prices or lower costs.

So how we deal with our suppliers has immense potential for reducing costs.

And reducing our costs will have a direct impact on increasing our profitability.

That's why I began by referring to what lies ahead as a landscape of opportunity.

And that's why I've shown you the map of the ground to be covered.

We know where to find the main roads to success.

We know the pitfalls to be avoided.

And we know the destination we want to reach.

All that remains now is to make sure we get there.

🔊 *Exercise 1 – Just a minute: avoiding* ums *and* ers

In the long-running BBC Radio 4 game show *Just a Minute,* panellists have to try to speak for a minute on a particular subject without hesitation, deviation or repetition. *Umming, erring* and *pausing* all count as hesitations that can be penalised, and much of the programme's humour derives from the sheer difficulty of speaking continuously for a whole minute. In this variant of the game, you don't have to worry about avoiding repetition, deviation or pauses. The sole challenge is to:

- ❏ Talk about any single topic for a whole minute without *umming* and *erring*.
- ❏ Whenever you find yourself about to produce an *um* or *er*, make yourself pause instead and then carry on. This will help you to become comfortable with the idea that regular pausing while speaking really isn't a problem when you're not engaged in conversation with other people.

🗨 Exercise 2 – Pauses in different places

To help to develop a sense for how pauses can affect the meaning and mood of a speech, use the sample speech at the beginning of this section:

- ❏ Go through it, pencilling in where you think it would be suitable to pause – using a single slash (/) for a short one and double slash (//) for a longer one.
- ❏ Experiment by putting the pauses in different places, and reading aloud to see how it affects mood and meaning.

🗨 Exercise 3 – Pauses of different length

This involves taking the previous exercise a step further by experimenting with pauses that last for different periods of time. Among other things, it shows how a pause that sounds long in conversation (e.g. half a second) is hardly noticeable in a speech or presentation. It's obviously impractical to speak and use a stopwatch at the same time, but there's a much simpler method of timing pauses. As soon as you stop speaking, start counting in your head as follows: 'one-one-thous-and-two-two-thous-and...'. Each sequence of four beats (one-one-thous-and) is equal to one whole second, so if you carry on speaking again after saying 'one-one' to yourself, you'll have paused for half a second.

❑ Take the text from the previous exercise, or prepare a new one. If you have not already done so, mark in some short pauses with a single slash (/) and some longer ones with a double one (//).

❑ Read aloud, counting two beats (one-one = half a second) at every single slash, and four beats (one-one-thousand = one second) at every double slash.

❑ If possible, record and listen to the result, and get feedback from someone else.

❑ Notice how, although you may feel strange delivering the speech in this way, it doesn't sound odd or artificial when you hear it played back.

🔈 Exercise 4 – Stressing different words

Take the text of a speech, which can be the same as the one you have already marked up with pauses, and underline or highlight at least one word in every sentence to be said with additional stress:

❑ Do this several times, reading it aloud with the stress on different words, to see what difference it makes to the meaning and mood of the sentences.

🔈 Exercise 5 – Varying intonation

You can also mark texts with guidelines to indicate where changes in intonation should occur. Some people put arrows pointing up and down (↑↓) to indicate points where they plan to shift their tone upwards or downwards. But it is easier and probably more effective to use a technique commonly used by actors when preparing their lines before rehearsals:

❑ Go through each sentence and think about what impression or meaning you want it to convey. Is it, for example, a factual statement or an opinion, or perhaps something you want to say ironically, seriously, challengingly, angrily, quietly, gently, etc.?

❑ Whatever you decide, write an appropriate word into the left-hand margin of the script, and then read the script aloud. The sight of marginal notes while reading is usually enough to prompt you to alter your intonation and deliver it in exactly the right way to convey the impression you're aiming for – just as the sight of a question mark is enough to prompt questioning intonation from a reader.

🔊 *Exercise 6 – Exaggerating conversational stress and intonation*

If you have completed all the exercises so far, you have already taken some important steps away from conversational mode. The final stage is to become comfortable with the idea of exaggerating your normal conversational intonation, and this can be done by bringing together all the techniques for marking up a script described in exercises 2–5 above:

❑ Mark pauses, pause lengths, prompt words in the margin and any words to be given extra stress.

❑ Take deep, slow breaths before the performance – and carry on using them when you pause during your speech. This will give you the fuel you need both to add the extra intonation and to speak more slowly.

❑ Read aloud and practise putting everything into effect at the same time. If, while you're reading it, you think it sounds somewhat 'over the top', then you have probably got it about right from an audience's point of view.

❑ If possible, record and listen to yourself. Better still, given that we are all our own most severe critics, get someone else to give you a second opinion on how it sounds.

🔊 Exercise 7 – Presenting in conversational mode

This involves doing almost the opposite of the previous exercise. However, even when speaking to a very small audience, it's not a good idea to sound too flat and monotonous, and a useful exercise is to carry on using the same fully marked-up script as in exercise 6 above. But:

❑ As you read it aloud, try to make it sound as if you were speaking to someone in a conversation.

❑ For useful guidance on this, listen closely to newsreaders on radio and television – or, if you can get access to them, speeches by Ronald Reagan, who was an outstanding exponent of how to make effective speeches in a chatty, conversational tone of voice – and then aim for a similar style of delivery.

❑ If possible, record and review your performance.

🔊 Exercise 8 – Using shorter options

If you *have not* yet realised that it *does not* sound as formal to use shortened forms like 'haven't' instead of 'have not', *I would* suggest that *you will* see the difference as soon as *you have* rewritten the words in italics in this paragraph. *You will* find that *it is* a very simple exercise that *will not* take you very long to complete. Once *you have* finished, *it is* a good idea to read this version and your revised one aloud. *You will* then be able to hear that yours *does not* sound quite as stilted as this one.

🔊 Exercise 9 – Using simpler words

Here is a small selection of the many words and phrases of the kind that are best avoided if you don't want to sound too formal or stilted. For each one, write down an alternative word with the same meaning that is more likely to be heard in everyday speech (e.g. *commence → start; endeavour → try; reimburse → repay*, etc.).

Ameliorate	In respect of	Remuneration
At this moment in time	In regard to	Prioritise
Circumvent	In accordance with	Predominant
Cognisant of	In excess of	Reimburse
Commence	In lieu of	Reiterate
Disseminate	In the event of	Scrutinise
Endeavour	Initiate	Subsequent
Enhance	Intimate	Supplement
Erroneous	Moreover	Supplementary
Expedite	Notwithstanding	Terminate
Forthwith	Ongoing	Thereafter
Facilitate	Optimal/optimum	Thereby
Feasibility	Parameters	Utilisation
Henceforth	Prior to	Whereas
Hitherto	Remittance	With regard to

● Exercise 10 – From passive to active

The following passage uses the passive 14 times (in italics).

❑ Rewrite in less formal-sounding language, deleting as many passives as possible.

❑ Then compare what the two versions sound like by reading both of them aloud.

Having been elected chairman of the Stylistic Enforcement Committee, I *have been asked* to ensure that everyone *is informed* about what *has been decided* about when the passive is *to be avoided*, and when it *may be used*. It *is recommended* that the use of passive *should be kept* to a minimum in situations where it is important that the speaker should not *be thought of* as trying to evade personal responsibility for actions that *have been taken*. However, if there is an advantage to be had by *being regarded* as neutral or detached, speakers *are permitted* to use the passive, on the grounds that it *can be relied* on to guarantee that such an objective *is achieved*.

● Exercise 11 – Dividing a long sentence into shorter ones

Divide the following sentence up into shorter ones that make the same point(s) in a clearer way. Then compare what the two versions sound like by reading both of them aloud.

One of the major challenges faced by anyone wishing to achieve significant improvements in their effectiveness at verbal communication is to develop an ability to select and combine suitable words, phrases and clauses together in such a way as to construct sentences that are not so long and complicated that listeners, who, unlike readers, do not have the luxury of being able to go through it a second time, have a reasonable chance of understanding the ongoing flow of talk and the various messages that the speaker is trying to get across.

🔊 Exercise 12 – Repetition

Divide the following into separate sentences, using repetition at the beginning or at the end of each one to emphasise the assurances being given to the company just taken over by Mergermongers Inc.

On behalf of the board of Mergermongers, I can assure you that we are not planning to close down factories and regional offices or strip assets and will be doing everything we can to avoid staff redundancies.

🔊 Exercise 13 – Simplification of content

When it comes to practising simplification, it's difficult to beat the kinds of exercises in précis that are, or at least used to be, a standard part of English lessons in schools. To get a feel for the problem of cutting out large amounts of detail, take a favourite book or film, and write a series of shorter and shorter summaries of the plot that still convey a recognisable outline of the story.

PART II
VISUAL AIDS AND VERBAL CRUTCHES

Reading from Slides and Talking with Chalk

Visuals Ancient and Modern

In the previous chapter, I suggested that the first thing people do when preparing a speech is to start writing. But this is not altogether an accurate description of how most speakers prepare presentations in the slide-driven era. Preparation now typically begins with putting some slides together with intent to *ad lib* about the contents of each one, and ends when the final slide is completed.

I. READING FROM SLIDES

1. Reliance on the written word

A 'slides first' approach to preparation runs a high risk of condemning the audience to suffer from the two main pitfalls associated with the language of the written word, long before the presentation actually takes place. First, because projectors enable words and

> Slides consisting of nothing but written words or numbers are the least helpful type of visual aid for an audience. They serve little useful purpose other than to remind speakers what to say next – at the very high price of putting audience attentiveness at risk, and, as often as not, confusing them with more information than they can comfortably take in.

sentences to be projected on to a screen, the speaker doesn't have to give much thought to the style of language to be used, let alone what it's going to sound like to the audience. The fact that so many slides amount to little more than lists of prompts for the speaker also means that people often spend too little time planning exactly what to say about each item, and end up having to make it up as they go along. The second drawback is that projectors also enable large quantities of detailed material to be displayed on the screen, tempting speakers into the trap of doing little or nothing to simplify and edit their content. The net result is that preparation that begins and ends with writing a set of slides is almost certain to result in a presentation that inflicts massive information overload on the audience, expressed in language that's likely to come across as unduly technical, formal or just plain rambling.

2. Gazing away

Armed with a collection of slides, the first priority of many speakers at the presentation itself is to get the projector switched on and the first exhibit in place as soon as possible. But slides work like magnets that draw people's eyes to the screen, inviting them to look away from the speaker – even though eye contact plays such an important part in maintaining audience attention (see Chapter 1). So the very first thing our speaker has done is to create an air of uncertainty as to where we should all be looking, while at the same time releasing us from some of the pressure to pay attention that comes with sustained eye contact. This raises the question of why anyone would want to deflect the audience's attention away from them, especially at the start of a presentation.

The answer is, or should be, that the risk will outweigh the disadvantages when you need to show the audience something that can't be easily communicated by words alone. Not surprisingly, then, the kinds of visual aid that audiences like best are those that help to clarify things for *them*, rather than ones that merely serve as a crutch for the speaker (see Chapter 5). Unfortunately, the overwhelming majority of slides that daily decorate the screens of conference rooms around the world fail this test: most of them consist of nothing more than lists of words and sentences that are, in effect, the speaker's notes.

3. Reading, listening or neither

For members of an audience, whose gaze has already been deflected from speaker to screen, the sight of written words provides another distraction that divides and threatens their continued attentiveness. As soon as we see writing, we can't help reading it, or at least trying to read it. So the speaker is now asking us both to break eye contact and to apply our brains to two things at once – reading and listening – regardless of any difficulty we may have in doing both effectively at the same time. Sometimes, the print is so small that we can't read it at all, and we become more and more irritated by being expected to do the impossible.

Nor is our mood much improved when we hear the words 'as you can see', or the more accurate, but no less annoying, 'you probably won't be able to read this'.

The torment of having to squint at unreadable slides has been eased by computer graphics and fonts big enough to be clearly visible. But now that we can read what's on the slide, we don't just look at the first line, but carry on reading, all the way down to the bottom of the screen. Now that we know what's coming next, the news value of what the speaker goes on to say is greatly reduced. Meanwhile, with our attention split between reading and listening, we often find that, by the time we get to the last line on the slide, we have lost track of where the speaker has got to. So we then start reading back up the screen – only to discover that the discussion has progressed no further than the first bullet point on the list. With five more to go, this slide alone could keep things going for another 10 or 15 minutes before we get to see the next one. In the days of the overhead projector, our fears about just how long the presentation was going to last were often amplified by the sight of mountains of acetates waiting to go on. Such visible warnings have been swept away by the arrival of computerised slides, and all we can do now is guess at just how many gigabytes lie in wait for us.

Whether reading the contents of slides, or reflecting on how long a presentation is going to take, members of an audience will inevitably find their attention being divided between the spoken and written word. But they're not alone, because slides made up largely of writing also cause problems for speakers. Some aren't sure whether to read them out word for word, or just leave them in the background for audiences to read at their leisure. Others announce a few moments of silence for people to read the slides for themselves. But just how long should you allow, and what are you supposed to do during the silence? Needless to say, none of these options impress audiences very much.

4. Cover up or build-up?

The same is true of what seemed, on the face of it, to be a perfectly rational response to the problem of audiences reading ahead, namely the practice of using a sheet of paper to cover up the bullet points on a slide and revealing them one by one. Ask audiences what they think about this, and the reaction is generally negative, ranging from mild irritation to intense annoyance. Some complain that they dislike the feeling of something being hidden from them; others that they feel they are being patronised. Yet ask these same people what they think about the computerised build-up of bullet points one by one, and you get a much more favourable response.

This raises the intriguing question of why audiences regard the animated build-up of bullet points as an acceptable way of preventing them from reading ahead. The most likely answer is that it works in a similar way to a type of visual aid with a long and distinguished track record both in holding audience attention and in getting points across effectively. This is the age-old practice of writing or drawing material on a blackboard, whiteboard or flip chart as you go along. And 'chalk and talk' is, of course, a medium through which most of us learnt a very great deal during all those years of formal schooling. In effect, the use of computerised techniques to build up bullet points or to animate graphs and diagrams, equips speakers with the capability to simulate what used to be done by writing and drawing on a board with chalk or a felt-tipped pen.

5. Innovation for better or worse?

The use of the past tense here may, of course, be a slight exaggeration, because a minority of speakers still do use chalk and talk – and almost always attract higher audience ratings than those who slavishly depend on textual slides. The advantages of chalk and talk are discussed in more detail in the second part of this chapter, but it's worth considering for a moment why it fell into disuse, and how it came to be replaced by a style of presentation that is so much less popular with audiences. The answer seems to lie in the convergence of two technological innovations: one was the invention of the overhead projector; the other was a very particular development in the evolution of photocopying machines.

It seems to have been forgotten that the overhead projector came into use to overcome a major problem in using chalk and talk when speaking to a big audience. Across a long distance, it's obviously difficult for people to see what is being written on the board. So overhead projectors were originally only to be found in large auditoriums and lecture theatres, where they were used in much the same way as blackboards. Part of the equipment was a roll of acetate for winding on whenever the portion showing on the screen was full, providing a convenient and effective alternative to writing or drawing on a blackboard.

Then came the development in photocopying technology that was to transform our whole approach to visual aids, and give birth to the new industry standard model of presentation. With the early photocopiers you could only make copies on paper, but the machines that came on to the market in the 1970s made it possible to copy directly on to acetate. Whether or not the research and development teams who invented these new machines deliberately set out to transform a whole generation's approach to presentation, this was to be their lasting legacy. It was also a lucrative break for the manufacturers of overhead projectors, whose sales increased dramatically as equipment came to be installed in smaller and smaller conference rooms – far away from their original natural habitat in the large auditorium. As more and more speakers took to using ready-made slides rather than chalk and talk, there was another bonus for the manufacturers: production costs could be cut by doing away altogether with the twin rollers for winding on the acetate rolls. These days, you hardly ever see any that still have them, and the few survivors hardly ever have a roll of acetate installed and ready for use. By the 1980s, acetate-friendly photo-copying machines had all but killed off the ancient art of chalk and talk, and spawned a new style of presentation that was to make life much more tedious for generations of audiences to come.

6. Why has the slide-driven presentation survived?

If the new style of presentation was an accidental result of techno-logical innovations that made life worse for audiences, why did it become so widely and firmly entrenched as the industry standard model? And why do people who don't much like being on the receiving end in an audience still conform to the model when making presentations of their own? The short answer to both these questions is ease and convenience for speakers. It was also positively encouraged by presentation skills training courses that taught it as good practice, not to mention computer graphics packages with an inbuilt bias towards the production of textual slides (see Chapter 5).

🔊 *Ease and convenience*

One of the great attractions of the slide-driven approach was that it offered an easy way of appearing to be prepared and professional. The mere fact that you had some slides to show was enough in itself to qualify it as a 'proper' presentation in the eyes of audiences, who were increasingly conditioned to expect nothing else. Regardless of how uninspiring the language was, or the sheer weight of information overload, such presentations were unlikely to be much worse than any of the hundreds of others to which the audience had been subjected. Add to this the prospect of being able to accumulate a collection of slides in a filing cabinet, or on a computer disk, and you had the further convenience of being able to mix and match as the occasion required, saving the time and effort that would otherwise be needed to start from scratch with new material for the next presentation.

🔊 *Standardisation*

Meanwhile, large corporations seized on the prospect of imposing a uniform and consistent message across different presentations by issuing standardised sets of slides to their workforce. European subsidiaries of American multinationals became used to receiving slides for translation from English into the local language. As far as the production of presentations was concerned, whether by speakers themselves or by anonymous slide writers at head office, this was all very convenient. But it showed little or no sensitivity for the end consumers who were condemned to listen to the presentations. Business people may have spent many thousands of hours extolling the virtues of putting the customer first, but seem to have spent little or no time attending to the needs of their audiences. As a result, there's nothing particularly unusual about hearing account managers giving presentations in reverential tones about 'bespoke solutions' and 'meeting your needs as the customer', while boring for England.

The only glimmer of hope was that local subsidiaries would occasionally resist having presentations imposed on them from on high, as occurred when an American computer manufacturer was launching new products. Its German branch set about translating every word on every slide that was sent to them from the USA. But their British counterparts were so appalled by the amount of detail on the slides that they established a special group, whose job was to scrap them and design presentations for UK audiences from scratch.

❧ Freedom from notes

In their sales literature, the manufacturers of overhead projectors used to proclaim yet another alleged benefit of the acetate revolution: *with our machines, you can speak without having to use any notes*. This was an extraordinary claim on two counts. In the first place, it can hardly have escaped their notice that one of the commonest uses to which their products were being put was to project speakers' notes on to screens. So they didn't free people from using notes: all that happened was that speakers stopped glancing down at their notes and started looking at the screen to find out what to say next.

A second curious aspect of the promise to liberate speakers from notes was the apparent belief that there was something wrong or shameful about being seen to be using notes. This ignored a rather obvious fact: in all traditions of public speaking, whether preaching, lecturing, political speechmaking or giving a best man's speech at a wedding, it is, and always has been, perfectly normal for speakers to use notes. There are even cases of people pretending to use notes, when in fact they don't have any at all. For example, in the later years of his life, the late Lord Stockton (former Prime Minister Harold Macmillan) would give after-dinner speeches from cards that, unknown to the audience, were completely blank. This was presumably intended to give the impression that he had prepared the speech specially for the occasion, and wasn't simply repeating one he had given so many times before that he knew it off by heart. As will be seen in Chapter 9, notes can be an important aid to presentation, and only become a problem for audiences if you spend all or most of your time looking down at them.

'Hard copy of slides available afterwards'

Another apparent advantage of the new orthodoxy was that it seemed to bring with it a means of insuring against the possibility that audiences might not take everything in at a single hearing. So it became common practice to distribute hard copies of the slides after a presentation, in the hope that the recipients would not only keep them and read them, but would also be able to understand the mass of shorthand headings and bullet points. Unfortunately, as anyone who has ever been issued with such a pack will know, it's rare indeed for all these hopes to be fulfilled. Some sets go straight in the waste bin, and others are filed away, never to be seen again. Even those that do get a second glance tend to be much less use than their authors would have hoped. This is because lists of bullet points are usually much harder to read than continuous prose, and invariably need further explanation to make sense.

Even if the speaker did this during the presentation, their elaborations are unlikely to be remembered by readers who come back to the material days or weeks later.

Teaching bad habits

Meanwhile, presentation skills training courses supported the institutionalisation of the industry standard model by teaching it as good practice. This was dramatically brought home to me on a consultancy project in which I had been invited to evaluate a company's in-house course. In the opening session, the tutor demonstrated one of his central recommendations by using 24 overhead slides in the first hour. The trainees were told always to follow his example: one bullet for every point they wanted to make; five bullets per slide; each bullet to consist of a full sentence, as one- or two-word headings were not enough. It wasn't just the rigidity of his rules that worried me. What baffled me most was that he didn't seem to think there was anything odd about expecting his audience to take in 120 'dos' and 'don'ts' in an hour – at a rate of two per minute. When I asked him what made him think that this was good practice, he replied: 'I've seen other speakers doing it like that.' Not surprisingly, perhaps, he also admitted that he'd never thought of asking audiences how they felt about it.

This may be an extreme example, but many people have told me that they have been on courses that teach the virtues of a slide-driven approach to presentation, without ever questioning its effectiveness from an audience point of view. The consolidation of the industry standard model was therefore speeded along by training programmes that were informed by observations of what more and more speakers were doing, and without any attempt to find out how well or badly it was going down with audiences. If anyone had bothered to inquire, they would have come up with a result that can be easily replicated by asking people a simple question: how many slide-driven presentations have you heard in which the speaker came across as really enthusiastic and inspiring? Having now posed this question to hundreds of people, I can report that most have to think quite hard to recall even a single instance, and no one has ever come up with a number higher than two.

7. Speaking from the screen

If successful presentations from words on a screen are such rare events, it presumably means that a dependence on slides makes things difficult for speakers as well as audiences. And there are at least two main reasons why it is a style of delivery that produces so few effective performances. The first is that, because the presentation has been half-written out on the slides, speakers rarely give enough thought in advance to exactly what, or how much, they are going to say about each bullet point. This puts them in the position of having to improvise on the spot; only the quick-thinking, articulate few are able to avoid coming across as rambling and disjointed.

A second, and perhaps more fundamental, source of trouble is that speaking from notes projected on a screen is a style of communication with no obvious parallels in any other area of our talking lives. It therefore feels strange and unnatural to us, and adds another dimension to our nervousness and unease. Part of the problem is that, like audiences whose attention is divided between reading and listening, speakers are also struggling to do two things at once. As if establishing good rapport were not challenging enough in itself, speakers also have to be confident (and competent) enough to manipulate electronic projection equipment at the same time as they are speaking. And, just as audiences are not sure whether to focus on the speaker or the screen, speakers too find their eyes being pulled in opposite directions from audience to screen and back again. If more of us were natural actors or competent technicians, perhaps it would be easier to make a better job of playing out such a complicated role. But the fact is that the world of presentations is populated by large numbers of unskilled actors and technicians, struggling to perform in a style that is by no means guaranteed to impress or inspire an audience. Under these circumstances, it's hardly surprising that confident and articulate conversationalists so often find themselves debilitated by nerves and anxiety, or that inspiring and enthusiastic slide-driven presentations are such rare events.

8. Verbal crutches or visual aids?

This title is deliberately intended to sum up the central dilemma when it comes to making effective use of visual aids. None of the discussion so far should be taken as meaning that they are inherently useless and have no place in presentations or speeches. The point is that the type of visual aid that poses the worst problems, both for audiences and speakers, is a sequence of slides made up of nothing but written words – the verbal crutches that are there as prompts for the speaker, distractions for the audience and repositories of information too extensive or too complex for them to be able to take in.

Not surprisingly, and as we shall see in the next chapter, the visual aids that audiences rate most highly are ones that are genuinely *visual*. The acid test of a good visual aid is that it helps the audience's understanding or appreciation, and is not merely there to help the speaker to remember what to say. If a particular style of visual aid goes down well with audiences, this is obviously good news for presenters. So too is the fact that the types of visuals that audiences like also happen to be ones that make it easier for you to communicate in a more natural and comfortable manner.

II. 'CHALK AND TALK'

When explaining to someone how to get to a particular destination, we quite often draw a map on a piece of paper at the same time. We write in the names of streets or landmarks along the way, and mark out the route with a pen. This method of showing people how to get from one place to another, how something works, or what something looks like, is commonly used in everyday conversation, and is a very efficient way of conveying many different kinds of information. The fact that this is such a natural and normal means of communication probably explains the enduring appeal of chalk and talk. Unlike the projection of completed lists on to screens, writing and drawing on a board or flip chart is a logical extension of an effective way of getting messages across that is familiar to everyone. Audiences obviously wouldn't be able to see what we're putting on the back of an envelope, so we simply do the same thing on a bigger scale, and on a vertical surface that everyone can see.

The fact that there is something more natural about using chalk and talk than speaking from lists projected on to screens may be the most general reason for its enduring popularity with audiences. But it also has a number of more particular advantages over the model of presentation that has largely replaced it. As was mentioned earlier, at least some of these can be simulated by exploiting the more dynamic features of programs like PowerPoint. Whether you are interested in trying your hand at chalk and talk, or in improving the impact of computerised slides, it's important to know what these benefits are.

1. Advantages of chalk and talk
🦗 *Focus of attention*
If the projection of slides inevitably divides the attention of the audience between looking at the speaker and looking at the screen, this is much less of a problem when you write or draw something on a flip chart. For obvious reasons, you are never more than an arm's length away from the thing you are inviting the audience to look at. Their focus of attention is therefore concentrated on a narrow visual field that includes both you and visual material. This means that they don't have to keep glancing repeatedly from side to side across the much wider gap that would be between you and the slide on a screen.

🦗 *Talking about what everyone is looking at*
A second advantage of writing things up as you go along is that it makes it much easier to achieve better coordination between what you are saying and whatever it is that you're asking the audience to look at. For example, while writing up a word, it's very easy to say the same word at the same time. It's also easy to describe a drawing or diagram as you are drawing it. This means that you are not putting the audience in the position of having to read up and down lists, trying to work out which item is the one you are

currently talking about. So another potential source of distraction associated with slide-driven presentations is neatly avoided.

🗨 Pace of delivery

Perhaps the most important advantage of putting things on a board or flip chart as you go along is that the pace of your delivery will be more closely in tune with the pace at which audiences can comfortably take in new information. A basic feature of the way spoken language works is that there has to be a close match between the speed at which we are able to produce talk and the speed at which we are able to understand it. If this were not so, it's difficult to see how it would be possible for conversationalists to produce turns as soon as the previous one has finished, and conversations would be punctuated by long delays while we worked out the meaning of what had just been said and what response to make to it. One of the problems with complex slides is that they suddenly confront audiences with much more information than can be taken in at a glance. But with chalk and talk it's impossible to put up large amounts of material all at once, so audiences don't have the problem of trying to take in a lot in a very short space of time.

🗨 Dynamic effects

Chalk and talk also opens up the opportunity to introduce elements of surprise that can make things more interesting for an audience. On one course, for example, a presenter started out by using a slide of the following graph to illustrate a point about the relationship between high-fibre diets and mortality rates. The gist of his argument was that, as the intake of fibre increases, mortality rates decrease – but only up to a point: too much fibre and death rates start to rise. The problem with putting the completed graph on a slide was that it gave the game away too soon: by the time he got to the interesting news about death rates increasing, it was no longer news to us, as we'd already seen the trend for ourselves from the shape of the curve. In a second exercise, he decided to draw the graph on a flip chart. After explaining what the axes represented, he marked in the downward curve while talking about the decrease in death rates, at which point he stopped drawing the line. Then, as he told us that there comes a point where death rates start to rise again, he drew in the upward part of the curve. The audience's response was unanimous: everyone agreed that withholding this piece of information until completing the graph was a much more interesting and effective way of presenting the data than when he had put up the completed version all at once.

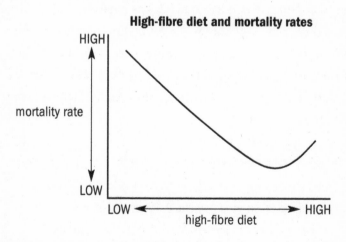

High-fibre diet and mortality rates

With a little advance planning, it's easy enough to produce such dynamic effects with chalk and talk. But it's also possible to simulate them by using the animated functions in programs like PowerPoint.

As was mentioned earlier, building up bullet points one by one is a way of simulating what speakers do when they write headings on a board. But you can also build graphs and charts up bit by bit, while giving a running commentary on what they show. At the click of a mouse, you can make lines and arrows move across the screen in different directions, as if drawn by an invisible hand.

Spontaneity and authority

Not all the advantages of chalk and talk can be simulated with computerised slides. For example, when you set to work on a flip chart, there's an element of spontaneity and immediacy involved. From an audience point of view, whatever is being written or drawn is being done here and now for the sole benefit of everyone in the room; it is not merely a pre-packaged list or chart that was prepared in advance by your secretary, or circulated from head office. Instead of being dependent on slides as prompts for what to say next, speakers who put things up on a flip chart as they go along come across as being in full control of their material. It conveys an air of confidence, authority and command over the subject matter, an impression that is so often sadly lacking from the slide-driven presentation.

> Writing or drawing on a board or flip chart has a very long history of helping audiences to follow an argument. It not only constrains speakers to develop their arguments at a comfortable pace for the audience, but can also convey an impression of authority, spontaneity and liveliness.

Even if you're afraid that you might forget what to put up next, you can easily achieve an appearance of spontaneity and authority with a little preliminary planning and a light touch with a very fine pencil. Headings, numbers or diagrams can be drawn in or written up very faintly in advance, so that they are visible to you but not to the audience. All you have to do then is to copy or trace the material at appropriate moments during the presentation, and the audience will marvel at your confident command over the subject.

Liveliness

In small meetings, and especially when sitting around a table, it's quite common to feel torn between staying in your seat or standing up. But having something to put up on a flip chart is a perfect excuse for getting to your feet. And once you are standing up and writing something on the chart, you can stay there for the rest of the presentation. This has advantages both for you and your audience. From your point of view, being seated makes it more difficult to break out of conversational mode into presentational mode, so that the presentation is likely to suffer from the kinds of problems discussed in Chapter 2. Movement from table to flip chart not only looks perfectly natural, but also helps to drain away some of the adrenalin and reduce tension and nervousness (see Chapter 11). Observations from workshops suggest that standing up results in a more animated presentation, with audiences often noting that the speaker's delivery became much livelier once they had got up from the table and started moving about.

🔍 *Low tech – low impact?*

The assumption that presentations have to be accompanied by slides has become so widely entrenched that people often worry that they might look unprofessional if they do something as apparently antiquated and makeshift as writing on a flip chart. But I know of no instance over the last 15 years in which someone who has tried out chalk and talk has come to regret it. The following two examples are typical of countless similar instances that could be mentioned. In one, a firm of human resources consultants had to present regular progress reports to their clients on the work they were doing for them. After one of our courses, they decided to give up using slides, as they had always done in the past, and started to use flip charts. In another case, someone whose job involved giving regular briefings to teams working in different parts of the country decided, in his own words, 'to take the risk' of using a flip chart instead of slides. In both cases the outcomes were the same: the speakers reported that they felt they had enjoyed much better rapport with their audiences – a view endorsed by the fact that the feedback had been much more favourable than when they had used slides.

2. Avoiding common pitfalls

🔍 *Writing too much or too slowly*

Using chalk and talk is, of course, not all plain sailing. If you write or draw too much on the chart at once, you run the risk of spending too long standing with your back to the audience. So it's important only to put up a little at a time, and to get it on the flip chart as quickly as possible. This means avoiding whole sentences and long words, using shorthand where necessary.

✐ Handwriting

Although people often worry about not having very neat handwriting, this doesn't seem to bother audiences very much. After all, what you put up on a board or flip chart is not being created as a permanent record, but is merely a temporary illustration or heading relevant to the particular point you are making. If you plan to draw graphs or tables that include numbers or words, it's a good idea to draw in the axes or grids beforehand, and so spare the audience from having to wait around and watch your artistic efforts. Then all you have to do is to fill in the curves on the graph, or put numbers or words into blank boxes at appropriate moments as you go along.

✐ Dud pens

Another pitfall to be aware of is that the conference rooms of the world are stocked with felt-tipped pens of different colours. Some of these, like green and red, are difficult to see from a distance, and can cause even bigger problems for people who are colour blind. Whenever possible, always use black or dark blue pens, reserving other colours for the occasional underlining or ringing of key points. Conference rooms of the world are also mined with booby traps in the form of pens that have run out of ink. Unlike chalk, which was cheap and wore down to almost nothing, felt tips look expensive enough to deter people from throwing them away. So you always need to check that they work before you start. Well-prepared speakers also play safe by taking their own supply with them.

3. The visualiser

Although the use of chalk and talk obviously works best in relatively small-scale settings where everyone in the audience can see the flip chart or whiteboard, the same results can also be achieved by writing on rolls of acetate on an overhead projector. A more versatile development of this is the visualiser, which consists of a video camera pointing downwards from about the same height as the reflecting lens on an overhead projector. It will project more or less anything placed under it up on to the screen, whether it's a slide, picture or even a page from a book.

On one occasion I saw a speaker, equipped with nothing more than a visualiser, a felt-tipped pen and a few sheets of A4 paper, receive a rapturous response from an audience of 800 people. On the sheets of paper, he drew pie charts and various other diagrams that got progressively more complicated as he warmed to his theme. As his subject was the history of pensions and the complexities and contradictions that have arisen over the years, the complicated diagrams that he ended up with were perfectly fitted to the argument he was presenting. His visual aids were, in other words, genuinely visual, and included no bullet points or lists of written material.

4. Conclusion

The slide-driven presentation that has become the industry standard model has resulted in a style of presentation that does little to inspire or enthuse audiences. The problem is at its worst when the slides consist of nothing but text or tables of numbers. Such heavy reliance on written words and numbers almost guarantees that the presentation will contain far too much information, and be presented in a form of language that is likely to be dull and boring. It also means that the audience's attention will be divided between trying to listen and read at the same time.

The history of the modern business presentation is a sorry tale in which the overhead projector, a technological development designed to overcome the problem of seeing chalk and talk from a distance, gave rise to a style of delivery that had much more to do with the convenience of speakers than with improving the lot of audiences. As a result, writing and drawing things on boards and flip charts fell into disuse, even though it remains popular with audiences.

But audiences are not averse to *all* kinds of slides. In fact, one of the biggest, and as yet under-used, advantages of computerised graphics is the ease with which you can create professional-looking pictorial images. The importance of this is that, as we shall see in the next chapter, it is the genuinely *visual* visual aids that audiences like the best.

Summary

1. Disadvantages of wordy slides

❏ Textual slides tend to lead into the two main pitfalls associated with the written word – uninspiring language and information overload – even before you give the presentation.

❏ When audiences have to read and listen at the same time, they won't be paying full attention to what you are saying.

❏ If you haven't planned what to say about each bullet point it's likely to sound as though you're stumbling your way through a series of lists.

❏ Eye contact can be seriously diminished by (a) speakers spending too much time looking at the screen and (b) audiences alternating their gaze between speaker and screen.

❏ Speakers can block the audience's view by standing between them and the screen.

❏ Speaking while trying to manipulate overhead and computerised technology can be a source of distraction and tension – so make sure you practise and familiarise yourself with the equipment.

2. Advantages of chalk and talk

❏ *Focus of attention:* Because you are at an arm's length from what you are writing or drawing, audience attention is not continually divided between having to look from speaker to screen and back again.

❑ *Coordination of the talk and the visual:* Writing and drawing while speaking ensure a close fit between what you are saying and the visual, which makes it easier for audiences to relate what they are hearing to what they are looking at.

❑ *Pace of delivery:* Having to develop your argument step by step makes it easier for audiences to follow than when they are confronted with a large amount of information all at once.

❑ *Spontaneity and authority:* It gives the impression that you are in control of your material – even if you are copying or tracing very fine pencil lines that had been put there beforehand.

3. Disadvantages of chalk and talk

❑ If you write too much or too slowly, it will (a) slow things down too much, and (b) result in spending long periods with your back to the audience.

❑ Felt-tipped pens may have run out. Check them beforehand, or take your own with you.

❑ Some colours can't be seen clearly at a distance, so avoid red and green in favour of black or dark blue whenever possible.

4. Simulating chalk and talk

By enabling you to build up bullet points and other images one by one, programs like PowerPoint make it possible to simulate some of the advantages of chalk and talk (for more on the pros and cons of PowerPoint, see Chapter 5).

Showing What You Mean

Visuals for Viewers

It pleases me well to observe a neat idea enter the head of a lecturer which he will immediately and aptly illustrate or explain by a few motions of his hand – a card, a lamp, a glass of water, or any other things that may be near him.
Michael Faraday

... in recalling their impressions they almost invariably say not 'we were told' but 'we were *shown*.'
Lawrence Bragg

(*Advice to Lecturers: An Anthology taken from the writings of Michael Faraday and Lawrence Bragg.* London: Royal Institution, 1974.)

Although audiences don't much like looking at endless lists of bullet points, there are, as Faraday notes, plenty of other things that they do like looking at. In particular, they like to be *shown* things that help them to understand what a speaker is talking about. This is borne out by the fact that the visual aids that most often attract positive ratings from audiences are ones that are genuinely *visual* or *pictorial,* rather than verbal or numerical. So the first part of this chapter offers a guide to the types of visual aids that viewers and listeners actually do find useful.

The good news is that the increasing availability of computerised graphics programs like PowerPoint not only make it possible to simulate some of the advantages of talk and chalk (see Chapter 4), but also have tremendous potential for generating the kinds of visual aids that audiences like. But realising that potential is not without its problems. One is that the production of pictorial slides, such as charts and diagrams, is much more complicated than producing lists of bullet points, which means that you have to be prepared to invest a good deal of time and effort in learning how to make the most of them. Another problem is that you often have to adapt the standard templates if you want them to be simple enough to help the audience, or clearly visible from the back row. But the most frustrating thing of all about PowerPoint is that it positively encourages speakers to produce the very types of slide and presentation that are least likely to impress audiences (see Chapter 4). The full extent of this problem is explored further in the second part of this chapter, which warns against an uncritical acceptance of the assumptions on which much of the program is based.

I. VISUAL AIDS LIKED BY AUDIENCES

1. Objects, props and demonstrations

A vivid image from the UK General Election of 1979 was a picture of Margaret Thatcher using a pair of scissors to cut a pound note in two. Inflation was a major issue in the campaign, and this was her way of showing how much the currency had suffered during the preceding years of Labour government. Forty years earlier, Prime Minister Neville Chamberlain had returned from his Munich meeting with Hitler brandishing a piece of paper, and declaring 'Peace in our time'. On the 10th anniversary of Margaret Thatcher's premiership, Paddy Ashdown, then leader of the Liberal Democrats, held up a 10-year-old newspaper in the House of Commons with the headline *'Thatcher says she'll quit after 10 years'*, and asked if she intended to keep her promise. The sequence was reported on most of the prime-time television news bulletins later that day.

These examples show that holding up an object while referring to it can be enough to strike a chord with an audience. In the context of a business presentation it might be something as simple as a report, a proposal or a handout that is going to be distributed afterwards. But the scope for using objects and props to illustrate a point is obviously more or less infinite. On one occasion I worked with a client in Spain, who held his audience in rapt attention after starting his presentation by setting fire to a 200 Peseta note. At a conference on product liability law, one of the speakers aroused the interest of his audience by holding up a rather nondescript-looking piece of metal during the introduction to his presentation. As he did so, he explained that, as the manufacturer of such clips, he was potentially liable to multi-million pound damages claims in the event of failure by any one of the thousands his company had produced. For the first several minutes, he kept the audience guessing, before revealing that the clips were used to fix the overhead lighting above motorways in position.

Whether you merely hold up a report, a product or, in more practical mode, take an engine apart to show how it works, the use of objects and props almost invariably gets a positive rating from audience members. Demonstrations, ranging from scientific experiments to home-made jam making, have always been an effective way of showing people how to do things that are complicated and difficult to describe in the abstract. But, as with all visual aids, there are some potential pitfalls. The first is that audiences tend not to be very impressed by the use of objects that are not obviously relevant to the point being made, especially if they appear too gimmicky, or are being used purely for the sake of livening up an otherwise boring presentation. Second, careful planning and practice are needed if you are to avoid embarrassing disasters. Audiences quickly lose confidence if your demonstrations fail to work, or if you seem unsure when handling your props. Third, you should be very wary of passing an object around for people to inspect for themselves. This is for the obvious reason that it will become a source of distraction that will continue for however long it takes for everyone to have a look at it – by which time you may find yourself struggling in vain to get their interest back.

2. Pictures

The much-quoted line 'A picture tells a thousand words' would perhaps be more accurate if it read 'a picture *can sometimes* tell a thousand words'. Carefully selected pictures certainly can enable

> The test of a good visual aid is whether it enables the speaker to explain something that would be difficult to get across in any other way. The ones that most regularly succeed in this, and are rated most highly by audiences, consist of genuinely visual or pictorial material rather than text or raw numbers.

you to show an audience something that would otherwise take a very long time to describe in the abstract, and, more often than not, they get favourable ratings from the audience. This has been true at least since the magic lantern shows became a popular form of entertainment in the days before the advent of movies. Later on, the development of 35mm photography widened the scope for talks based on a series of colour transparencies. Some of the best classes I ever attended were by an art teacher who revelled in talking us through slides of famous paintings. The same was true of an inspired Women's Institute lecturer, who used sets of colour transparencies to illustrate her talks on the dry stone walls of the Lake District. The key to both these speakers' success was that they understood the need for careful selection of the slides, and equally careful advance preparation of the accompanying commentary.

☜ Editing pictures

The main drawback of pictures as visual aids will be familiar enough to anyone who remembers the days when colour photography first became a mass pastime. Prints were expensive, and the main medium was the 35mm slide that had to be projected on to a screen, or viewed in rather unsatisfactory hand-held viewers. It was an era when the return of friends and relations from holidays was a source of dread and foreboding, bringing with it the awful prospect of having to sit in the dark for as long as it took for them to show every slide from every roll of film they had shot on their travels. As if that were not bad enough, they would accompany their pictures with rambling commentaries, punctuated by apologetic explanations along the lines of 'you might not be able to see this very well, but it's me holding up the Leaning Tower of Pisa'.

So a first priority in using pictures must always be ruthless editing. As for how many slides you should use per minute, or for a five or 10-minute presentation, the answer is that it could be one or 21, depending on the point you want to get across. I once saw a doctor give a brilliant 15-minute talk on a particular illness, in which his only visual aid was a simplified picture of the internal organs of the human body. On another occasion, I saw an architect show 20 pictures of different buildings in not much more than a minute. The doctor needed to be able to point to various details on the picture from time to time during his presentation; the architect wanted to give his audience a general impression of what his buildings looked like. Completely different approaches succeeded in getting the points across to the audience, which underlines the fact that it's a mistake to think that there is some golden rule about the ideal number of slides per minute that all presenters should follow.

Sequencing pictures

Some years ago, I went to a talk on renovations that had been carried out on a medieval village church. The speaker started out by showing about 20 pictures of crumbling stone and other parts of the fabric that had been in need of repair. He then went through another 20 slides with pictures of what each trouble spot looked like, now that the repairs had been completed. For reasons that will become clear in the next chapter, contrasting 'before' with 'after' had the potential to be an extremely effective way of dealing with the subject. But the trouble was that it wasn't until the twenty-first slide that we got to see what the very first problem looked like after it had been repaired, and not until the twenty-second one that we could see how the second problem had been dealt with – and so on. This meant that, by the time we saw the pictures of the renovated parts of the fabric, it was more or less impossible to remember how bad they had been in the first place. His comparisons would have worked far better if he had shown the 'before' and 'after' pictures immediately after each other. Then we could have seen at a glance what a good job they had done, and perhaps even been persuaded to donate more money for the next phase of renovation. The obvious lesson to take from this is that careful planning of the sequence in which the slides are to be shown is essential in order to get the key points across to the audience with maximum clarity.

✒ Clipart and cartoons

As with objects and props, it's important not to use pictures simply for the sake of using them. This has become an ever-present temptation thanks to the huge libraries of banal Clipart images that are built into so many software packages. A related hazard is the cartoon, and I have often been asked whether it is a good idea to liven up a presentation by inserting these from time to time. The answer is that I have hardly ever seen it work. One reason is that they are often only marginally relevant to the subject matter, and therefore make you look as if you know you are boring the audience, and are desperately hoping that the cartoon will some-how help to retrieve the situation. Another problem is that the humour of many cartoons depends on the caption underneath, which is often printed in letters so small that no one can read it. Even if they can read it, they will do so at different speeds, which means that they're unlikely to get the point and laugh at exactly the same time. Worse still, they may not get the point or not think it funny enough to be worth a laugh.

Looking out for pictorial possibilities

So long as pictures are relevant to the subject matter, they can usually be relied on to go down well with audiences. It's therefore a good idea to be continually on the lookout for illustrative mate-rial that you might be able to use. Some things that may not seem to be obviously pictorial in the first place can often make more of an impact by being turned into pictures. For example, I have seen scores of slides proudly displaying a list of clients to whom the speaker's company has supplied goods or services. When asked about the purpose of these, no one has ever said that they are expecting the audience to remember them all. Usually, the aim is to create a favourable impression by showing that well-known organisations have enough faith in the speaker's company to buy their products or services – in which case, a slide made up of famil-iar corporate logos is a more vivid way of conveying the general impression they want to make.

3. Video

The almost universal availability of video has made it very easy to use moving pictures to illustrate talks and presentations. An example of this that went down extremely well with an audience was a short clip from a Grand Prix motor race. It showed the cars coming towards the camera in neat formation until a wheel came off one of them and caused a multiple pile-up. As the scene unfolded, the speaker gave the following perfectly timed comments:

Video scene	Commentary
Cars travelling in neat formation	We know from experience that everything can appear to be going smoothly and according to plan ...
Wheel comes off leading car	Then something unforeseen happens, and before you know where you are ...
Cars crashing into each other	one unfortunate event can have a whole series of knock-on effects that quickly result in total chaos.

The speaker's subject had nothing whatsoever to do with motor racing, but the sequence provided a vivid introduction to some of the key management issues facing her company.

This example shows that, as with still pictures, the effective use of video depends on careful planning of what examples to include, the sequence in which they are to be shown, and the commentary to be associated with each one. If several clips are involved, it's always best to copy them all, in the order in which they are to be played, on to a single demonstration tape or PowerPoint show. Then all you have to do is press a button as and when required. Otherwise, the audience will be condemned to watch your fumbling efforts to change from one tape to another. It's even more disastrous if you have to wind a tape backwards and forwards to find the next clip. This actually happened at an international conference, when an American professor had made the mistake of assuming that the counter numbers on his video recorder back home would correspond with those on the machine in the confer- ence hall. Unfortunately for him, they did not, and almost half the time allocated for his presentation was taken up by his ever more frantic attempts to find the particular examples he wanted to talk about – and all this at a conference on communication studies!

When using video, it's usually best to keep the clips short, and the 30-second television commercial is a useful guide to optimal length. If you play longer clips, the danger is that the audience will start to feel as though they are at a film show, rather than a pres- entation. Once that happens, you may well find yourself losing the impetus, and have problems getting them back into the mood for listening to a talk. And, if it was a lively and well-produced piece of video, there's the added risk of coming across as dull and amateurish compared with what they've just been watching.

4. Maps

Sometimes speakers put up slides with lists of towns or countries they have visited, or where their company has branches. Listed in alphabetical order, these are not a particularly effective way of depicting geographical spread. Nor is it likely that an audience will remember them, or indeed that the speaker intends them to do so. Usually, the aim is to give an overall impression of the number of branches and/or their geographical coverage, in which case the obvi- ous solution is to use a simple map with towns or countries marked on it. If you are intending to discuss each of the places in more detail along the way, you can use programs like PowerPoint to bring the place names up one by one, which prevents the audience from being distracted by other locations that you have not yet talked about.

One of the most impressive map users I have ever seen was an expert on the Russian economy, whose only visual aid was a huge map that extended several metres across the front of the conference room. Whenever he needed to refer to a particular town or region, he would dash from one end of the map to the other wielding an old billiard cue to point at the relevant parts of the map. By so doing, he managed to convey an infectious sense of eccentric enthusiasm that invariably attracted high ratings from his audiences.

5. Organisation charts

Another kind of map is the organisation chart. This can be very helpful to audiences, because describing in the abstract how the various parts of an organisation fit together is not always easy. But it's very important to keep such charts as clear and simple as possible. This can be quite a challenge when working with some of the templates included in packages like PowerPoint. Its organisation chart building system not only features small fonts, but also gives you the opportunity to fill in no fewer than four lines of text per box. The various options for linking different parts of the organisation then open up the possibility of producing charts that look as complicated as electrical circuit diagrams. Taken together, these features of the program amount to an incentive to produce organisation charts that are far too detailed and difficult to read from a distance. It is, however, possible to simplify them and to make them less distracting by building up the boxes or layers one by one as you go along.

Before deciding whether to embark on describing an organisation at all, it's always worth giving some serious thought to the question of just how interesting or relevant such information is likely to be to the audience. It is, for example, very common for speakers who are presenting to prospective clients to start with a detailed description of the company, its mission statement, corporate values, etc. It's also not uncommon for prospective clients, who may have to listen to several similar descriptions in a single morning, to become quite impatient about having to endure yet another one. Before starting out on just such an introduction, one presenter was completely taken aback when a prospective client said, 'I hope you're not going to waste our time by telling us how many people you employ and who reports to whom.' Unfortunately, this was exactly what he was planning to do, so the opening moments of his presentation were taken up with a desperate search for the first slide that didn't deal with the organisation.

6. Diagrams and flow charts

When it comes to discussing complex arrangements, processes or theoretical models, various kinds of diagrams come into their own. But, as with organisation charts, they have to be kept simple. Figure 1 shows the interconnections between the bodies involved in rail safety following the privatisation of the railways in the UK. Under normal circumstances, it would represent a dramatic failure of the simplicity test. However, if the object of the exercise were to show how absurdly complex the arrangements are, as was in fact the case here, then the use of such a complicated diagram with so many arrows and acronyms becomes a very effective way of making the point.

This diagram was made possible by the fact that PowerPoint provides an extensive collection of boxes, arrows, multi-layered triangles and concentric circles. Used in moderation, these can help when discussing various abstract models and relationships, but they can also result in the production of charts and diagrams of such complexity that audiences will end up being more confused than enlightened. You can greatly reduce the chances of this happening by careful advance planning of what you're going to say about each item and the order in which to say it. It then becomes quite easy to work out how to draw the diagram on a board or flip chart, or how to build it up on a slide while explaining how the various parts relate to each other. This is illustrated by Figure 2, which is based on one used by a business school professor in a lecture on emotional intelligence. The complete diagram contains a considerable amount of information, complete with abstract concepts, such as 'drivers', 'enablers' and 'constrainers', all of which need further explanation for it all to make sense. The most effective way to do this is to build up each of the elements one by one, explaining each individual item as it appears on the

Figure 1: Diagram

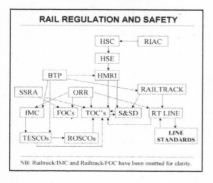

Figure 2: Chart

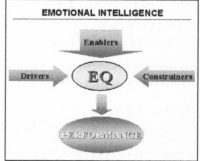

screen. Compared with displaying the whole diagram all at once, this is much more likely to keep the audience on track, and prevents them from being distracted by wondering what all the other things mean.

7. Graphs

Many presentations include discussions of numerical or financial information, which are often accompanied by slides made up of tables of numbers. If slides with writing on them invite the audience to read and listen at the same time, slides with numbers on effectively invite them to do some mental arithmetic at the same time as trying to listen. But the most frequent use of numbers in presentations is to show trends, relationships and proportions, all of which can be much more effectively depicted in graphical form than with raw numbers. Graphs, bar charts and pie charts all get higher ratings from audiences than tables of numbers – but only if you keep them simple and explain them clearly as you introduce them.

Here again we come up against the problem of computer graphics templates that push presenters towards making some common mistakes that are not particularly helpful to audiences. In the case of graphs, for example, the lines in the PowerPoint template are so thin and use such faint colours that they are hardly visible even from a short distance away from the screen. It is therefore worth making the effort to learn how to replace them with thicker lines and stronger colours.

8. Bar charts

Audiences also tend to react positively to the use of bar charts when listening to discussions of various types of numerical data.

On the PowerPoint template, the bars stand out more clearly than the wispy lines on some of its graphs, but the fonts are too small to ensure visibility from the back row. The audience also has the problem of trying to make instant sense of 12 bars, in three different colours over four periods of time.

Part of the problem with PowerPoint's graph and bar chart templates is that they are exactly the same as the ones in Microsoft's flagship word-processing and spreadsheet packages, Word®* and Excel®.* This is no doubt the result of a deliberate strategy aimed at integrating functions between different programs within the Microsoft Office suite of programs. But their inclusion in PowerPoint implies that there is no difference between the needs of readers of written reports, and the needs of an audience at a presentation. But there is, of course, a very big difference. When reading a report, you can take as much time as you like to study a chart, absorb what the axes represent and relate the colours to the key, scanning backwards and forwards from one part of the page to another, rereading and rechecking where necessary. For an audience, it's impossible to do this at a glance and from a distance, especially if you're trying to listen to the speaker while struggling to read small print at the same time.

The designers of these templates are not alone in believing that the contents of such charts will be instantly accessible to an audience. Many speakers act under the same assumption when they launch straight into a discussion of the figures as soon as the chart goes up on the screen, and without bothering to say anything about what the axes, bars and colours actually represent. If you

---

* Excel, Word and PowerPoint are registered trademarks of Microsoft Corporation.

don't do this, the audience is likely to be distracted by trying to do it for themselves, and will find your argument more difficult to follow. You can show even greater sensitivity to their needs by exploiting other functions within PowerPoint to adapt charts to make them simpler and easier to understand. Obvious first steps are to increase the size of the fonts and to use fewer numbers and letters along the axes. If you tell the audience what the different colours mean, you can safely get rid of the key that appears on the template, which will prevent the audience from being distracted by trying to read it. PowerPoint also makes it possible to add in the bars one by one, so that you can get the audience to focus on one set of figures at a time before clicking the mouse to reveal the next one – and so on until the chart is complete.

9. Pie charts

Proportions are best illustrated by pie charts, again so long as they are kept as simple as possible. The basic PowerPoint template passes the simplicity test, but it also brings with it the temptation to slice the pies into so many segments that they end up being too complicated to be of much use to an audience.

10. Blank slides: a non-visual exception

The main theme of this chapter has been that the visual aids that go down best with audiences are ones made up of pictorial and graphical material, rather than written words and sentences. But few subjects call for the continuous display of one such slide after another, and you often see speakers leaving a slide on the screen long after they have finished talking about it – at which point it becomes a potential distraction. The best solution is to insert a blank slide at those points where you have things to say that don't require any visual support. Some speakers recognise this by inserting slides with nothing on them but a corporate logo or some other image. However, so long as there is something on the screen, audiences have a reason to look away and break eye contact with the speaker. The obvious way to prevent this is to insert a slide that is completely blank. With PowerPoint, all you have to do is to apply a black background to a slide, and it will appear to the audience as though there is nothing on the screen at all.

Blank slides are also useful at the beginning and end of presentations. As was mentioned in the Introduction, audiences don't much like having to watch on-screen displays of an arrow searching through files for the one they need for today. So it's well worth getting the slide show ready on the computer before anyone else arrives in the room. If your first slide is a blank, the audience will be completely unaware that there is already a slide on the screen, and all you have to do is decide when to press the button to bring up your first exhibit. It's also a good idea to blank out the screen towards the end of a presentation. This not only serves as an implicit signal that the end is near, but also ensures that the audience's full attention will be on the speaker during the all-important concluding remarks.

11. Handouts: a textual exception

Although all presentations should aim at simplifying the content as much as possible, there are some subjects where it's difficult to avoid dealing with detailed material altogether, as when a speaker needs to take an audience through financial or other statistical data. The same is true of the kind of linguistic examples described in Chapters 6 and

Once speakers abandon their dependence on textual slides in favour of visual aids that are more sensitive to the needs and preferences of audiences, they immediately experience better rapport with their listeners.

7, many of which are extracts from actual speeches. Whether in a book or a lecture, written transcripts enable people to see and understand the patterns under discussion. When speaking to an audience, this means that you have to make a choice between projecting the transcripts on to a screen or printing them out on handouts for distributing around the room. And the more effective option is to give members of the audience their own individual copies.

I first learnt about the superiority of handouts over slides for handling detail from the experience of giving and listening to presentations on academic research into various aspects of talk. Before the advent of acetate-friendly photocopiers, it was standard practice to hand out transcripts before taking the audience through the analysis, but these new machines held out the promise of saving paper and reducing duplicating costs. However, I know of no one who tried putting transcripts on overhead projector slides who ever did again, and everyone quickly reverted to using handouts. From the speaker's point of view, one of the problems of putting the excerpts on the screen was that some of them extended over several slides, which caused much awkward fumbling while trying to go through a single example. When sitting in an audience, it was much more difficult to concentrate on the details and follow the speaker's argument at a distance than with direct access to your own personal copy of the handout.

Two common fears associated with handouts are first that everyone will start reading, and second that the resulting loss of eye contact will divert the audience from listening to what you are saying. A partial solution to the first of these is not to hand anything out until you're ready to start talking about it. Once they get a copy in their hands, people will, of course, start reading it. So the answer is to move quickly to take control, firmly directing their attention to the first detail to be discussed. This will typically involve telling them to look at the first example, the number in the top left-hand box in the table, or whatever happens to be relevant to your first topic. At this point, you will become aware of a sudden and complete loss of eye contact with the audience, which, under other circumstances, would be cause for serious panic. But when using a handout, it is a promising sign that you have engaged the audience's attention on the detail you want to discuss. And it's even more encouraging if they seem interested enough to start writing notes on the handouts.

II. THE POTENTIAL AND PITFALLS OF POWERPOINT

1. PowerPoint plus points

In a world where the visual aids that audiences like best are pictorial rather than textual, computerised graphics programs like PowerPoint have tremendous potential for responding to audience needs, and bringing about a general improvement in the effectiveness of speeches, lectures and presentations. Its main advantages can be summarised under the following headings:

☜ *Pictures*

It is extremely easy to incorporate photographs and other types of picture, which can be used in just the same way as 35mm projectors were used in traditional slide shows.

☜ *Graphics*

It provides great scope for producing graphs, charts, diagrams and all the other types of pictorial material that audiences find useful – though you do have to be prepared to simplify and modify the templates if necessary.

☜ *Build-up*

The capacity to build up bullet points and animate charts enables you to simulate and benefit from some of the advantages of chalk and talk discussed in the previous chapter.

☜ *Slide changing*

The ease with which you can change slides at the push of a button makes for much smoother transitions than the shuffling of acetates (with its associated delays and distractions).

2. PowerPoint minus points

Judged by the number of speakers who use PowerPoint to produce the types of visual aid most likely to appeal to audiences, its potential is still a very long way from being fully realised. Most PowerPoint presentations still depend on slides that merely replicate the tedious lists and tables that dominated the era of the overhead projector – the main difference being that they look neater and more professionally produced than their acetate ancestors. This raises the question of why so little has changed. Why are presenters still so keen on using verbal crutches rather than visual aids? And why are so many still so reluctant to use slides in which material is built up step by step?

On being exposed to the points made in this and the previous chapter, most delegates on courses say that the observations closely reflect their own experiences of sitting in audiences, and the main thrust of the argument tends to attract more or less unanimous agreement. However, there are some recurring 'but' clauses: they would love to make more use of pictures and charts, but only know how to create slides made up of lists; they would like to use the build-up and animated functions, but haven't yet found out how to do it. And those who do have the necessary expertise often say that they would make even more use of such slides if only it didn't take up so much time to design and prepare them. None of these problems would arise if the templates and guidance built into PowerPoint made it easier for users to generate the types of pictorial and dynamic visuals favoured by audiences. On this crucial front, the program arguably falls short of what might be reasonably expected from a market-leading software package.

✎ *Bias towards detail*

As was noted earlier, PowerPoint's templates for charts and diagrams are identical to those in Word and Excel, which are designed for written reports aimed at readers. But for audiences, the default fonts, lines and colours tend to be too small, too faint and too watery. Perhaps worst of all, the templates serve as a positive incitement to users to overload their audiences with far more information than can be easily digested on a single slide. At the same time, they lull presenters into an awful sense of false security about the quality of their slides. After all, if Microsoft decrees that this is an ideal graph or bar chart, it must be so. But the unfortunate fact is that these model templates often need considerable modification to be made accessible and useful to audiences.

🔍 Bias towards lists

Although working with graphical templates may require a good deal of skill on the part of the user, producing lists is extremely easy, even for complete beginners. Start PowerPoint running, and the first thing you get is an invitation to 'Choose an Auto Layout' from a set of 24 alternatives. With text featuring in no fewer than 17 of these (71 per cent), it's hardly surprising that users have no qualms about producing so many slides with so many words on them.

An even stronger incentive to concentrate on writing textual slides is built into the collection of 24 model presentations that come as part of the package. These are ready-made sets of slides on different subjects (e.g. 'Marketing Plan', 'Financial Overview', 'Recommending a Strategy', etc.), and consist mainly of bullet points giving advice on how to construct the various types of presentation. The idea is that you can select whichever one is suitable for your purpose and insert your own subject matter into the templates. If the aim is to propagate total conformity to the industry standard model of presentation, the collection must be hailed as a spectacular success.

Unfortunately, however, guidance on the creation of slides that are sensitive to the needs and preferences of audiences is conspicuous only by its absence. One of the slide sets is for a website, and is therefore omitted for present purposes. The remaining 23 presentations include a total of 214 slides, of which the overwhelming majority (94 per cent) consist of nothing but text, at an average of 20.5 words per slide. A further two slides (1 per cent) feature tables with words and columns of raw numbers. The vast majority are therefore indistinguishable from the static lists of bullet points that have been the norm since the days of acetates and overhead projectors. This implies a degree of reluctance on the part of Microsoft's designers to use one of the most positive features of their own software – the build-up function – which only makes an appearance in one of the 23 sets of slides.

Bias against pictures and charts

With the model presentations giving such overwhelming priority to textual slides, it's hardly surprising that PowerPoint users rely on them so heavily. But what of the remaining 5 per cent of specimen slides that do include some of the types of visual that audiences are actually likely to find useful? These include two graphs, one bar chart, two pie charts and eight diagrams. Of these, only the two pie charts (1 per cent of the total collection) appear on their own with minimal text to distract the audience's attention. But the single example of a bar chart assumes that audiences will have no difficulties in taking in three of them at the same time.

As for the rest of the slides containing visual material, they feature text above, below, to the side of, or within the graphical images. So, as a model of how to make the most of the graphical and pictorial capabilities of PowerPoint, the few slides that do include charts (one in 20) implicitly discourage the creation of simple, uncluttered visual slides of the kind most likely to help speakers to get their points across.

🔊 *Bias against change*

This review of the assumptions built into PowerPoint goes a long way towards explaining why, in spite of its potential for producing pictorial and build-up slides, so little has changed since the days of the overhead projector. If Microsoft's designers themselves make so little use of the program's pictorial possibilities – let alone the scores of other dynamic functions that are not used at all in any of the model presentations – is it any wonder that so many presenters still persist in using so many excessively wordy slides? After all, if this is the market leader in presentational software, its designers must presumably be reliable authorities on what constitutes an effective presentation. Following their templates and models must therefore be a sure-fire way to produce presentations that will go down well with audiences. Unfortunately, the sad fact is that the evidence from listening to what audiences think about different types of slide points in exactly the opposite direction.

Short of a massive overhaul of the program, releasing the positive potential of PowerPoint can only be done by approaching it with caution, and a willingness to make major changes to its standard templates. That means rejecting its in-built bias towards heavily textual slides, and learning how to simplify its graphs, charts and diagrams. It's also worth making an effort to master its other pictorial and dynamic capabilities, and especially some of its build-up and animated functions – while bearing in mind that not all of these are guaranteed to impress an audience. For example, it's as well to resist the temptation to use some of the more bizarre build-up options that make words and objects swoop into position from every possible angle of the screen, accompanied by the sound of machine-gun fire, screeching brakes or breaking glass.

3. Life after death from 1,000 slides

This discussion of visual aids started by showing that the modern business presentation has been hijacked by a style of slide-driven delivery that puts the needs of speakers above those of audiences, and has no precedent in the long history of public speaking. At the heart of the story has been a dismal and widespread failure to understand that writing and speaking are fundamentally different forms of communication, and that reading and listening are two quite distinct forms of mental activity (see Chapter 3). Otherwise, a style of presentation that confuses the two (by assuming that it's reasonable to expect audiences to read and listen at the same time) would never have evolved in the first place.

The main offenders are slides consisting of nothing but words, sentences or tables of numbers. But there are, of course, plenty of other types of visual aid that can be a tremendous help in clarifying key points and making presentations lively and interesting. For hundreds of years, people have learnt a great deal though the medium of chalk and talk, which still gets high ratings from contemporary audiences. Some of its virtues can be readily simulated using the dynamic features of computerised graphics programs, which also open up a new world of pictorial possibilities. In deciding on what visual aids to use, the only real test is whether it will benefit the audience. If its main or only function is to aid the speaker, as is the case with the vast majority of textual slides, then it has failed the test and should not be used.

At first sight, it might seem that to abandon the industry standard model of presentation is far too radical a step to take, and that speakers would end up being paralysed with uncertainty about how to proceed in the absence of their familiar old security blanket.

Fortunately, the news from years of experience in training and coaching points in a much more optimistic and liberating direction. Once people abandon their dependence on textual slides in favour of visual aids that are more sensitive to the needs and preferences of audiences, they immediately experience better rapport with their listeners. Visual aids prepared with the audience in mind also greatly reduce the chances of inflicting too much information on the audience. Taken together, these represent an important move towards mastering the language of public speaking.

The next challenge is to find an escape route from the boring language that typically adorns the word-filled slide, and from the rambling and hesitant commentaries it tends to prompt from speakers. The way forward lies in developing a practical under-standing of forms of language that effective speakers have used for thousands of years to get their messages across with impact. This is the focus of the next two chapters, which look at the enduring power of rhetoric and imagery as techniques for inspir-ing audiences.

Audiences like to be *shown* things that help them to understand what the speaker is talking about, so the visual aids most likely to attract positive ratings are ones that are genuinely *visual* or *pictorial*, rather than textual or numerical.

1. Visual aids that go down well with audiences

(provided they are as clear and simple as possible)

- ❑ Objects, props and demonstrations
- ❑ Pictures
- ❑ Video
- ❑ Maps
- ❑ Organisation charts
- ❑ Graphs
- ❑ Bar charts
- ❑ Pie charts

Non-visual exceptions:

- ❑ Blank slides (e.g. black background)
- ❑ Using handouts during a talk

2. Advantages of PowerPoint

Pictures: It's extremely easy to incorporate photographs and other types of picture.

Graphics: It provides great scope for producing graphs, charts, diagrams and all the other types of pictorial material that audiences find useful.

Build-up: The capacity to build up bullet points and animate charts enables you to simulate some of the advantages of chalk and talk (see Chapter 4).

Slide changing: Being able to change slides at the push of a button makes for much smoother transitions than when shuffling acetates on and off an overhead projector.

3. Disadvantages of PowerPoint

Bias towards too much detail: Many of the templates are too detailed (e.g. four sets of three bars on a single chart) and use fonts that are too small to be seen at a distance.

Bias towards lists: A very high proportion of the templates encourage users to produce lists of bullet points.

Bias against build-up: Only one of the 23 model presentations uses the build-up function.

Bias against pictures and charts: None of the templates in the model presentations includes pictures, and only 5 per cent of them contain graphs, charts and diagrams, most of which are too cluttered to be of much use.

Bias against change: The industry standard model of presentation is implicitly encouraged, in spite of the fact that PowerPoint's pictorial and dynamic functions have such great potential for generating slides that appeal to audiences. Making the most of PowerPoint therefore means learning to use these functions and how to adapt its templates.

Part II Exercises

🔖 *Exercise 1 – Building up bullet points*

❑ As building up a list of bullet points one by one is almost always preferable to putting them all up at once, you should aim to become proficient at creating such slides on PowerPoint or whatever program you normally use.

❑ In general, the fewer the words per bullet point, the less of a distraction they will be, so stick to one- or two-word headings as far as possible.

❑ PowerPoint contains a wide range of options that enable you to bring words swooping in from all angles, to the accompaniment of a similarly wide range of sound effects. On the whole, audiences don't seem to be very impressed by these, so concentrate on learning to use the most unobtrusive options, such as 'appear' and 'wipe down' – and think twice before using any sound effects at all.

❑ Most people tend to press the button too early so that the bullet appears before they start talking about it, giving the impression of not being sure what to say until the next heading is on the screen. 'Later rather than sooner' should be the motto, as saying the word just before it comes up makes you appear more in control of your material – so it's worth practising this approach to timing.

🔊 Exercise 2 – Chalk and talk

Deciding what to put on a board or flip chart requires careful advance planning, which you can do on a piece of paper before practising it on a larger scale. One of the problems with flip charts is that they are quite narrow, which can make it difficult to prevent diagrams like organisation charts from spilling off the page. Take some simple subject matter, such as those listed below, work out a simple way of drawing it up and then plan what to say while you are doing so. For some of them, you might also like to try using a pencil to create a faint outline that can be traced in with a felt-tipped pen.

❑ A map of how to get to your house.

❑ Part of your family tree.

❑ A plan of a football pitch or tennis court.

❑ A graph.

❑ A list of single word headings.

🔊 Exercise 3 – Selecting and editing pictures

Take a set of 20 or 30 photographs that have yet to be put into an album (e.g. from your latest holiday). The object of the exercise is to select the best few pictures with a view to showing them to someone in a way that both avoids skipping randomly from one scene to another and back again, and spares them from having to look at blurred, under-exposed or other poor-quality prints.

❑ Edit them down to a maximum of one-third of the original number.

❑ Put them into a logical sequence.

❑ Plan in advance what to say about each one.

✎ *Exercise 4 – Computer graphics*

As genuinely visual images are the ones that go down best with audiences, it's extremely important to develop your expertise at using the functions of PowerPoint, or your preferred program, that generate such slides. Whether you decide to go on a course or teach yourself, you should give priority to learning and practising the following:

❑ How to import pictures from a scanner, disk or the internet – it's also well worth learning to use a photo-editing program that enables you to edit and alter pictures in various ways.

❑ How to produce each of the different types of slide liked by audiences, as listed in Part I of Chapter 5.

❑ How to modify the templates where necessary – e.g. eliminating unnecessary details, changing font sizes, colours, thickness of lines, etc.

❑ How to build up maps and charts (e.g. putting up place names on a map, bars on a bar chart, etc., one by one).

❑ How to make lines and arrows move, so that graphs and charts can be made to look as though they are drawing themselves up on the screen while you are talking about them.

✎ *Exercise 5 – Mastering the blank slide*

One of the reasons speakers go on projecting point after point at their audiences is that once they have switched PowerPoint on, they dare not switch it off again. Release yourself from this slavish dependence by becoming familiar with the blank slide.

❑ Create your first truly blank slide (select 'new slide'; 'blank format'; 'black background'). Notice how there is nothing on the screen, and it appears to the audience that the PowerPoint show has been switched off.

❑ Look at the visual aids you used in your last presentation. How many of them were really necessary? Now delete all but the ones containing vital visual information.

❑ Insert blank slides into the gaps between the useful slides you have left. The audience will now be able to focus their attention on your spoken words, rather than on the screen. When you need to take them through some more visual information again, they will automatically be drawn back to the projected images you want to talk about.

PART III
WINNING WITH WORDS

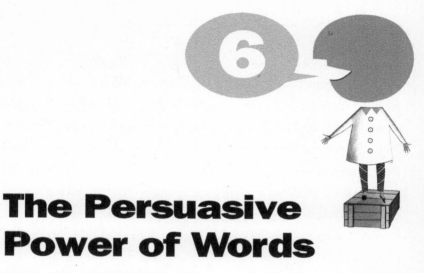

The Persuasive Power of Words

The Use of Rhetorical Techniques

So far, I have concentrated on the challenge facing speakers in holding the attention of audiences, and on how to overcome the worst excesses of the modern slide-driven style of presentation. It is now time to turn to the biggest questions of all. Is there anything you can do to get your messages across with greater impact? Are there any techniques that all successful speakers use to inspire, persuade and enthuse their audiences? And, if so, can anyone learn to use them to become a more effective communicator? The good news is that the answer to all these questions is an emphatic *yes*.

I. RHETORIC AS A TOOL KIT

If we had gone to school in the earliest days of ancient Greek civilisation, we would have learnt about little else than rhetoric. This is because schools of rhetoric were the first form of institutionalised education in classical Greece. To participate effectively in a small-scale democracy, people had to be able to speak in public, to argue a case and, above all, to persuade others to agree with what they were saying. So the Greeks, and later the Romans, spent a great deal of time studying rhetoric and oratory. They set about classifying different techniques and teaching them to those who would eventually become active in politics, the law and government. The study of rhetoric remained central to a classical education until quite recently, and visitors to Oxford may have noticed a sign above one of the doorways in the Old Schools that reads '*Schola Astronomiae et Rhetoricae*'.

1. Rhetoric as a positive asset

Nowadays, of course, rhetoric is no longer widely taught, and the word itself has had such a bad press that it tends to be regarded mainly as a term of abuse. It is more likely to be used to dismiss some statement as hollow, inaccurate or lacking in substance than to refer to a set of linguistic techniques that have been with us for thousands of years. But there's nothing particularly new about rhetoric attracting criticism. Schools of rhetoric may have been the first in ancient Greece, but they were quickly followed by schools of philosophy, led by scholars like Plato, who criticised students of rhetoric for being more interested in persuasion and plausibility than in the pursuit of truth. As a result, philosophy, logic, mathematics, and ultimately the development of science and technology, were born out of a reaction against the study of rhetoric. But it's essential for anyone who wants to master the language of public speaking to put all the negative associations with the word 'rhetoric' firmly to one side. There is nothing to be gained, for example, from taking the same attitude as the young Member of Parliament,

> The same rhetorical techniques that were originally identified by the ancient Greeks are still very much alive and well today. They are part and parcel of the way effective speakers speak, and are to be heard in action wherever people are arguing, and whenever someone is trying to be persuasive or convincing.

who told a colleague of mine that he wanted his speeches to be persuasive, but didn't want to use any rhetoric – which makes about as much sense as saying that you want to make an omelette without using any eggs.

If I have learnt anything from more than 20 years of research into audience reactions to different kinds of speeches and presentations, it is that the same rhetorical techniques that were originally identified by the ancient Greeks are still very much alive and well today. They are part and parcel of the way effective speakers speak, and are to be heard in action wherever people are arguing, and whenever someone is trying to be persuasive or convincing. As such, they are the indispensable building blocks of the language of persuasion. Whether we look at what prompts applause in political speeches, the sound bites played on prime time news broadcasts or even famous advertising slogans, the structure of many of the sentences conforms exactly to that recommended by the classical writings on rhetoric. And one thing that great speakers past and present have in common is a shared ability, whether consciously or unconsciously, to use these same rhetorical techniques to get their key messages across.

2. Simplicity and accessibility

At this point, you may be starting to worry that all this talk about the classical interest in rhetorical techniques means that they must be obscure, complex or difficult to understand. Nothing could be further from the truth. As we shall see, the techniques are not only very simple, but are also strangely familiar to us. In fact, most people already use them to a greater or lesser extent, both in conversation and in speeches, without actually realising what they are doing. In one sense, then, the real challenge is to become more aware of what they are, and then to make much more use of them than before.

The fact that these techniques for getting messages across are so simple brings with it some further good news. After many years of teaching them to very different audiences, I never cease to be amazed at just how quickly people latch on to them and learn to use them for themselves. Just as impressive is the fact that the techniques seem to be infinitely adaptable: as will become clear in later chapters, you can use them to increase the impact of any kind of speech whatsoever, regardless of subject matter, objectives or type of audience.

In this chapter, the main focus is on the techniques that are most likely to trigger applause in political speeches. This is partly because this was where my research into effective speaking first began to deliver results, and partly because applause and cheering are the most overt ways for an audience to show approval. It provides concrete evidence that the listeners are not only awake, but are also so much in agreement with what the speaker just said that they produce an immediate and positive response.

3. Same message, different impact

A very general feature of language is that, for anything anyone might ever want to say, there is a range of different ways of saying the same thing. However, although the various alternatives may convey more or less the same meaning, they can have a very different impact on those who hear them. While one version comes across as dull, bland and unmemorable, another might strike a chord with the audience, prompt applause and perhaps even be remembered afterwards. For example, the meanings of the three lines in options A and B below are more or less the same, but you'll see at a glance that one version is rather more striking than the other:

Option A

I can't decide whether or not to commit suicide.

Nobody is going to make me change my economic policies.

I hope that racial discrimination in America will disappear within a generation.

Option B

To be, or not to be. **Shakespeare** (*Hamlet*)

You turn if you want to. The lady's not for turning. **Margaret Thatcher**

I have a dream that my four little children will one day live in a nation where they will not be judged by the colour of their skin, but by the content of their character. **Martin Luther King**

I have now shown these alternatives to well over 1,000 people, and there is always total agreement on which version has the greater impact: the B versions are more stirring than the A versions. However, in spite of this unanimity, very few notice that the B versions also have something in common as far as their rhetorical structure is concerned. All of them involve the use of a contrast – between 'you turning' and 'the lady not turning', between 'to be' and 'not to be', and between 'the colour of their skin' and 'the content of their character'. As such, they are famous examples of the use of the first type of rhetorical technique you need to know about if you are to get your points across with greater impact.

II. RHETORICAL TECHNIQUES

1. Contrasts

The effectiveness of this technique was well known to classical writers on rhetoric, who referred to some of its different forms under headings like *antithesis*, *enantiosis* and *antitheton*. But most people find the concept much easier to grasp by using the term 'contrast'. From research based on videotapes of more than 500 political speeches, we know that the contrast has lost none of its force, and is responsible for prompting a large proportion of the applause enjoyed by politicians. Lines that strike such an immediate chord with an audience stand a better chance of surviving beyond the moment of delivery than those that are listened to in silence. This increases their chances of being remembered, reproduced in newspapers and prime time radio and television news programmes – and, in a minority of cases, being preserved for posterity in dictionaries of quotations. So, for at least 2,000 years, many of the quotations that have survived have involved the use of a contrast:

It is more blessed to give than to receive. **The Bible** (Acts 20:35)

I come to bury Caesar,
not to praise him. **Shakespeare** (*Julius Caesar*)

Live as if you were to die tomorrow.
Learn as if you were to live forever. **Mahatma Ghandi**

Those who cast the votes decide nothing.
Those who count the votes decide everything.
Joseph Stalin

Two thousand years ago. man's proudest boast was 'civis
     Romanus sum'.
Today, in the world of freedom, the proudest boast is 'ich
     bin ein Berliner'. **John F. Kennedy**

That's one small step for man;
one giant leap for mankind. **Neil Armstrong**

I stand here before you not as a prophet
but as a humble servant of you, the people. **Nelson Mandela**

Although all these statements make a contrast between two things, they do so in rather different ways, and it is important to be aware of what some of the commonest and most adaptable forms are.

🎤 *Contradictions: 'not this but that'*

Of the examples seen so far, the two Shakespearian quotations and the ones from Margaret Thatcher and Martin Luther King took the form of 'Not [A] but [B]' or '[A] but not [B]'. Simple though it may seem, following a negative with a positive, or vice versa, has a very impressive history when it comes to summing up points in a punchy way:

Dignity consists
not in possessing honours,
but in the consciousness that we deserve them. **Aristotle**

Advice is judged by results,
not by intentions. **Cicero**

The test of our progress is
not whether we add more to the abundance of those who have
    much;
it is whether we provide enough for those who have too little.
Franklin D. Roosevelt

The ultimate measure of a man is
not where he stands in moments of comfort,
but where he stands at times of challenge and controversy.
Martin Luther King

The house we hope to build is
not for my generation
but for yours. **Ronald Reagan**

September 11th was not an isolated event,
but a tragic prologue. **Tony Blair**

In general, deciding whether the positive or negative should go first
depends on which part of the contrast you want your audience to
identify with, or which one you are planning to develop in what
you go on to say next. In all but one of the above examples, the
negative comes before the positive, and this is by far the commonest form of contradictory contrast. It no doubt reflects the fact that
speakers will usually want to focus attention on the positive implications of the point they are making before going on to say more
about it. But occasionally, as in the case of Margaret Thatcher's
'You turn if you want to. The lady's not for turning', it will be the
negative to which the speaker wants to give special emphasis.

● *Comparisons: 'more this than that'*
Grammar not only includes rules for generating negatives, but also
equips us with comparative forms that enable us to say that one thing
is better, bigger, faster, taller, etc., than something else. This provides
another rich resource for contrasting one thing with another:

I count him braver who overcomes his desires
than him who overcomes his enemies. **Aristotle**

For better or for worse, for richer or for poorer ...
Marriage vows

The man who reads nothing at all is better educated
than the man who reads nothing but newspapers.
Thomas Jefferson

Better to remain silent and be thought a fool
than to speak out and remove all doubt.
Abraham Lincoln

I have taken more out of alcohol
than alcohol has taken out of me. **Winston Churchill**

I've learned in Washington, that it's the only place where
sound travels faster than light. **Ronald Reagan**

Opposites: 'black or white'

Having begun his Forum speech with a positive–negative contradictory contrast – 'I come to bury Caesar, not to praise him' – Mark
Antony went on to make a contrast between the two opposites of
good and evil:

> The evil that men do lives after them.
> The good is oft interred with their bones.
> **Shakespeare** (*Julius Caesar*)

'Good' and 'evil' and 'life' and 'death' are examples of the many
hundreds of words in the language that have directly opposite
meanings, and which are to be found in the antonym section of
dictionaries of synonyms and antonyms. The range is vast, and is
not confined to any particular parts of speech:

Nouns: truth–falsehood, happiness–misery, health–illness, etc.
Verbs: attack–defend, live–die, sit–stand, etc.
Adjectives: kind–cruel, hot–cold, bright–dull, etc.
Adverbs: always–never, quickly–slowly, honestly–dishonestly, etc.
Prepositions: up–down, before–after, above–below, etc.

The fact that there are so many words with opposite meanings provides us with immense scope for producing stark and dramatic-sounding contrasts:

Fair is foul, and foul is fair. **Shakespeare** (*Macbeth*)

Small opportunities are often the beginning of great enterprises.
Demosthenes

Glory is fleeting,
but obscurity is forever. **Napoleon**

Liberalism is trust of the people tempered by prudence.
Conservatism is distrust of the people tempered by fear.
William Ewart Gladstone

The inherent vice of capitalism is the unequal sharing of blessings;
the inherent virtue of socialism is the equal sharing of miseries.
Winston Churchill

Injustice anywhere is a threat to
justice everywhere.
Martin Luther King, Jr

There is nothing wrong with America
that cannot be solved by what's right with America.
Bill Clinton

What the electorate gives,
the electorate can take away. **Tony Blair**

🔊 *Phrase reversals*

Finally, there is a particularly elegant type of contrast, in which some of the same words in the first part of the contrast are used in reverse order in the second part:

Thou shouldst eat to live;
not live to eat. **Socrates**

Wise men talk because they have something to say;
fools, because they have to say something. **Plato**

The optimist sees opportunity in every danger;
the pessimist sees danger in every opportunity.
Winston Churchill

Tradition does not mean that the living are dead.
It means that the dead are living. **Harold Macmillan**

I was born in the slum,
but the slum was not born in me. **Jesse Jackson**

Management is doing things right;
leadership is doing the right things. **Peter Drucker**

When John F. Kennedy became president of the USA in 1961, he wanted his inaugural speech to be more memorable than what he considered to have been the rather bland efforts of his immediate predecessors. So he instructed his staff to study the speeches of some of the great figures of the past. Some of the most famous quotations from Kennedy suggest that they may have been particularly taken with the following line from an earlier Democrat president:

> We cannot always build the future for our youth,
> but we can build our youth for the future.
> **Franklin D. Roosevelt**

This reversal of key words in the second part of a contrast was used in some of the most widely quoted lines from Kennedy's inaugural speech:

> Ask not what your country can do for you;
> ask what you can do for your country. **John F. Kennedy**

> Let us never negotiate out of fear.
> But let us never fear to negotiate. **John F. Kennedy**

> Mankind must put an end to war,
> or war will put an end to mankind. **John F. Kennedy**

🔎 *Repetition, balance and anticipation*

In looking at differences between the written word and the spoken word (see Chapter 3), we saw that various forms of repetition can be very effective when we are speaking, even though it's something we try to avoid when writing for readers. A common feature of about half of the above examples of different types of contrast is that words or phrases from the first part are repeated in the second part. As a result, the two parts of such contrasts are not only of similar length, but also sound very similar. From a listener's point of view, this makes it very easy to focus on those elements that change, and instantly get the point of the contrast. And, for an audience on the lookout for a slot where they can applaud, the contents of the first part of a contrast contain implicit instructions as to when the second part of the contrast will come to an end, and when the applause can start.

There is another way that contrasts can create a sense of anticipation and increased attentiveness on the part of an audience. In many of the above examples, the first part of the contrast sets up a puzzle or question in the mind of the listener. If we are not supposed to ask what our country can do for us, just what is it that we are supposed to ask? If September 11th was not an isolated event, what was it? Having placed such questions in our minds, the speaker supplies an immediate answer with the second part of the contrast. This brings us to a second important rhetorical technique.

2. Puzzles and questions
🔍 Puzzle–solution formats

Posing an implicit puzzle during the first part of a contrast is not the only way to intrigue an audience enough for them to start wondering what's coming next. Another is to be more direct, and say something puzzling enough to prompt them into actively trying to anticipate a solution, rather in the same way as good writing will make readers want to see what is on the next page. With audiences, the equivalent is to increase their attentiveness to a point where they will be listening out closely for the solution, which, if it is clever or witty, is likely to elicit a positive response:

PUZZLE: On my way here I passed a local cinema and it
            turned out you were expecting me after all,
SOLUTION: for the billboards read: 'The Mummy Returns'.
            Margaret Thatcher

Ronald Reagan was well known for his self-deprecating sense of humour, which, on occasions would hark back to his earlier career as a film actor. The speech announcing his intention to run for the presidency included a puzzle–solution sequence that started by prompting the audience to reflect on the source of his mixed emotions. His solution was followed by immediate laughter and applause:

PUZZLE: This is a moment of quite some mixed emotions
            for me.
SOLUTION: I haven't been on prime time television for quite a
            while. **Ronald Reagan**

Some years later, another veteran communicator, former British Prime Minister Harold Macmillan, used a puzzle–solution format to commend something Ronald Reagan had done. Before telling his audience what it was, he gets them wondering what it might have been:

PUZZLE: Then President Reagan did a very wise thing.
SOLUTION: He dismissed all the academic economists in
            Washington. **Harold Macmillan**

In each of these sequences, the solutions to the puzzles prompted the audience to laugh as well as applaud, and are examples of how the format can be effectively used for humorous purposes. But puzzles can equally well be posed in order to focus the audience's attention on a more serious message that's about to be delivered:

PUZZLE: The world is very different now.

SOLUTION: For man holds in his mortal hands the power to abolish all forms of human poverty, and all forms of human life. **John F. Kennedy**

🔍 Rhetorical questions

The simplest and commonest type of puzzle is to ask the audience a question or series of questions. The fact that questions in everyday conversation put us under pressure to come up with a response means that, even though members of an audience know that they are not actually going to have to answer the speaker's question, it will still make them sit up and start wondering what's coming next.

Of all nature's gifts to the human race, what is sweeter to a man than his children? **Cicero**

Shall I compare thee to a summer's day? **Shakespeare**

What is conservativism?
Is it not the adherence to the old and tried against the new and untried? **Abraham Lincoln**

What stands in our way?
The prospects of another winter of discontent?
Margaret Thatcher

Answers to rhetorical questions can, of course, be extended beyond a single word or sentence, as in this extract from Churchill's speech on taking office as prime minister:

You ask, what is our policy?
I will say: 'It is to wage war, by sea, land and air, with all our might and with all the strength that God can give us: to wage war against a monstrous tyranny, never surpassed in the dark lamentable catalogue of human crime. That is our policy.

You ask, what is our aim?
I can answer in one word. It is victory. Victory at all costs. Victory in spite of all terrors. Victory, however long and hard the road may be, for without victory there is no survival. **Winston Churchill**

One of the commonest uses of rhetorical questions is for making a link from a section that has just been completed to the one that's coming next:

So much for the past.
What about the future?

So much for the problems.
What solutions can we offer?

People often tell me that they're afraid to ask rhetorical questions in case it prompts some heckler in the audience to reply with a hostile or embarrassing put-down. In fact, this hardly ever happens, because most members of an audience assume that any question they hear is a rhetorical one that requires no immediate response from them. Indeed, this assumption is so strongly entrenched in a listener's frame of mind that, in situations where you really do want a reply from members of the audience, you have to make it very clear to them that this particular question is not merely rhetorical, but is a real one that you actually want someone to answer.

3. Lists of three

🗨 Types of three-part list

In conversations, speeches and various other forms of communication, by far the commonest type of list has three items in it (including the one at the beginning of this sentence). Lists of three also regularly trigger applause in political speeches, and are to be found in many famous quotations. They can be made up of:

Three identical words:

> I shall fight, fight and fight again to save the party I love.
> **Hugh Gaitskell**
> No, no, no. **Margaret Thatcher**
> Education, education, education. **Tony Blair**

Three different words:

> I am the way, the truth and the light. **New Testament**
> Veni, vidi, vici (*I came, I saw, I conquered*). **Julius Caesar**
> Liberté, egalité, fraternité. **French revolutionary slogan**

Three phrases:

You have all the characteristics of a popular politician: a horrible voice, bad breeding, and a vulgar manner. **Aristophanes**

Government of the people by the people for the people. **Abraham Lincoln**

I stand before you today the representative of a family in grief, in a country in mourning before a world in shock. **Lord Spencer**

Three clauses:

Happiness is when what you think, what you say, and what you do are in harmony. **Mahatma Gandhi**

Strengthened by their courage, heartened by their valour and borne by their memory, let us continue to stand for the ideals for which they lived and died. **Ronald Reagan**

Three sentences:

Dogs look up to us.
Cats look down on us.
Pigs treat us as equals. **Winston Churchill**

The time for the healing of the wounds has come.
The moment to bridge the chasms that divide us has come.
The time to build is upon us. **Nelson Mandela**

🔹 Giving the impression of completeness

One of the attractions of three-part lists is that they create an impression of completeness. Lists with only two items in them sound inadequate, and hardly seem to constitute a proper list – to the extent that we have various words and phrases we can add whenever we are having trouble finding a third item in a list. 'Thingummyjig', 'whatchumacallit', 'you know', 'and so on' and 'etcetera' can all be slotted into third position to make it sound as though the list is now complete.

Research into conversation has shown that, on those occasions where one of the speakers gets as far as a second item in a list but then gets stuck struggling to find a third one, the other conversationalists are prepared to wait for a second or so to allow them time to search for the word. This suggests that, until the arrival of a third item, we don't consider the previous turn to have come to an end. However, in cases where speakers produce lists of four items, they tend to be interrupted by another speaker immediately after the third one, so that the fourth one is drowned out by the next speaker's turn. This suggests that, in conversation, we are used to treating the third item in a list as a signal that the previous turn has finished, and that someone else can now start speaking. The equivalent in large-scale gatherings is that audiences regard third items as marking places where they can start to applaud.

🔹 Putting the longest item last

An intriguing feature of many well-known three-part lists is that they have a third item that is longer than the first two. This can take the form of longer words, or more words, in third position, as in the following examples:

Father, Son and Holy Spirit. **New Testament**

Faith, hope and charity. **New Testament**

The inalienable right to life, liberty and the pursuit of happiness. **American Declaration of Independence**

... we cannot dedicate, we cannot consecrate, we cannot hallow this ground. **Abraham Lincoln**

Ein Volk, ein Reich, ein Führer. **Adolf Hitler**

There are at least two reasons why you might want to put a longer item in third position. For one thing, third items are often the most important, as is sometimes made explicit when a speaker says 'Third, and most importantly ...'. If your third point is the most important of the three, making it longer is a simple way of implicitly highlighting its greater significance compared with the first two. The audience then has to spend more time listening to the third point than to each of the earlier ones. A second reason why longer items in third position can be useful at political rallies is that it often results in the audience starting to applaud *before* the speaker has got to the end of the list. This gives the impression that the audience agreed so strongly with the point being made that they couldn't wait to show their approval, and are now interrupting the speaker with their applause. The last part of the list then has to be delivered against a rising tide of popular acclaim, as happened in the following example of a list with a third item longer than the first two. In this particular case, the applause got under way just before the word 'united':

We're on the same side, the same team and Britain United will win. **Tony Blair**

The applause also started well before the end of a longer third item in the example from one of Tony Blair's predecessors that was discussed in Chapter 3:

You learn that they have no children in local schools.
You learn that they have no relatives on YTS.
You learn that they don't have a loved one waiting in pain on a National Health Service list. **Neil Kinnock**

4. Combined formats

In one of the above examples, Tony Blair's repetition of the word 'education' was actually prefaced by a question that announced that his answer would come in three parts. As such, it combined two techniques, the puzzle(**P**)–solution(**S**) format and a three-part list, in the same sequence:

P →   Ask me my three priorities?

S →   (1)→   Education,
                (2)→   Education,
                (3)→   and education. **Tony Blair**

This is an example of how different rhetorical techniques can be combined together in different ways, and brings us to one of the most important weapons in the speaker's armoury: the combined format. If the use of a single rhetorical technique to package a message has a positive impact on an audience, using more than one at the same time should in theory have an even greater impact. And there are at least two grounds for supposing that the combined format, in its various permutations, is indeed the most powerful rhetorical technique of them all.

🔴 Combining for greater impact

Messages packaged using a combination of rhetorical techniques are more likely to prompt longer and louder bursts of applause than normal. It may seem odd to talk about a normal or standard burst of applause, but the fact is that, with extraordinary regularity, clapping tends to come to a stop after about eight seconds (except at the end of a speech or musical performance, when it typically goes on for very much longer). Nor is this standard length of response a local cultural peculiarity of Britain or Europe. After Ayatollah Khomeni came to power in Iran, clapping was banned as a decadent western practice, and replaced by the chanting of slogans such as 'Down with the American imperialists'. Some Iranian students who studied tapes of the Ayatollah's speeches told me that the chants not only tended to occur after he had used the same rhetorical techniques as those described in this chapter, but also usually lasted for about eight seconds.

> If the use of a single rhetorical technique to package a message has a positive impact on an audience, it follows that combining more than one at the same time is likely to have an even greater impact.

This standard length of bursts of applause is so regular that we tend to notice any significant deviations from it: applause that lasts only three or four seconds sounds feeble and lukewarm, while bursts of 12 or 15 seconds sound much more enthusiastic than usual. From a politician's perspective, the important point about this is that media reporters are also likely to notice the longer bursts, with the result that the lines that triggered them stand a better chance of being singled out and played on prime time news programmes as the sound bite of the day.

A second reason for regarding combined formats as the most powerful of all is that they appear to be used more frequently by politicians with reputations as really outstanding orators than by more average run-of-the-mill speakers. This was true of Winston Churchill, John F. Kennedy and Martin Luther King, and was an observation that first came to my notice when studying speeches by veteran British Labour politician Tony Benn. His powers of oratory were such that he was able to follow his retirement from the House of Commons by giving one-man shows to packed auditoriums all over the United Kingdom. It therefore seems that one of the underlying factors that distinguishes the superstars of oratory from their lesser competitors lies in an ability to combine rhetorical techniques in interesting ways. In the following example, a 90-year-old Harold Macmillan treated the House of Lords to a puzzling contrast, one part of which contains another contrast, and the second part a three-part list. The solution (**S**) to the puzzle (**P**) deploys another contrast to bring it to a powerful conclusion.

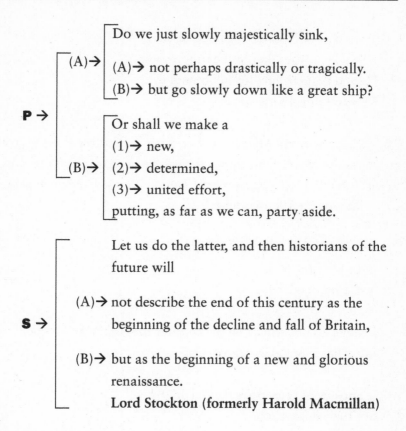

P →
  (A)→
    Do we just slowly majestically sink,
    (A)→ not perhaps drastically or tragically.
    (B)→ but go slowly down like a great ship?
  (B)→
    Or shall we make a
    (1)→ new,
    (2)→ determined,
    (3)→ united effort,
    putting, as far as we can, party aside.

S →
    Let us do the latter, and then historians of the future will

    (A)→ not describe the end of this century as the beginning of the decline and fall of Britain,

    (B)→ but as the beginning of a new and glorious renaissance.
    Lord Stockton (formerly Harold Macmillan)

There are, then, a number of ways in which the various rhetorical techniques can be combined together, and some of the main ones are summarised below.

◗ *Lists of contrasts*

Speakers don't have to stop at using one contrast, but can produce several in a row:

> We observe today not a victory of party but a celebration of freedom,
> symbolising an end as well as a beginning,
> signifying renewal as well as change. **John F. Kennedy**

> Hatred paralyses life; love releases it.
> Hatred confuses life; love harmonises it.
> Hatred darkens life; love illumines it.
> **Martin Luther King**

This example from Martin Luther King uses three consecutive contrasts, but more than three can also be used to good effect, as when John F. Kennedy accepted nomination as the Democrat candidate for the US presidency:

> The new frontier of which I speak is
> not a set of promises:
> it is a set of challenges.
>
> It sums up not what I intend to offer the American people,
> but what I intend to ask of them.
>
> It appeals to their pride,
> not their pocketbook.
>
> It holds out the promise of more sacrifice
> instead of more security. **John F. Kennedy**

On entering 10 Downing Street after winning her first general election in 1979, Mrs Thatcher quoted four contrasts from St Francis of Assisi:

> Where there is discord,
> may we bring harmony.

Where there is error,
may we bring truth.

Where there is doubt,
may we bring faith.

Where there is despair,
may we bring hope. **Margaret Thatcher**

An even longer list of contrasts is to be found in a famous passage
from the Bible, in which there are no fewer than 23 repeats of the
words 'a time'.

To everything there is a season,
a time for every purpose under the sun.
A time to be born and a time to die;
a time to plant and a time to pluck up that which is planted;
a time to kill and a time to heal ...
a time to weep and a time to laugh;
a time to mourn and a time to dance ...
a time to embrace and a time to refrain from embracing;
a time to lose and a time to seek;
a time to rend and a time to sew;
a time to keep silent and a time to speak;
a time to love and a time to hate;
a time for war and a time for peace. **Ecclesiastes 3: 1–8**

● *Lists of questions*

Posing one rhetorical question after another can also build up an audience's sense of anticipation, as was done very effectively in Ronald Reagan's speech to veterans on the fortieth anniversary of the Normandy landings:

> ... you risked everything here. Why? Why did you do it? What impelled you to put aside the instinct for self-preservation and risk your lives to take these cliffs? What inspired all the men of the armies that met here?

> We look at you, and somehow we know the answer.
> It was faith and belief; it was loyalty and love.
> **Ronald Reagan**

● *Combining lists and contrasts*

The following is an example of how to include three contrasting items (*culmination–vindication, campaign–crusade, a few weeks–a hundred years*) in each part of a contrast:

> Those 'yes' votes in Scotland and Wales were
> not the culmination of a campaign of a few weeks.
> They were the vindication of a hundred year crusade.
> **Paddy Ashdown**

Sometimes the first part of the contrast (**A**) can be made up of three items, as in the following two examples:

A →
    (1)→ When I was a child, I spake as a child,
    (2)→ I understood as a child,
    (3)→ I thought as a child;

B →
    but when I became a man, I put away childish things. **1 Corinthians 13:11**

A →
    (1)→ This was not a mandate for dogma,
    (2)→ or for doctrine
    (3)→ or a return to the past,

B →
    but it was a mandate to get those things done in our country that desperately need doing for the future of Britain. **Tony Blair**

🗨 *Puzzles with contrastive solutions*

One way of solving a puzzle (**P**) is with a solution (**S**) in the form of a contrast, as in this famous quotation from the nineteenth century:

P →
    The difference between a misfortune and a calamity is this:

S →
    (A)→ If Gladstone fell into the Thames, it would be a misfortune.

    (B)→ But if someone dragged him out again, that would be a calamity. **Benjamin Disraeli**

The same technique was used by Winston Churchill to show his awareness of how difficult it is to make an after-dinner speech:

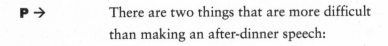

P →   There are two things that are more difficult than making an after-dinner speech:

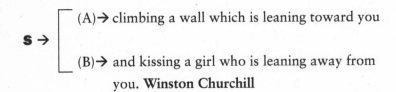

S →

(A)→ climbing a wall which is leaning toward you

(B)→ and kissing a girl who is leaning away from you. **Winston Churchill**

At the start of the 1987 election, a puzzle (**P**) with contrastive solution (**S**) from Margaret Thatcher was replayed on prime time news broadcasts:

P →   So from the Labour Party expect the iceberg manifesto.

S →

(A)→ One-tenth of its socialism visible,

(B)→ Nine-tenths beneath the surface.
Margaret Thatcher

The Labour Party must have felt it an important enough point to be worth responding to, and it was not long before the then leader, Neil Kinnock, addressed it head on with another kind of combined format, in which the solution (**S**) to the puzzle (**P**) came in the form of a three-part list.

Puzzles with solutions in three parts

P →   In a way she was right – it is a bit of an iceberg manifesto.

S →
(1)→ It's really cool,
(2)→ and it is very tough,
(3)→ and totally unsinkable. **Neil Kinnock**

Sometimes the three parts of the solution to a puzzle can be longer than just a few words, and, as in the following example, may involve embedded contrasts as well:

P →   There are those who are asking the devotees of civil rights, 'When will you be satisfied?'

S →
(1)→ We can never be satisfied as long as our bodies, heavy with the fatigue of travel, cannot gain lodging in
(A)→ the motels of the highways and
(B)→ the hotels of the cities.

(2)→ We cannot be satisfied as long as the Negro's basic mobility is
(A)→ from a smaller ghetto
(B)→ to a larger one.

(3)→ We can never be satisfied as long as
(A)→ a Negro in Mississippi cannot vote and
(B)→ a Negro in New York believes he has nothing for which to vote. **Martin Luther King**

In neither of the above examples does the speaker give advance notice to the audience that there are going to be three parts to the solution, but some puzzles make this explicit right from the start:

P →   There are three kinds of lies.

S →   (1)→ Lies,
       (2)→ damned lies,
       (3)→ and statistics. **Benjamin Disraeli**

🎤 *Three-part lists where each item contrasts with the one before it*
It can also be very effective to contrast a second item with the first, and the third one with the second:

You can fool some of the people all of the time,
and all of the people some of the time,
but you cannot fool all of the people all of the time.
Abraham Lincoln

This is not the end.
It is not even the beginning of the end.
But it is perhaps the end of the beginning. **Winston Churchill**

Recession is when your neighbour loses his job.
Depression is when you lose yours.
And recovery is when Jimmy Carter loses his. **Ronald Reagan**

🎤 *Three-part lists with a third item that contrasts with the first two*
A very simple and adaptable technique that can be used to get

almost any key point across, is to contrast a third item with the first two:

> I am not an Athenian
> or a Greek,
> but a citizen of the world. **Socrates**

> ... we pledge our best efforts to help them help themselves ...
> not because the Communists may be doing it,
> not because we seek their votes,
> but because it is right. **John F. Kennedy**

> We don't hide our space programme.
> We don't keep secrets and cover things up.
> We do it all up front and in public. **Ronald Reagan**

What makes this so easy to use is that all a speaker has to do is start by deciding what the main point to be made is to be, and then find two negatives to go in front of it (or, if the point is in the negative, two positives):

> We will negotiate for it [peace],
> sacrifice for it,
> we will never surrender for it, now or ever. **Ronald Reagan**

This technique is also widely found in the history of fable and the world of humour. In the parable of the Good Samaritan, for example, the first two travellers pass by on the other side, but the third takes care of the injured victim. The first two parts of the story establish a pattern that is then broken by the third, and it is in this contrast with the first two that the moral of the story lies. Traditional children's stories, like the Three Little Pigs and Three Billy Goats Gruff, have the same structure and work in exactly the same way.

The same is true of large numbers of jokes, where the punch line comes in third position, the humour coming from the contrast with the expectation established by the first two parts of the joke. So dominant is this three-part structure that one of the countries of the British Isles is left out in the large collection of jokes that begin with the line, 'There was an Englishman, an Irishman and a Scotsman ...'. The absence of a Welshman almost certainly has less to do with anti-Welsh sentiment than with the power of the rule of three. Nor do unexpected lines only have a humorous impact when they come in the third line of jokes that have been announced as such in advance. They can also have a similar impact when they complete a list that starts out with two serious-sounding items, as in the following list of the virtues of life in the USA:

> ... freedom of speech,
> freedom of conscience,
> and the prudence never to practise either. **Mark Twain**

5. Conclusion

This chapter has concentrated on ways of putting words, phrases and sentences together that have a long and well-proven record of striking chords with audiences. However, before looking in more detail at how to use them in speeches and presentations, we need to consider another very important set of techniques with just as long and distinguished a history as the rhetorical structures described above. In fact, we have already had a glimpse of them in some of the quotations, which have referred to things like 'building a future', 'a winter of discontent', 'climbing a mountain', 'icebergs' and 'sinking ships'. Yet none of the speakers who used these images was talking literally about building, winter, mountain climbing, icebergs or disasters at sea. Nor, of course, would any hearer or reader of these words and phrases seriously think that they were. And the reason for this is that we are all very familiar with using and understanding various forms of imagery.

Summary

Although the word 'rhetoric' tends to have negative connotations nowadays, it originally referred to the study of verbal techniques for packaging messages in striking and persuasive ways.

These are still as effective today as they ever were, and provide a simple toolkit for translating otherwise bland statements into more striking and punchy forms. Examples of the main types and sub-types are listed below.

1. Contrasts

Contradictions: 'not this but that'
The house we hope to build is not for my generation but for yours. **Ronald Reagan**

Comparisons: 'more this than that'
The man who reads nothing at all is better educated than the man who reads nothing but newspapers.
Thomas Jefferson

Opposites: 'black or white'
There is nothing wrong with America that cannot be solved by what's right with America. **Bill Clinton**

● *Phrase reversals*

Ask not what your country can do for you; ask what you can do for your country. **John F. Kennedy**

2. Puzzles and questions

● *Puzzle–solution format*

PUZZLE: On my way here I passed a local cinema and it turned out you were expecting me after all

SOLUTION: for the billboards read: 'The Mummy Returns'.
    Margaret Thatcher

● *Rhetorical questions*

Shall I compare thee to a summer's day? **Shakespeare**

3. Lists of three

● *Three identical words*

Education, education and education. **Tony Blair**

● *Three different words*

Liberté, egalité, fraternité. **French revolutionary slogan**

● *Three phrases*

Government of the people by the people for the people. **Abraham Lincoln**

● *Three clauses*

Happiness is when what you think, what you say, and what you do are in harmony. **Mahatma Gandhi**

Three sentences

Dogs look up to us.

Cats look down on us.

Pigs treat us as equals. **Winston Churchill**

4. Combinations

Any of the first three techniques can be combined in various ways that are likely to have an even greater impact than any single one used on its own (e.g. lists of three contrasts or questions, puzzles with solutions that come as a contrast or in three parts, lists of three in which the third item contrasts with the first two, etc.).

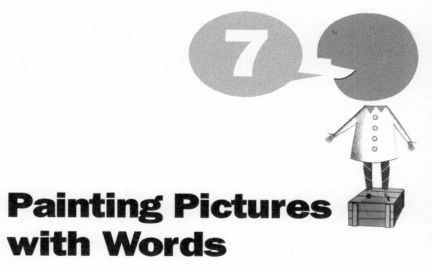

Painting Pictures with Words

The Use of Imagery and Anecdotes

A picture may sometimes tell a thousand words, but words can just as easily be used to create a thousand images. Whether it's *'an iron curtain descending'* across Europe (Winston Churchill), *'a wind of change blowing* across Africa' (Harold Macmillan) or *'a great beacon light of hope shining* across America' (Martin Luther King), we know instantly that the speaker is not speaking literally, and have no trouble in seeing exactly what is meant. And *'seeing'* the point is a crucial part of the process, because the use of imagery requires listeners to make the connection between the visual image and the reality to which it refers, and then to draw their own conclusions. The mental effort involved in doing this, coupled with the satisfaction that can come on seeing the point, may well be at the heart of why the use of imagery is such an effective way to strike chords with an audience.

Imagery involves important similarities with two of the key principles discussed in previous chapters. The first is that, by enabling us to encapsulate complex ideas in a brief and economical way, it provides a means of achieving the kind of simplicity of expression that plays such an important part in effective communication. A single word, phrase or sentence can often be enough to get across a point that would otherwise take many more sentences to explain. Imagery can also be seen as another type of contrastive technique, as it involves making an implicit or explicit comparison between a particular image and the actual subject matter under discussion.

1. Imagery, poetics and the oral tradition

If rhetoric has a history dating back more than 2,000 years, the history of imagery goes back even further to the world of preliterate societies. Writing may have been a major breakthrough in our capacity to store and transmit complex knowledge in detail (see Chapter 3), but it was possible to store limited forms of knowledge within the oral tradition. A common feature of preliterate societies is that poetry and story telling play an important part as repositories of cultural and religious information. In the case of verse, metre, rhythm, rhyme and alliteration combine with imagery to provide a means of storing knowledge in a form that is easy to remember and pass on from one generation to another. It's widely believed, for example, that the Greek poet Homer never actually existed, and that it was the name given to the team of scribes who wrote down what had been circulating within the oral tradition for generations before the advent of writing. The same is true of the Old Testament, which only started to be written down in around the tenth century BC, and is, of course, a vast storehouse of imagery, proverbs, poems (psalms) and stories. But, whether

> Before the invention of writing, poetry and story telling enabled knowledge to be stored in a purely oral form that was easy to remember and pass on from one generation to another. When it comes to striking chords with an audience, similes, metaphors and analogies are still as effective as they ever were.

conveyed in poems or prose, the point about stories and fables is that they are so easy to remember that they can be told and retold time and time again. The importance of parables in the establishment of world religions like Christianity is powerful evidence of just how successful well-chosen stories can be in illustrating and communicating core beliefs to a very wide audience over a very long period of time.

2. Everyday imagery

Before looking at some of the most important types of imagery, it is extremely important to be aware that there is nothing difficult or mysterious about putting it to work in speeches and presentations. An ability to use imagery effectively is not a specialised art that is a monopoly of great speakers or writers, but is a thoroughly normal and regular feature of everyday speech. Regardless of whether anyone actually knows what a simile or metaphor is, everyone makes regular use of them. In fact, many images are so much a part of the language that we are hardly even aware that we are speaking metaphorically. We sometimes *bite off more than we can chew*, find things *as easy as pie*, sleep *like a log*, or run *like the wind*. There are those who *live in the fast lane* and *spend an arm and a leg* on maintaining their lifestyle, while others *live from hand to mouth* without *two pennies to rub together*. On occasions, we *make mountains out of molehills, rub people up the wrong way* or *pull their legs*. We also sometimes *beat about the bush, get our wires crossed, jump to conclusions* and may even *break someone's heart*. And, once *embarked* on *pulling together* a *catalogue* of examples, we have to be continually *on guard* against the temptation of *scraping the barrel* or *going over the top*.

Although everyone may be perfectly at ease in using imagery in everyday speech, many speakers tend to edit it out when it comes to addressing an audience. This is especially true of business presentations, where a reluctance to use imagery is a feature of the 'cloak of formality syndrome' discussed earlier (see Chapter 3). It's as if people feel that they have to speak in a much more official and analytical way than usual, and must therefore avoid using anything that smacks of colourful language. What they don't realise is that something all effective speakers have in common is a capacity to use imagery in interesting and imaginative ways. Nor should it be thought that you have to avoid imagery when speaking analytically about facts and information. This is even true in the language of science and technology, which is littered with metaphors and analogies. Magnetic *fields*, sound *waves* and *cells* have been with us for generations, and we now think nothing of using search *engines*, *robots* and *spiders* to *surf the net, navigating our way* through an information *superhighway* in *cyberspace*, using computers that are vulnerable to *infections* from *viruses, worms* and *Trojans*.

3. Types of imagery

🗨 *Similes*

Sometimes called 'open' or 'overt' comparisons, similes make it clear that the thing being talked about is *like* something else:

> My love is like a red, red rose
> That's newly sprung in June:
> My love is like the melodie
> That's sweetly played in tune. **Robert Burns**

> I'll be floating like a butterfly and stinging like a bee.
> **Muhammad Ali**

At one stage during his eulogy at the funeral of Queen Elizabeth, the Queen Mother, the then Archbishop of Canterbury developed the imagery established by an initial simile:

> Like the sun, she bathed us in her warm glow. Now that the sun has set and the cool of the evening has come, some of the warmth we absorbed is flowing back towards her. **Archbishop George Carey**

But similes can just as easily be used to criticise or poke fun at someone:

> Being attacked by Sir Geoffrey Howe is like being savaged by a dead sheep. **Denis Healey**

Margaret Thatcher must have wished that this were true, because it was an attack from the same Geoffrey Howe that was to mark the beginning of the end of her premiership. In his resignation speech to the House of Commons, he described what it had been like working with her, and used a cricketing simile with devastating effect:

> It's rather like sending your opening batsmen to the crease, only for them to find, the moment the first balls are bowled, that their bats have been broken before the game by the team captain. **Geoffrey Howe**

Sporting images are very adaptable for getting a wide variety of messages across in a way that is likely to appeal to a wide audience, provided, of course, that national differences are taken into account. British speakers, for example, can't rely on cricketing images to make much sense to audiences from parts of the world where they don't play the game. A curious exception to this is that American sporting metaphors, such as 'getting to (or past) first base', have been adopted in parts of the English-speaking world where there is little or no interest in baseball.

You can also use similes in combination with the rhetorical techniques discussed earlier, as in the following example of three in a row:

> A hippie is someone who walks like Tarzan, looks like Jane and smells like Cheetah. **Ronald Reagan**

There is considerable scope for using them to set up the first part of a puzzle–solution sequence:

Socialism is like a dream.
Sooner or later you wake up to reality. **Winston Churchill**

Being powerful is like being a lady.
If you have to tell people you are, you aren't.
Margaret Thatcher

Government is like a baby.
An alimentary canal with a big appetite at one end
and no sense of responsibility at the other. **Ronald Reagan**

One of Churchill's most famous wartime quotations was produced in response to a simile that had been used by French generals in 1940.

When I warned them [the French Government] that Britain would fight on alone whatever they did, their generals told their Prime Minister and his divided Cabinet, 'In three weeks England will have her neck wrung like a chicken.' Some chicken! Some neck! **Winston Churchill**

Whereas similes make it quite clear that one thing is being compared with another, metaphors achieve similar effects in a rather less obvious way.

Metaphors

Metaphor involves using a comparative image without using words such as 'as' or 'like' to make it explicit that this is what you are doing; it leaves it to listeners to get the point for themselves.

This may only involve a word or two, as in various famous insults and nicknames: Churchill referred to Mussolini as 'the bullfrog of the Pontine marshes'; Margaret Thatcher was variously described as 'the iron lady', 'Atilla the Hen' and the 'immaculate misconception'; according to Gore Vidal, Ronald Reagan was 'a triumph of the embalmer's art'; and, when Tony Blair became leader of the Labour Party, his opponents dubbed him 'Bambi'. These examples highlight something every schoolchild knows and every teacher fears, namely that nicknames based on metaphors that sum up some particular characteristic of a person tend to stick.

But metaphors are just as useful for paying people compliments, as when we talk of someone being a 'tower of strength', 'solid as a rock' or as in Newton's famous acknowledgement of his debt to previous scholars:

If I have seen further, it is by *standing on the shoulders of giants*. **Isaac Newton**

Just as we know that Newton was not claiming literally to have stood on the shoulders of giants, we also know that the speaker in the next example was not talking about going for a walk though a few valleys and up a mountain:

There is no easy *walk to freedom* anywhere, and many of us will have to pass through the *valley of the shadow of death* again and again before we reach *the mountaintop of our desires*. **Nelson Mandela**

Nor, when we hear speakers referring to 'today' and 'tomorrow', do we think that they are referring to Tuesday and Wednesday, rather than the present and the future.

> You cannot escape the responsibility of *tomorrow* by evading it *today*. **Abraham Lincoln**

In one of his wartime speeches, Churchill spoke of a better future as 'broad sunlit uplands' in the first part of a contrast, and of 'sinking into the abyss of a new Dark Age' in the second part:

> If we can stand up to him, all Europe may be free and the life of the world may move forward into *broad, sunlit uplands*. But if we fail, then the whole world, including the United States, including all that we have known and cared for, will *sink into the abyss of a new Dark Age*. **Winston Churchill**

Two decades later, Martin Luther King used almost identical images the other way around:

> Now is the time to rise from the *dark and desolate valley of segregation* to the *sunlit path of racial justice*.
> **Martin Luther King**

These examples, together with the earlier ones from everyday speech, point to the almost infinite scope for using similes and metaphors to get your points across. But you don't always have to stop after a few words or sentences, and can sometimes expand on them in greater detail.

🔈 Analogies

Although there is a certain amount of scholarly disagreement about the precise difference between similes, metaphors and analogies, one view, which is the one taken here, is that analogies are extended similes and metaphors used to simplify and explain some more complicated state of affairs. Margaret Thatcher, for example, revelled in making parallels between the management of the British economy and her experience as a housewife managing a domestic budget. More generally, analogies are widely used in the teaching of science and medicine. Discussions of electricity often use the analogy of water flowing through pipes, the heart can be thought of as a pump, the liver as a filter and so on.

But it's only ever possible to develop analogies so far, as there usually comes a point where the comparison starts to break down in the face of details that don't quite fit. At that point, an analogy can become counterproductive, unless the aim is to push it to its limits for deliberately humorous purposes. A classic case of this was Alan Bennett's spoof sermon in the 1960s satirical review *Beyond the Fringe*, which included the following extended analogy:

Life, you know, is rather like opening a tin of sardines. And I wonder how many of you here tonight have wasted years of your lives looking behind the kitchen dressers of this life for that key. I know I have. Others think they've found the key, don't they? They roll back the lid of the sardine tin of life, they reveal the sardines, the riches of life, therein, and they get them out, they enjoy them. But, you know, there's always a little bit in the corner that you can't get out. I wonder – I wonder, is there a little bit in the corner of your life? I know there is in mine. **Alan Bennett**

But you can sometimes successfully extend analogies to develop more serious themes at greater length. One of the most outstanding exponents of this was Martin Luther King, whose speeches bristle with vivid imagery drawn from the Bible and elsewhere. Indeed, of all the orators I have ever studied, his mastery of metaphor and analogy was second to none, as can be seen by reading almost any of his major speeches. Cashing a cheque at a bank might seem at first sight to be a rather unpromising analogy, but he managed to develop it in a way that vividly summed up the issues that had given rise to the civil rights movement, and the mass demonstration in Washington in 1963. As well as the banking imagery, the sequence includes other metaphors, repetition and a series of powerful contrasts:

In a sense we have come to our nation's capital to *cash a cheque*. When the *architects* of our republic wrote the magnificent words of the Constitution and the Declaration of Independence, *they were signing a promissory note* to which every American was to *fall heir.*

This note was a promise that all men would be guaranteed the inalienable rights of life, liberty, and the pursuit of happiness. It is obvious today that America has *defaulted on this promissory note* insofar as her citizens of colour are concerned. Instead of honouring this sacred obligation, America has given the Negro people a *bad cheque which has come back marked 'insufficient funds'.* But we refuse to believe that the *bank of justice is bankrupt.* We refuse to believe that there are *insufficient funds in the great vaults of opportunity* of this nation.

So we have come to cash this cheque – a cheque that will give us upon demand the riches of freedom and the security of justice. We have also come to this *hallowed spot* to remind America of the fierce urgency of now.

This is no time to engage in the *luxury of cooling off* or to take the *tranquillising drug of gradualism.* Now is the time to *rise from the dark and desolate valley of segregation to the sunlit path of racial justice.* Now is the time to *open the doors of opportunity* to all of God's children. Now is the time to *lift our nation from the quicksands of racial injustice to the solid rock of brotherhood.*
Martin Luther King

🔊 *Mixing and modifying metaphors*
One of the risks of extending an image is that speakers sometimes confuse one metaphor with another without realising it:

Security is the essential *roadblock* to achieving the *road map to peace.* **George W. Bush**

The result can be amusing for listeners, even though this may not be what the speaker was intending. Many of the verbal slips, regularly published in the 'Colemanballs' section of the magazine

Private Eye, involve inadvertently mixed metaphors, as in the following quotations from British football managers:

> If you can't stand the *heat in the dressing-room*, get out of *the kitchen*. **Terry Venables**

> We *threw our dice into the ring* and *turned up trumps*. **Bruce Rioch**

> I have *sown a few seeds* and *thrown a few hand grenades* and I am now waiting for *the dust to settle* so that I can see how *all the jigsaw bits come together.* **Gary Johnson**

In the case of metaphors that are so well known that everyone has heard of them, you can sometimes modify them to get a point across in a humorous way:

> A sheep dressed in sheep's clothing. **Winston Churchill** (about Clement Attlee)

> He was born with a silver foot in his mouth. **Ann Richards** (about George Bush Sr.)

> Every silver lining has a cloud. **Anonymous**

Similar witty effects can be achieved by extending famous metaphors, as in:

> Familiarity breeds contempt – and children. **Mark Twain**

A government that robs Peter to pay Paul can always depend upon the support of Paul. **George Bernard Shaw**

A stitch in time would have confused Einstein. **Anonymous**

4. Anecdotes

From the earliest days of infancy, we are exposed to story telling, and our command of language develops so quickly that we soon become very skilled at telling stories to others. Even very young children are able to describe their birthday party, or what happened at play school. Indeed, if they were unable to tell the story of what kind of insect had just stung them, or how some injury occurred, their chances of survival would be significantly reduced. And if people didn't like listening to stories, it would be impossible to understand the enduring popularity of literature, the theatre and the cinema, not to mention the domination of television schedules by soap operas and other drama programmes.

Just as an ability to use metaphors and similes is not confined to great writers and speakers, so too is a capacity to tell stories something we are all very used to doing in everyday speech. A great deal of conversation involves us in telling each other stories about what happened at the weekend, where we went on holidays or how things went when we last saw the doctor. When it comes to speaking in public – whether teaching a class, preaching a sermon, making a political or after-dinner speech or giving a business presentation – people with reputations as effective speakers invariably excel at using illustrative anecdotes to get key points across. In fact, it can be such an effective technique that I have often thought that large organisations ought to employ corporate anthropolo-

> The two key rules for the effective use of anecdotes are first that they should be relevant to the point being made, and second that they should be brief – i.e. not much more than a minute or so.

gists, whose job would be to collect stories about successes and failures that could be used to liven up executive presentations.

It is not that any old anecdote will do, or that there are no limits on how long you should spend telling a story. The two key rules for the effective use of anecdotes are first that they should be relevant to the point being made, and second that they should not go on for too long. The trouble is that being brief and to the point is easier said than done, and requires you to be very disciplined about what details to include or exclude. This problem arises from the fact that descriptions of events can always be endlessly extended and elaborated. I saw a striking example of this while involved in a research project into group therapy sessions at a psychiatric hospital. At one of them, the doctor asked a patient, who'd just been home for the weekend for the first time since being admitted, to describe how it had gone. The story began as follows:

I got up, had a shower and went downstairs to the cafeteria and had my breakfast: porridge, bacon and eggs and toast. Then I went back upstairs, brushed my teeth, packed my bag, and spent ages trying to find my hair brush. Then I went downstairs, through the hall and out through the revolving doors at the main entrance. I walked down the drive to the hospital gates, and realised I didn't know what time the bus left. So I went across the road to the bus shelter to read the timetable. Then I had to wait about 15 minutes before a bus came. When it arrived, I thought should I go upstairs or downstairs ...

A minute or more into the story and he was only just getting on to the bus home. In the end, the psychiatrist had to press him to get on with it, and to tell the group what had happened when he finally arrived home and met up with his wife and family.

By contrast, and even though it is a story with three parts, the parable of the Good Samaritan is a model of economy, the main part of the story taking a mere 166 words:

A certain man went down from Jerusalem to Jericho, and fell among thieves, which stripped him of his raiment, and wounded him, and departed, leaving him half dead. And by chance there came down a certain priest that way: and when he saw him, he passed by on the other side. And likewise a Levite, when he was at the place, came and looked on him, and passed by on the other side. But a certain Samaritan, as he journeyed, came where he was: and when he saw him, he had compassion on him. And he went to him, and bound up his wounds, pouring in oil and wine, and set him on his own beast, and brought him to an inn, and took care of him. And on the morrow, when he departed, he took out two pence, and gave them to the host, and said unto him, Take care of him; and whatsoever thou spendest more, when I come again, I will repay thee. **Luke 10: 30–35**

In 1952, suspicions about misappropriation of campaign funds forced a young Richard Nixon to defend himself on national television. Often featured in collections of famous American speeches, it became known as the 'Checkers speech' because of one short anecdote:

> One other thing I probably should tell you, because if I don't they'll probably be saying this about me, too. We did get something, a gift, after the election. A man down in Texas heard Pat on the radio mention the fact that our two youngsters would like to have a dog. And believe it or not, the day before we left on this campaign trip we got a message from Union Station in Baltimore, saying they had a package for us. We went down to get it. You know what it was? It was a little cocker spaniel dog, in a crate that he had sent all the way from Texas, black and white, spotted, and our little girl Tricia, the six year old, named it Checkers. And you know, the kids, like all kids, love the dog, and I just want to say this, right now, that regardless of what they say about it, we're gonna keep it.
> **Richard Nixon**

One of the most famous British speeches of the 1960s was Enoch Powell's controversial analysis of what he saw as the dangers of mass immigration. It contained much vivid imagery, including the line, 'Like the Roman I seem to see the River Tiber foaming with much blood', that led to its becoming known as the 'Rivers of Blood' speech. He also claimed to be watching a nation 'busily engaged in heaping up its own funeral pyre', and that race relations legislation would 'risk throwing a match on to gun powder'. But the main thrust of his argument was established early in the speech with an anecdote that began as follows:

> I am going to allow just one of those hundreds of people to speak for me. Eight years ago in a respectable street in Wolverhampton a house was sold to a Negro. Now only one white [woman old-age pensioner] lives there. This is her story. She lost her husband and both her sons in the war. So she turned her seven-roomed house, her only asset, into a boarding house. She worked hard and did well, paid off her mortgage and began to put something by for her old age. Then the immigrants moved in. With growing fear, she saw one house after another taken over. The quiet street became a place of noise and confusion. Regretfully, her white tenants moved out. **Enoch Powell**

Another master of the well-chosen anecdote was Ronald Reagan, whose potential as a major player on the political stage first attracted widespread attention with his 'Rendezvous with Destiny' speech in support of Barry Goldwater's nomination as Republican candidate for the US presidency in 1964. Sometimes known simply as 'The Speech', it included several fine examples of how to use anecdotes to get key points across briefly and succinctly:

> Not too long ago two friends of mine were talking to a Cuban refugee, a businessman who had escaped from Castro, and in the midst of his story one of my friends turned to the other and said, 'We don't know how lucky

we are.' And the Cuban stopped and said, 'How lucky you are! I had someplace to escape to.' In that sentence he told us the entire story. If we lose freedom here, there is no place to escape to. **Ronald Reagan**

Some of Ronald Reagan's speeches as president also featured anecdotes that were perfectly fitted to the occasion and the audience. For example, his address to Second World War veterans on the fortieth anniversary of the Normandy Landings included the following:

I think I know what you may be thinking right now – thinking 'we were just part of a bigger effort; everyone was brave that day'. Well, everyone was. Do you remember the story of Bill Millin of the 51st Highlanders? Forty years ago today, British troops were pinned down near a bridge, waiting desperately for help. Suddenly, they heard the sound of bagpipes, and some thought they were dreaming. Well, they weren't. They looked up and saw Bill Millin with his bagpipes, leading the reinforcements and ignoring the smack of bullets into the ground around him. Lord Lovat was with him – Lord Lovat of Scotland, who calmly announced when he got to the bridge, 'Sorry, I'm a few minutes late,' as if he'd been delayed by a traffic jam, when in truth he'd just come from the bloody fighting on Sword Beach, which he and his men had just taken. **Ronald Reagan**

I have included these anecdotes in full in order to underline the point that the most effective story-tellers keep them brief. It is obviously difficult to be precise about the perfect length, but the evidence from famous speeches that both had an impact when delivered and were remembered later suggests that the most effective anecdotes hardly ever take much more than a minute to deliver.

5. The sound of words

Within the oral tradition, imagery and story telling were not the only things that enabled ideas and information to be stored and passed on to others. Just as important, especially when it comes to remembering poems, is the sound of the words themselves and the part played by things like alliteration, rhythm and rhymes.

In moderation, the use of alliteration, in which a series of words start with the same sound, is the most adaptable of these techniques when it comes to making speeches, and some of the earlier quotations featured examples of this:

Veni, vidi, vici. **Julius Caesar**

Fair is foul and foul is fair. **Shakespeare**

It appeals to their pride, not their pocketbook.
John F. Kennedy

Other famous examples include:

We cannot fail or falter. **Winston Churchill**

Let us go forth to lead the land we love. **John F. Kennedy**

This sweltering summer of the Negro's legitimate discontent. **Martin Luther King**

One alliterative contrast, 'the ballot or the bullet', originally attributed to American Black Power leader Malcolm X, was revived some years later to sum up the key political choice facing paramilitary groups in Northern Ireland. And it was a simple alliterative phrase, 'the people's princess', that became the most widely quoted sound bite from Tony Blair's speech on the morning after the death of Diana, Princess of Wales.

Although alliteration may have a positive impact when used in moderation, you have to be careful not to overdo it. One accomplished orator who has, on occasions, pushed the use of rhyme and alliteration to the limits is Jesse Jackson, whose speech to the Democratic National Convention in 1984 included the following sequence of three poetically constructed contrasts:

Dream of doctors who are concerned more with public health than private wealth.
Dream of lawyers more concerned about justice than judgeship.
Dream of preachers who are concerned more about prophecy than profiteering. **Jesse Jackson**

The same speech also included an alliterative sequence of five words beginning with the same sound:

My constituency is the desperate, damned, disinherited, disrespected and the despised. **Jesse Jackson**

At another stage in the speech, a series of rhymes came in quick succession:

Today's students can put dope in their veins or hope in
their brains.
If they can conceive it and believe it, they can achieve it.
They must know it is not their aptitude but their attitude
that will determine their altitude. **Jesse Jackson**

The trouble with sequences containing such frequent repetition of
rhyme or alliteration is that the audience is almost certain to be
distracted by them and have their attention diverted away from
the content of the messages to the form of words and the creative
effort that must have gone into producing them. Such poetic lines
may work well enough as advertising slogans, as in 'A Mars a day
helps you work, rest and play', or 'Soft, long and very strong', but
can come across in speeches as so contrived as to be distracting
and counter-productive. When it comes to poetic elements, then,
the safest strategy is to be very wary about using rhyme, and only
to use alliteration occasionally and in moderation.

6. Quotations

Many of the examples of similes, metaphors and analogies referred
to in this chapter are to be found in dictionaries of quotations,
which are, of course, widely used by speakers as a source of inspira-
tion. They provide a rich resource, not only of imagery that might
be worth borrowing and reusing, but also of lines suitable for quoting verbatim during a speech or presentation. As with other forms
of imagery, the main rule in selecting a quotation is that it should be
relevant to the point a speaker is trying to get across. This was not
the case in the opening of Alan Bennett's spoof sermon in *Beyond
the Fringe*, some of the humour of which came from the fact that it

quickly became apparent that there was no connection at all between the opening quotation and what followed:

The 29th verse of the 14th book of Genesis: 'My brother Esau is an hairy man but I am a smooth man.'
Alan Bennett

Bennett's humour was based on the fact that quoting from a religious text is a standard way of starting a sermon. But you can also use quotations to good effect at the beginning of almost any other kind of speech, lecture or presentation, so long as you stick to the relevance rule. If it sounds as though you are just using a quotation for the sake of using a quotation, the audience is unlikely to be impressed. It's therefore very important not to use dictionaries of quotations indiscriminately. A near disaster of this kind was narrowly averted when a client of mine, who was chancellor of his local university, sent me the text of a speech he was planning to give at a graduation ceremony. The first page contained four quotations about education, not one of which had any connection whatsoever with university education, graduation days or any of the themes covered in the rest of the speech. They were, in other words, as irrelevant as the opening quotation in Bennett's spoof sermon, and underline the danger of undisciplined searches through dictionaries of quotations.

One final warning about the use of quotations is that it is important to make it clear that they were originally someone else's words rather than your own, otherwise the effect can be quite disastrous, as happened when American Senator Joe Biden, a candidate for the Democratic presidential nomination in 1987, borrowed some lines from a speech made by Neil Kinnock and used them as if they were his own:

Kinnock's original version	Biden's borrowed version
Why am I the first Kinnock in a thousand generations to be able to get to university? Why is Glenys the first woman in her family in a thousand generations to be able to get to university?	Why is it that Joe Biden is the first in his family ever to go to university? Why is it that my wife who is sitting out there in the audienceis the first in her family to ever go to college?
Was it because our predecessors were thick? ... Of course not. It was because there was no platform upon which they could stand.	Is it because our fathers and mothers were not bright? ... No, it's not because they weren't as smart ... It's because they didn't have a platform upon which to stand.

Shortly after this remarkable similarity was noticed and exposed by the media, Biden's campaign for the Democratic nomination collapsed.

7. Naturally gifted speakers?

Almost all the examples in this and the previous chapter have been taken from famous speakers or writers from different periods of history. The advantage of using well-known sources is that it underlines the fact that all persuasive speakers, regardless of their nationality or political views, use the same techniques to get messages across in punchy and vivid ways. The disadvantage of citing famous speakers is that it's likely to prompt a worrying question that often arises when people are first being exposed to these techniques. It's all very well, they say, to use quotations from the great and the good, but they're all gifted speakers blessed with a natural ability to produce punchy lines without giving it a second thought, whereas we aren't so gifted and therefore stand no chance of getting our messages across with anything like the same impact.

One of the first occasions when I came up against this issue was during a radio interview about the televised experiment at the 1984 SDP Conference, in which I had helped a novice speaker to win a standing ovation. The show's producers had asked Ken Livingstone, who was then leader of the Greater London Council, what he thought about the rhetorical techniques we had used. His reply went as follows:

Public speakers are born,
not made.
People shouldn't worry about all these techniques;
they should just be themselves. **Ken Livingstone**

The irony in this is that here was someone using two consecutive contrasts in order to reject the usefulness of rhetorical techniques. In other words, he was using one of the most powerful techniques in the rhetorical armoury to say, in effect, that persuasive power should be left in the hands of people like him who happen to have had the good fortune to speak that way naturally.

A much more democratic and less élitist view is that the goal should be to liberate the techniques that gifted speakers are blessed with, and to make them available for anyone and everyone to use them for themselves. After 20 years of running courses and coaching programmes based on this principle, I am in no doubt that a command over rhetoric and imagery does not have to remain the monopoly of a gifted few, but can be acquired quickly and easily by anyone. The next chapter starts to look at how this can be done.

Imagery, poetry and fables are central to the oral tradition, and provided a way of storing and communicating knowledge before the invention of writing. They are just as powerful today as they ever were, and are important weapons in the armoury of effective speakers.

1. Types of Imagery

Similes

Sometimes called 'open' or 'overt' comparisons, similes make it clear that the thing being talked about is *like* something else:

> I'll be floating like a butterfly and stinging like a bee.
> **Muhammad Ali**

Metaphors

Metaphor involves using a comparative image without words like 'as' and 'like' to make it explicit that this is what you are doing:

> If I have seen further, it is by standing on the shoulders of giants. **Isaac Newton**

Unless you deliberately intend to be humorous, beware of mixing metaphors:

> If you can't stand the heat in the dressing room, get out of the kitchen. **Terry Venables**

● *Analogies*

These involve extending a simile or metaphor, and provide a vivid way of simplifying and clarifying a subject:

> *So we have come to cash this cheque – a cheque that will give us upon demand the riches of freedom* and the security of justice. We have also come to this *hallowed spot* to remind America of the *fierce* urgency of now. This is no time to engage in the *luxury of cooling off* or to take the *tranquillising drug of gradualism* ... **Martin Luther King**

2. Anecdotes

- ❏ Carefully selected stories are an extremely effective way to illustrate key messages.
- ❏ They must be kept short and to the point (as a rough guide, anything much more than a minute and you risk turning them into shaggy dog stories).

3. The sound of words

- ❏ Used in moderation, alliteration can help to make a particular message more noticeable and memorable.

We cannot fail or falter. **Winston Churchill**

People's princess. **Tony Blair**

- ❏ Too much alliteration or rhyme is likely to be so obvious that it deflects the audience's attention away from the message to the technique itself, and can therefore be counter-productive.

My constituency is the desperate, damned, disinherited, disrespected and the despised. **Jesse Jackson**

**Part III
Exercises**

🔴 *Exercise 1 – Repackaging a message*

After showing people video clips illustrating the techniques discussed in Chapters 6 and 7, I often get them to do an exercise that demonstrates just how quickly it's possible to learn how to use them for themselves. The results after only five minutes of redrafting are usually very impressive, with hardly anyone failing to improve on the original version. So this is the ideal point in the book for you to try out the same exercise.

Rewrite the following sentence, making *as much use as possible* of rhetorical techniques and imagery. Feel free to use poetic licence, and don't be afraid to write things that might initially strike you as being too dramatic or 'over the top' (as it often happens that the more use people make of the techniques, the better the response they get from the rest of the group).

Recent years have seen a widespread proliferation in the incidence of medical negligence cases, in which Health Authorities have incurred increased costs as a result of the greater legal sophistication with which cases are being argued.

The next few chapters deal in more detail with this process of translating messages into more striking forms of words, and more exercises along these lines will be found at the end of Part IV.

🔎 Exercise 2 – Analysing famous speeches

The scripts of famous speeches are widely available in books and on websites.

- ❏ Read through them and make a note of any sequences that strike you as particularly powerful or impressive.
- ❏ Go through your selection to see how many involved the use of the rhetorical techniques and forms of imagery described in Chapters 6 and 7.

PART IV
PUTTING PRINCIPLES INTO PRACTICE

Translating Messages to Increase Impact

Political Speeches and Business Presentations

The first exercise at the end of Part III involved using rhetorical techniques and imagery to translate the following sentence into a more interesting form of words:

> Recent years have seen a widespread proliferation in the incidence of medical negligence cases, in which Health Authorities have incurred increased costs as a result of the greater legal sophistication with which cases are being argued.

One alternative version, produced after only five minutes, started by posing a puzzle (**P**) about a new epidemic, and developed it with a contrast between another two medically related metaphors ('disease' and 'plague'). The solution (**S**) to the puzzle then turned out to be 'medical negligence cases', which have three characteristics, the third of which is the longest of the three (see discussion of combined formats, pages 199–210):

P →
> Health Authorities are faced with a new kind of epidemic.
>
> (A)→ A once-rare disease has turned into
> (B)→ a plague of litigation.

S →
> Medical negligence cases are now
> (1)→ more frequent,
> (2)→ more expensive
> (3)→ and more expertly argued than ever before.

The fact that people can learn to use these techniques so quickly means that they have grasped an important fundamental principle: the production of memorable and persuasive lines involves what is essentially an exercise in translation into the language of public speaking. And the idea of *translation* is central to developing an ability to get messages across with greater impact. When

> The idea of translation into the language of public speaking is central to developing an ability to get messages across with greater impact. Becoming an effective speaker means going beyond deciding what to say to working out how to say it in a way that's most likely to appeal to an audience.

planning a speech or presentation, all too many speakers make the mistake of stopping at the point where they have decided on the message they want to get across, without giving much thought to other possible ways of making the same point. But becoming an effective speaker means going beyond deciding *what* to say to working out *how* to say it in a way that's most likely to appeal to your audience.

This chapter uses real examples to show how the toolkit described in Chapters 6 and 7 can be used to get political and business messages across. The section on political speeches is based on my own experience of writing them, and describes some of the thought processes that went into the construction of particular lines. The discussion of business presentations draws on real examples produced by people who had attended one of my courses.

I. POLITICAL SPEECHES

1. Modifying messages

The first opportunity I had to find out whether my research into what prompts applause in political speeches could be put into practice came when Gus Macdonald, then with Granada Television, came up with the idea of making a programme in which I was challenged to train a complete novice to make a speech at a political party conference. Like many voters in the early 1980s, Ann Brennan had become so disaffected by the Labour Party's lurch to the left that she had joined the breakaway Social Democrats. But she had reservations about the new party's image, feeling that it was too intellectual and middle class to attract traditional working class Labour supporters like herself. She had never made a speech before in her life, but was keen to have a go at getting her point across at the party's annual conference.

💬 *The emperor has no clothes*

When working on the opening lines, she left us in no doubt about what she thought of the rather dense paper on the concept of inequality that was to be the subject for the debate in which she would be speaking. When she said 'I hardly understand a word of it', the question arose as to whether she would be willing to say this in her speech. The answer was that she certainly would, as the paper was typical of the kind of intellectual élitism that she felt was preventing the SDP from engaging with the wider electorate.

Once you are clear about what message you want to get across, the first thing to do is to consider whether or not the initial wording is worth keeping. If not, the next step is to search through the rhetorical toolkit for something that might help to improve it. In the case of 'I hardly understand a word of it', the sense could have been retained by translating it into a simile, along the lines of 'Reading this paper is like reading the small print on a life insurance policy', or perhaps the more anecdotal 'While I was reading this paper, I fell asleep five times, and didn't wake up until the next morning'. But in this particular case, we wanted to retain as much of her message and style of speaking as possible, so we settled on an opening line that posed a puzzle about why she should be feeling unequal in a debate about equality. The solution came in the next two sentences, with her own original words in the third and final one:

P →   (1)→ I feel very unequal in this debate.

S → (2)→ I've been through the background paper, and

(3)→ I hardly understand a word of it. **Ann Brennan**

It produced an instant burst of applause, which suggested that she was not alone: many in the hall apparently thought the same, and were pleased to hear someone speaking the truth about the emperor's new clothes. The positive response also demonstrated how important it is to get off to a good start. The audience had suddenly come alive, and literally moved forward to the edge of their seats, ready to listen to what she was going to say next.

🔊 *Including a prop as a visual aid*

This opening sequence was followed with more lines that involved a slight modification of something else that Ann had said about the background paper, namely, 'It's not the kind of thing you could distribute on the doorsteps around King's Cross.' If she had kept exactly to these words, it would certainly have been easy enough for the audience to understand, but might have been too direct and serious to have made much of an impact. So we agreed on a somewhat lighter approach that would both get the audience to use their imagination and introduce a touch of humour. The sequence also showed how effective it can be to use props as visual aids (see Chapter 5). Holding a copy of the paper in the air, she developed her criticism of it with another simple puzzle–solution format:

P →   Imagine going around King's Cross with this.
         [Audience laughter]

S →   They'd end up thinking you were a Jehovah's Witness.
         [Audience laughter and applause]

The basic message had stayed the same, but the modified version almost certainly generated a more positive response than if she had used the original words.

These examples show how you can increase the impact of a particular message by making quite minor modifications to the original wording, and by using rhetoric to aid the process of translation. However, as will be seen in the next section, you can use more poetic licence to produce lines that are much further removed from the wording of the original message, yet still retain the same meaning.

2. The language of leadership

To merge or not to merge?

Having fought the 1987 general election as an alliance of two separate parties, the Liberals and SDP began debating whether to merge and become one party. Paddy Ashdown, who was later to become leader of the merged party, was a strong supporter of the merger and planned to speak in favour of it at the Liberal Assembly that had been called to decide on the matter. Like many others, he was depressed that squabbling and division within and between the two parties were frittering away the earlier successes of the Alliance (whose share of the popular vote in the 1987 general election had come within two percentage points of Labour). One of his key messages could therefore be summed up as follows:

> Internal squabbling is damaging the potential of the third force in British politics.

The use of these exact words to make the point would have sounded like such a bland statement of the obvious that it would have been unlikely to have impressed anyone. So the search for other possible ways of conveying the message began by noting that the sentence includes two facts: (1) there's a lot of squabbling going on, and (2) it's damaging to the future of the two parties. This is always a promising start, because the presence of two components raises the possibility of being able to make a contrast between them. And in this case, the use of some kind of contrast did seem to be on the cards. Early possibilities included 'Voters don't want to see us squabbling; they want to see us becoming more successful', and 'we should stop squabbling and start building on our potential'.

It's very important to be aware that this process of trying out alternative versions can set the brain off in different directions that are often extremely helpful in pushing the creative process along. A particular word, or the sound of a word, may stand out and make you think of other similar ones that sometimes turn out to be an improvement on the original. For example, in this particular case, 'squabbling' sounds like 'babbling', and 'babbling' made me think of the original source of the word – the Tower of Babel. The sound of a word had therefore not only led to a powerful biblical image – of people speaking to each other in different languages – but to one that neatly summed up the problem the Liberals and SDP were up against. The phrase 'Tower of Babel' also triggered thoughts of another common metaphor: 'tower of strength'. With two towers now in mind, was there any way of making a contrast between them that would stay close enough to the gist of the original version of the message? The answer came from one of the versions considered earlier in the process, and the components fell easily into place. The contrast between 'stop' and 'start building' was taken from 'We need to stop squabbling, and start building on our potential', so that the line was finally rephrased and delivered as:

> We need to stop sounding like the Tower of Babel,
> and start building a tower of strength. **Paddy Ashdown**

The applause it prompted showed that it had struck a chord with the audience. At the end of the speech, it emerged that the BBC television commentator had also noticed it, as it was the only line that he singled out and quoted – even though he read far more into it than had ever been intended in the first place: 'And with that reference to turning a Tower of Babel into a tower of strength, Mr Ashdown is giving a clear indication of his intention to run for the leadership of a new merged party.' Although he did eventually run for the leadership, no such thoughts had been in our minds when we were trying out alternative ways of getting the point across. But the fact that it stood out enough to be noticed by the commentator was a nice example of the power that a rhetorically packaged message can have.

Parties of yesterday, today and tomorrow

After the two parties had agreed to merge into the Social and Liberal Democrats, Paddy Ashdown decided to announce his candidacy for the leadership of the new party. Developing the potential of a third force in British politics was still very much at the top of his agenda: the Tories had just won their third consecutive general election, and Labour had yet to abandon some of the left-wing policies that had made them look old-fashioned and unelectable. At that particular time, then, it looked as though the Tories were firmly entrenched in government for the foreseeable future, Labour might go into terminal decline and the new third party might overtake them to become the second biggest party. So here was a message that was about the recent past, the current situation and the outlook for the future – which immediately opened up the possibility of dividing it into three sentences. At the same time, a political system with three main parties is a perennial gift for the speechwriter, and it didn't require too much creative effort to translate the message into three statements, in which the second and third contrasted with the one before it. The word 'party' was repeated in each line, and 'yesterday', 'today' and 'tomorrow' were used as metaphors for past, present and future:

The Tories may be the party of today.
Labour is certainly the party of yesterday.
It falls to us to be the party of tomorrow. **Paddy Ashdown**

Simple though the sequence is, it stood out enough to be selected from the 40-minute speech for replaying on all the prime time news programmes later that day.

🗨 *Back in business*

A few weeks later, it became clear that Ashdown was going to win the leadership contest, and the question arose as to what he should say when the result was announced. The basic message he wanted to get across was along the lines of:

After the months of internal squabbling since the election, there is a danger that the public is forgetting that we exist, and no longer sees us as a force worthy of being taken seriously.

Put like this, the message was unlikely to make much of an impact. It not only exhibits some of the characteristics of the written word (see Chapter 3), but its focus on the party's problems also made it far too negative for wider public consumption. Something more upbeat was clearly needed.

The search for a more positive alternative began with the idea of 'carrying on the good work' that had been achieved before the recent election. And, as happened in the case of the Tower of Babel, one of these initial words triggered another related one, setting off a train of thought that went as follows:

'Work' suggested 'business'…
    …'business' suggested the alliterative phrase 'back in business'…
    …'back in business' suggested the phrase 'means business'.

Now that we had two very similar-sounding phrases, 'back in business' and 'means business', the question was whether or not it would work to contrast them with each other. Luckily it did, and the final version managed to translate the main gist of the original message into words that were much shorter, punchier and more colloquial:

We have to show the British people that we're
not just back in business,
but really mean business. **Paddy Ashdown**

It also played well with the media, where it was the most widely quoted line from the speech, supplying news programmes with headlines like: 'Paddy Ashdown becomes the new leader of the Democrats and says that they're not just back in business but really mean business.'

3. The creative process

I have gone through these examples in some detail in order to show how the techniques described in Chapters 6 and 7 can be used as a resource in translating messages into more interesting and punchy forms of words. Once you know what the options are, it's like having a manual that can be consulted to check on whether any of them would work to get a particular point across. This not only points you in the right direction for ways of saying things that are known to be effective, but also has the advantage of restricting your choice to a relatively small number of techniques. If there were no such limits, the nature of language is such that the possibilities would be more or less infinite, and the sheer

The number of techniques with a proven track record at impressing audiences is small enough for people to be able to master them fairly easily, and to search through them quickly when looking for a punchier way to say something.

range of alternatives would be so great that there would be no way of knowing where to begin or end the search. Fortunately, the number of techniques with a proven track record at impressing audiences is small enough for people to be able to master them fairly easily, and to search through them quickly when looking for a more punchy way to say something.

The creative process also involves a good deal of trial and error, and a first attempt hardly ever becomes the final version. Words and phrases bring other similar ones to mind that sometimes lead in a fruitful direction, and sometimes down blind alleys. The important thing is to be willing to follow these trains of thought to see where they take you. There are obviously no right or wrong answers, but our experience of sitting in audiences puts us all in a good position to know a punchy line when we see one.

4. The position-taker: a powerful political technique

There is one particularly useful technique that has the highest success rate of all when it comes to prompting applause in political speeches. This was not included in Chapter 6 because it is somewhat less adaptable for use in speeches and presentations outside the political arena, its main use being for launching powerful attacks on opponents. Although this is central to the everyday discourse of politics, it tends to have a lower priority for speakers in most other contexts.

The position-taker is a close relation to the puzzle–solution format, as it involves a two-part sequence that starts by building up a sense of anticipation in the minds of the audience about what's coming next. In the first part, the speaker describes something about which the audience will expect him or her to be strongly for or against. In the second part, the speaker praises or condemns the situation just described – at which point the audience applauds.

STATEMENT: Time and again, Labour Parties have been elected and tried to implement capitalist policies better than the Tories.

POSITION-TAKER: We want to see no more of that with the next Labour government. **Arthur Scargill**

Sometimes, the statement part of the sequence can be extended for some time before finally taking a position on it, as in the following example, the first part of which includes a list of three:

STATEMENT: The unspoken assumption behind policies of withdrawal from the community and unilateral disarmament is that others will continue to bear their burdens and pick up ours as well; that others would continue to accept our products even though we refuse to accept theirs; that others would ensure the defence of Europe and provide a shield behind which we could shelter.

POSITION-TAKER: What a contemptible policy for Britain. **Margaret Thatcher**

II. BUSINESS PRESENTATIONS

In courses on business presentations, I make extensive use of video clips from political speeches to illustrate the techniques that make for effective speaking. One of the advantages of this is that politicians are professional communicators. As some of them are widely recognised as better communicators than average, we can learn from observing how they do it. But a disadvantage is that it sometimes prompts doubt and scepticism on the part of people whose main speaking commitment is the business presentation. After all, they point out, political messages are very different from business messages: they are much more emotive, they involve attacks on their opponents that are far more hostile and insulting than is acceptable when talking about business competitors. Unlike political speeches, management presentations are more concerned with cool analysis and the communication of facts and information. So just how appropriate is it to use the same techniques to get business messages across?

Those who raise these issues hardly ever seem to realise that, in getting their point across, they have made rather effective use of a contrast between perceived differences between political messages on the one hand, and business messages on the other. They also underestimate just how many business presentations are concerned with persuading an audience, whether it is about the benefits of a product, a proposal, a change in strategy, or just simply that the speaker is doing an excellent job for the company.

However, regardless of the particular objectives, the important point is that rhetoric and imagery can work at different levels. Certainly they are very effective techniques for packaging emotive messages that are intended to inspire and sway an audience. But they are just as useful for breaking up complex material into the kinds of short, digestible chunks that audiences find easy to follow. They therefore help to overcome two of the biggest problems that audiences face. First, by enabling you to say things simply, they reduce the chances of overloading audiences with too much complex information. And second, by packaging messages in ways that are known to go down well with audiences, you're more likely to hold their attention and interest, and may even enthuse and inspire them.

Armed with the knowledge that *how* a message is packaged can make a world of difference to an audience, and with the toolkit described earlier, anyone can start to compose punchy lines for themselves. The evidence for this comes from the experience of seeing people do it on hundreds of courses, and what is so impressive is just how quickly they learn. In fact, I have never run a course on presentation and public speaking that lasted for more than two days, and many have been shorter than that. To underline the point, the extracts in this section are all real examples that were produced by course participants, who had been exposed to the techniques described earlier for no more than one day.

1. Contrasts

In this first example, the original version of the message was formulated in the kind of written formal-sounding language that was typical within the company in question:

> In this presentation I'm going to talk to you about the need
> to set objectives and formulate an action plan in response

to significant anticipated growth in the number of new products announced by International Digital Technology from 497 in the last full year to a tentatively projected figure of a thousand per annum three years hence.

In translating this into a punchier form, the speaker singled out the key point about the dramatic increase in the number of new products, and used a simple contrast:

A →   In 1998, IDT launched around 500 new products.

B →   By 2002, this number will have increased to a staggering one thousand new products during the year.

(Name of company, numbers and dates changed to protect anonymity.)

When it comes to highlighting dramatic changes over time, a simple contrast between two dates and two facts is an extremely simple and economical way of getting the point across. Rather than spoon-feeding the audience with lots of irrelevant data that they are unlikely ever to remember, it allows them to draw their own conclusion. The following is an almost identical example from a talk by a famous management guru:

A →   In 1970 it took 108 guys five days to unload a timber ship.

B →   That same activity today takes eight people one day.
           Tom Peters

The next example came right at the end of a presentation in which the speaker wanted to leave his audience with the following basic message:

> The various points I have outlined in this presentation point to the need for us to do even better in the future.

He chose to reformulate this using a comparative ('more this than that') contrast, and 'today' and 'tomorrow' as metaphors for the present and future:

	So the important thing
A →	is not how good we are today,
B →	but how much better we need to be tomorrow.

As with many of the other examples in this book, there is great scope here for changing a word or two to get across whatever particular message you want to convey. In this case, for instance, the line would work just as well if it included various other comparisons, as in these variations on the same theme:

A →	... not how profitable we are today,
B →	but how much more profitable we need to be tomorrow.

A →	... not how successful we are today,
B →	but how much more successful we need to be tomorrow.

The following rather neutral-sounding statement does little to dramatise the pressing importance of the situation:

In order to continue in business, the company is being forced to rationalise various aspects of its organisation.

By translating it into a contradictory contrast ('not this but that'), the speaker was able to convey a greater sense of urgency:

A → Rationalisation is not an option.

B → It's an absolute necessity for survival.

2. Puzzles and questions

🔊 *Moving smoothly between sections of a presentation*

Once they have put aside their fear of being interrupted by hecklers (see Chapter 6), most speakers find that the easiest technique to master is the puzzle–solution format, and the posing of a rhetorical question. As was mentioned earlier, questions are particularly useful for pointing the way forward to the next section of a presentation. This not only gets the audience to start thinking about what's coming next, but also relieves them from having to listen to repetitive and overworked lines like those in italics in the left hand column below. The alternatives on the right use questions to do the same job:

Moving on now to our strengths ...	If those are our weaknesses, what are our strengths?
The next slide shows a list of steps involved in preparing for the strategic review.	So what steps are we taking to prepare for the strategic review?

In the first of the above examples, the word 'strengths' in the question contrasts with the 'weaknesses' in the previous clause. As the following examples show, this is quite a common feature of this type of bridge between two sections of a presentation:

I've taken you through the figures for last year, but what are our plans for the next one?

That's what our business looks like in the UK, but how is it shaping up in the rest of Europe?

I've outlined the problems, but what about the solutions?

So much for the above the line campaign, but what are we doing in-store?

Attracting attention in the first place

The above examples use questions to get the audience interested at the start of a new section. In the same way, puzzles and questions can be used right at the beginning of a presentation to engage the attention of the audience. The speaker in the following example had to introduce some of his colleaguesto a campaign aimed at increasing customer awareness of the high quality of their company's goods and services. He decided that the best way to get into the subject was by beginning with a puzzle:

I'd like to start by posing a question.

P → Is there any point in being good at something if people don't know you're good at it?

S → The obvious answer, in business at least, is no ...

From an audience point of view, a riddle of this kind is obviously much more likely to attract their interest and attention than having to listen for a hundredth time to a list of agenda items prefaced by the commonest opening line of all: 'In this presentation I'm going to talk about ...'

I was once asked to coach the finance director of a multinational company for a presentation at an annual management conference. In previous years, he had received very poor ratings from delegates because he had rambled incomprehensibly through slides containing nothing but tables of numbers so small that no one but him could read them. Having persuaded him of the importance of getting off to a good start, he tried to find the word 'finance' in the index of various dictionaries of quotations. Interestingly, it was nowhere to be found in any of them. So he looked up 'money' instead, and came up with a puzzling simile from Somerset Maugham:

P →   Money is like a sixth sense.

S →   Without it you can't make full use of the other five.

He then changed 'money' to 'finance', and used it as the opening line of his presentation, following it up with three metaphors, and a contrast outlining the overall structure of what was to come:

    In our business finance has other roles as well.

1 →   It's a map for seeing where we are,

2 →   a compass for putting us in the right direction,

3 →   and the fuel for getting us to our destination.

    So I want this morning to take a look at

A →   where we are today

B →   and where we're going tomorrow.

Many of those who had suffered his presentation at the previous year's conference said that, as soon as they heard this opening sequence, their fears began to slip away. Some even went as far as to rate it as a 'hundred times better' than his earlier discursive ramblings about tables of illegible numbers; the less exaggerated evaluations were unanimous in giving him higher ratings than he'd ever had before.

3. Three-part lists

As the last example shows, lists of three can also be effectively used in business presentations, and are second only to rhetorical questions in the ease with which people are able to start producing creative lines of their own. They quickly discover that it's possible to condense all kinds of different subjects into three headings, often managing to put the longest item in third position:

> The strategy has three main purposes:
> to boost the industry's confidence,
> to enhance the credibility of the council
> and to open the way for new initiatives in consumer
>   promotions.

They learn that audiences will assume that there are three things coming up, whether or not this is announced in advance, and that it certainly isn't necessary to introduce each point with 'firstly', 'secondly' and 'thirdly'.

Our company enjoys a high reputation on several fronts:
the quality of our products and services,
our contribution to the UK economy
and our determination to succeed in a rapidly changing
    business environment.

People also discover that various forms of repetition they would
never dream of using when writing a letter or proposal actually
sound quite natural when spoken aloud, even when the repeated
words and phrases come very close together in each part of the
list, as in the following examples from different presentations by
different speakers:

To be a truly global player, you need a truly global service
provider,
with *the right* expertise,
the right knowledge
and *the right* understanding to meet your needs.

Customers *will gain*, the company *will gain* and staff *will gain*.

They are *out of* touch, *out of* date and *out of* work.

4. Combined formats

Some years ago, I worked with a director of an electricity supply
company. He was preparing for a public meeting at which he had
to speak on the rather delicate issue of his company's policy on
disconnecting customers who were either unable or unwilling to
pay their bills. He was very aware that the attitude of many in the

audience would be along the lines of 'it's all very well for you, but you don't know what it's like to be so poor that you can't pay for the basic necessities of life'. He decided to address the issue head on by starting his speech on a personal note aimed at showing that he did understand the problems faced by low-income families and individuals. The sequence began with a contrast between two lists of three:

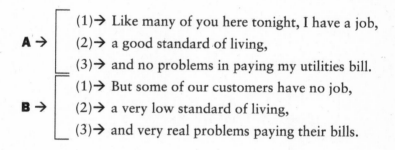

A →
(1)→ Like many of you here tonight, I have a job,
(2)→ a good standard of living,
(3)→ and no problems in paying my utilities bill.

B →
(1)→ But some of our customers have no job,
(2)→ a very low standard of living,
(3)→ and very real problems paying their bills.

The scope for combining different techniques to get points across in business presentations is no less than in political speeches, and the following different types of combination are further examples produced by speakers who had only just been exposed to the basic principles.

Contrast followed by three-part list

A → We've got to move from informing people
B → to involving people.

1 → And that means clear priorities,
2 → clear targets
3 → and clear measures of performance.

🗨 *Contrast, the second part of which is a three-part list:*

A →   We'll succeed not by luck,

              (1)→ but by listening,

B →   (2)→ talking

              (3)→ and responding to customers.

🗨 *Puzzle solved by two contrasting similes and a three-part list:*

P →   How do we compare in the great scheme of things?

              (A)→ We're like a David

              (B)→ to Microsoft's Goliath,

              (A)→ a TVR

              (B)→ to General Motors.

S →   (1)→ Small in size,

              (2)→ big on quality

              (3)→ and successful niche players in the global
                        marketplace.

5. Imagery and anecdotes

As is clear from some of these examples, there is no problem about using metaphors and similes in business presentations. Anecdotes too can be used as illustrative examples to get key points across in a vivid and memorable way, a point that has been underlined by the results of research by Tim Clark and David Greatbatch* into presentations by business gurus such as Tom Peters, Rosabeth

---

* Greatbatch, D. and Clark, T. (2002). 'Laughing With the Gurus'. *Business Strategy Review*, 13:10-18.

Moss Kanter and Gary Hamel. A main finding was that all of them make very extensive use of carefully selected stories, many of which are designed to prompt laughter from the audience. They show how the gurus play on the laughter to make the audience feel part of an 'in-group' that shares the line of criticism or praise being meted out by the speakers to different styles of management. And humour tends to be deployed at those points where an audience might disagree with them, so that it has the effect of deflecting any possible dissent. As a result, the world's leading management gurus are never booed from the stage and typically generate very positive audience reaction and a high feel-good factor.

The effectiveness of using illustrative examples receives further support from a study of audience reactions to presentations, in which I used two cameras to generate a split-screen image, with the speaker in one half of the screen and members of the audience in the other. Among other things, this showed that almost every time a speaker used the phrase 'for example ...', people's heads or eyes would move upwards in anticipation of what was to come. This would often happen just after the presenter had said something involving an abstract concept or made a generalisation or some other point, the meaning of which was not immediately self-evident. Following it up with an illustrative anecdote shows a degree of sensitivity and responsiveness to the audience's problem of understanding, and is therefore likely to be well received.

One case that clearly demonstrated how effective anecdotes can be in getting key messages across occurred at a conference on crisis management. The speaker who got the highest audience ratings by far was the only one who didn't use slides with long lists of *dos* and *don'ts*. Instead, he told two contrasting anecdotes to illustrate alternative ways in which an organisation can approach its dealings with the media. In one case, a refusal to release information to the press resulted in reporters trying to find out what had happened from neighbours and others outside the organisation. As a result, the coverage relied heavily on rumour and innuendo, and reflected badly on the organisation in question. In the second case, a more open and cooperative approach resulted in media coverage that took the side of the organisation in crisis, and had a positive impact on its public image.

6. Conclusion: liberating speakers to be themselves

The aim of this chapter has been to demonstrate that the techniques described earlier can be quickly grasped and put to work by political speakers and business presenters. None of the examples has been invented, and all the ones from business presentations were produced by relative novices within a few hours of learning about the potential power of rhetoric and imagery. Perhaps most encouraging of all is the fact that, once equipped with the necessary toolkit, beginners discover creative abilities within themselves of which they had not previously been aware. They also find that planning presentations becomes less of a chore to be dreaded, and can even be quite enjoyable.

At first sight, it might be thought that the result of everyone using the same set of techniques would be a collection of communicational clones, who would all end up sounding exactly the same. The evidence, however, points in exactly the opposite direction, probably because there is such immense flexibility in the way the techniques can be used. The situation is not much different from that of a community of people who speak a common language. As speakers of English, we may all speak the same language, but none of us applies the rules of grammar, syntax and turn taking in exactly the same way. These subtle differences play an important part in the way we come to be regarded by others as unique individuals, each with a slightly different personality. In the same way, the techniques described in this book can be thought of as building blocks of a language of public speaking and persuasion. As such, they too can be and are used by different speakers in slightly different ways, thereby ensuring that no two people ever sound identical.

Nor is the applicability of this approach limited to a narrow range of specialist topics or areas. Over the years, I have seen it being successfully adapted and used by managers from almost every conceivable sector of the economy, by people working in health, social services, education and research and by speakers at family and social occasions (see Chapter 10). Once participants on courses have witnessed each other making the transition from a slavish dependence on slides to a more confident and eloquent reliance on the power of the spoken word, they never express doubts about the dangers of cloning or question the relevance of such techniques for conveying messages about their own specialist area of interest. But what they do report with great regularity is that they feel liberated, and that much more of their own personality is coming across than when they were trying to conform to the industry standard model of presentation. And at the heart of the transformation is the experience of achieving better rapport than ever before with audiences that show no signs at all of falling asleep.

Political and business messages can be translated into more striking forms by using the techniques described in Chapters 6 and 7.

1. The creative process

- ❑ The search for alternatives always involves trial and error, and a first attempt hardly ever becomes the final version.
- ❑ A word, phrase or idea can set off trains of thought that help the creative process along – even the sound of a particular word may stand out and make you think of others that can be used to improve on the original.
- ❑ You can often put a key statement into the first or second part of a contrast or the third item in a list.
- ❑ Whenever there are two related points, it's worth considering whether they can be translated into a contrast.
- ❑ Rhetorical techniques are especially useful at pivotal points in a speech – e.g. beginnings, endings, summing up the gist of a section, bridging from one section to another, etc. (For more on overall structure, see Chapter 9).

2. The position-taker

This is an adaptable and very effective technique for packaging political messages, and involves two stages:

1 talk about something that the audience will expect you to take a strong position on, e.g. 'Time and again, Labour Parties have been elected and have tried to implement capitalist policies better than the Tories ...';

2 then state your position, e.g. '...We want to see no more of that with the next Labour government.' **Arthur Scargill**

Putting it all Together

Structure and Preparation

The previous chapter showed how to put the principles described in Part III into practice to get political and business messages across, and the next chapter focuses on how to use them when making social and duty speeches. But it isn't just the structure of sentences that makes a big difference to the impact speakers have on audiences; the overall structure of the speech or presentation as a whole also plays a crucial part in the process. Without shape and careful planning, it is doomed to failure. If rhetorical techniques, imagery and anecdotes are to succeed in highlighting your main points, you need to create a coherent structure. This will not only help the audience to follow your thoughts and argument, but will also make it easier for you to stay on track and say the things you want to say – all of which applies to every kind of speech or presentation, whether in political, business, social or any other settings.

This chapter therefore outlines an approach to preparation that gets away from the assumption that it's enough simply to get some slides together as a prelude to *ad-libbing* through a list of bullet points. Sometimes, people who have been used to this 'slides-first' method of preparation worry that any alternative approach will take far more time and effort than they have available. The approach taken here has been developed in direct response to such fears, and provides a systematic method of preparation that's specifically designed to enable you to plan well-structured presentations that will achieve maximum impact in a minimum amount of time. The many people who have tried it out over the years have found not only that it can be mastered very quickly, but also that it enables them to produce effective speeches and presentations much more quickly than they had previously thought possible.

It involves a seven-step process that not only helps with the creation of a tight, easy-to-follow sequence, but also prepares you for the moment when you deliver it:

1   Analysing the audience
2   Brainstorming the topic
3   Creating the structure
4   Saying it creatively
5   Creating the visual aids
6   Rehearsal
7   Preparing for question time (optional)

1. Analysing the audience

Although preparing a speech obviously involves planning what to say, it's useful to think of the process as one of planning listening time for your audience. Just as you would never plan a business meeting without thinking of your clients, you should also never plan a speech or presentation without thinking about your audience. And, as was emphasised in earlier chapters, the capacity of an audience to remain attentive and to understand the points being made are things that can never be taken for granted. In particular, you need to take into account who is going to be in the audience, how many are going to be present and what kind of message is likely to be appropriate.

Who's in the audience?

A famous example of what can happen as a result of neglecting some or all of these considerations was a speech by Tony Blair to the annual conference of the Women's Institute in June 2000. An overtly political speech about the government's agenda was greeted by heckling and slow hand-clapping, with some members disapproving so strongly that they actually walked out. His main mistake was a failure to realise that the Women's Institute takes great pride in being a non-political organisation. Many of those in the audience were therefore annoyed that he had used their conference as a platform for making a party-political speech. Others objected to the fact that he spoke for much longer than the 20-minute slot he had been allocated.

Another case of a politician misreading his audience resulted in the only occasion on which I ever heard Paddy Ashdown being jeered during a leader's speech to a Liberal Democrat conference. What he (and those of us who had helped to write the speech) had forgotten was that the party's position on environmental issues meant that, in public at least, members are very keen on public transport, and very hostile towards private cars. He opened with a joke about something that had happened on the way there, and began with the words, 'As I was driving to Nottingham...' His mistake was to use the word 'driving', which was enough to provoke boos and jeers from some sections of the audience – displays of disapproval that would almost certainly not have happened if he'd used some alternative form of words, such as, 'On the train to Nottingham ...' or 'On the way here ...'.

These failures to take the audience into account are in marked contrast to the experience of a group of directors who had to make presentations at a conference for the 200 most senior managers in the company. They had been so concerned by the negative audience ratings at the previous meeting that, in preparation for the next one, they commissioned a survey of their workforce to find out about their main priorities and concerns. Their presentations then dealt directly with the points raised in the survey, and were rewarded by vastly more positive ratings than at the previous year's conference.

These examples underline the importance of taking the composition and interests of your audience into account right from the start of the planning stage. Included in this should be an estimate of how much they are likely to know about the subject matter. The contents of a talk on nuclear energy will obviously be very different, depending on whether the audience is made up of physics graduates or of people who know little or nothing about science. When the choice is as stark as this, the problem of where to pitch the presentation is fairly easy to solve. More difficult is to know how to approach it if the audience is made up of a mixture of specialists and non-specialists. The safest solution is to pitch it towards the non-specialists, as the specialists in the audience will, like the speaker, be aware of the different levels of expertise among those present. They are therefore likely to make allowances for a speaker's attempt to make things intelligible for everyone.

How big is the audience?

The bigger the audience, the greater the diversity of backgrounds and levels of knowledge will tend to be, which means that the anticipated size of an audience will have a bearing on the level at which the subject matter should be pitched: in general, the larger the audience, the simpler the content should be.

The numbers likely to be present will also have a bearing on other issues, such as what kinds of visual aids will be appropriate, and whether or not to rely on notes or to use a full script. With small audiences, it is rarely appropriate to read a speech verbatim from a text. But many speakers feel safer speaking from a text when addressing 50 or 100 people. When timing is of critical importance, a fully scripted speech also has the advantage of making it more likely that the presentation will end on time.

What message for this audience?

From listening to the comments of participants on training programmes, it would seem that many presentations in the business world are given every day with little or no thought being given to why they are being given in the first place. Indeed some people say that when they start to think seriously about what the point of many of their presentations is, they realise that it's often not at all clear, other than that they are simply part of the way things have always been done. To avoid such uncertainty, a final and crucial step in analysing the audience is to decide on the core message to be conveyed to this particular audience.

This involves you in being clear about two important points. First, what is the purpose of your talk? And second, what is the main message you want to get across to them? For example, you may want to show that management is caring, concerned and responsible, while delivering a difficult message about staff discipline. Or you may want to show that you're a forward-thinking, confident account manager, while talking about the year-end sales figures to a particular group of customers.

People often ask how many points per hour they should aim to get across. To this, the late Professor Sir Lawrence Bragg, who had an outstanding reputation for making scientific lectures accessible to lay audiences, had an interesting answer:

> I think the answer should be 'one'. If the average member of the audience can remember with interest and enthusiasm one main theme, the lecture has been a great success ... There should be one main theme, and all the subsidiary interesting points, experiments or demonstrations should be such that they remind the hearer of the theme. (*Advice to Lecturers: An Anthology taken from the writings of Michael Faraday and Lawrence Bragg.* London: Royal Institution, 1974.)

Winston Churchill expressed a similar view that echoes earlier discussions of the rule of three:

> If you have an important point to make, don't try to be subtle or clever. Use a pile driver. Hit the point once. Then come back and hit it again. Then hit it a third time with a tremendous whack. **Winston Churchill**

At first sight, these may seem to be excessively pessimistic views about how much can be conveyed in a lecture or speech. However, given the problems of audience attentiveness and understanding discussed earlier, the best we can probably ever hope for is that people will go away with a grasp of the main theme or gist of what we were talking about. This is why it's so important to be absolutely clear right from the start about what, if nothing else, you want this particular audience to take away with them at the end. This then makes it possible to set about preparing and structuring in a way that will make it more likely that you succeed in getting that central theme across.

A concrete example of learning this lesson the hard way comes from my experience of giving talks about my research into the techniques that trigger applause in political speeches. The first time I ever spoke on the subject in public was at an academic conference, at which I inflicted about 70 excerpts from speeches on the audience in the course of one hour. After giving similar talks to other audiences, it gradually dawned on me that, however many examples I used, and however intriguing the subtle variations and deviant cases might be, the gist of the argument that audiences were going away with was always the same, namely that applause was triggered by a small number of rhetorical techniques. So I decided that it would be more helpful to structure a presentation that would make it easy for them to get that particular point, rather than leaving them to infer the gist of the argument for themselves from an excessive number of examples. This eventually resulted in a presentation that uses three short video clips to illustrate each of the main techniques. Pared down to only 12 excerpts, there's no doubt that audiences get a much clearer idea of what the techniques are and how to use them than in the days when examples were coming at them at a rate of more than one a minute.

2. Brainstorming

After analysing the audience, the next step in preparation is to think about the topics that might be relevant to getting your key message across to the target audience. This begins with a brainstorming exercise, which involves making a list of all the possible topics that might be included in the presentation. Once you have done this, there's a good chance that there will be far too much material, or that some of it may not be suitable for your target audience. So, in the interests of simplification and tailoring the material to your listeners, you can often start deleting some of the items straight away. As was noted in Chapter 3, one of the main problems for audiences is having to put up with speakers trying to get far too much information across in the time available. So you have to be prepared to cut your material to an extent that you may find quite painful.

🐟 Sectionalising

Brainstormed lists will typically consist of many more than the three or four sections that would make a suitable structure, so the next step is to organise the various items under a smaller number of headings. The way to do this is to go through the list with an eye to which items fit together, and which ones would be better placed in some other section. At the end of this stage, you should be left with a small number of main headings, with related topics listed under each one.

Sequencing

The order in which you write items down on a brainstormed list is likely to influence the order in which you put the different sections. But this won't necessarily be the best sequence for making sure that the key theme gets across to the audience. You therefore need to give careful thought to the order in which you are going to present each of the sections. For the audience to understand the first section, for example, it may be necessary for them to be familiar with the points made in the second one, in which case the order should obviously be reversed. Another section might involve drawing conclusions from all the others, in which case it should come last. In general, the aim should be to organise the various parts of the structure into a coherent argument that you can develop in logical steps throughout the course of the presentation. And it is particularly effective if the whole thing can be made to sound like a story with a clear moral at the end of it.

3. Creating a structure

A glance at almost any written document, whether a book, newspaper, letter or project proposal, is usually enough for us to get an initial understanding of its overall structure. Chapters, headlines, headings, paragraphs and lists of contents all help us to anticipate how the text is organised, and perhaps which sections to read carefully and which ones to skip.

Audiences too can make better sense of a presentation if they are clear from the start about what it is going to cover, and the order in which the different items will be dealt with. Having a sense of what to expect gives them a set of milestones that enables them to track where the talk has got to, and, importantly, to anticipate when it is likely to finish. Without such guidelines, there is the awful prospect that it might go on for ever. The trouble is, of course, that members of an audience have no idea about how the contents of a talk are going to be organised, unless or until the speaker does something about it. This is no doubt why so many manuals and courses recommend what is sometimes referred to as the military model of structure, which instructs speakers to 'tell them what you're going to tell them; tell them; and then tell them what you told them'.

In effect, this is saying that there should be an introduction, a main body and a summary, which is certainly good advice as far as it goes. But experience suggests that, from an audience point of view, there are advantages in dividing presentations into a five-part structure, in which the introductory and concluding sections are divided into two:

❑ Pre-introduction
❑ Introduction
❑ Main body
❑ Summary
❑ Conclusion

❦ The pre-introduction

If it's important for audiences to have a sense of what's to come, it's obviously crucial that they should be fully attentive at the point when you introduce your subject matter. Right at the start, however, you can't rely on audiences to be completely focused on what you are saying. They may still be rattling coffee cups, or chatting between themselves at the point when you start. In any event, it usually takes a few moments for them to adapt to a new speaker, so the danger of launching straight into the introduction is that not everyone will have settled down enough to take it in. And, if they miss crucial information about the structure of what's to come, they may find the talk more difficult to follow later on. An effective pre-introduction therefore involves saying something that has no other purpose than to catch the attention of the audience and set the mood for what follows. Then, by the time you get to the introduction proper, there is a much greater chance of the audience paying full attention to it than if you had launched straight in with it during your first few words.

Pre-introductions provide considerable scope for creativity. Some of the examples from business presentations in the previous chapter were in fact pre-introductions. The contrast between two dates and two facts presents the audience with a stark fact aimed at getting their interest, while only hinting at what might be to follow:

> In 2000, IDT launched around 500 new products. By 2004, this number will have increased to a staggering 1,000 new products during the year.

Two of the puzzles were also pre-introductions designed to catch the audience's attention:

> I'd like to start by posing a question. Is there any point in being good at something if people don't know you're good at it?

> Money is like a sixth sense. Without it you can't make full use of the other five.

A suitable quotation, references to current affairs, something said by an earlier speaker or an anecdote can all be pressed into service to get the interest and attention of the audience. And, as was seen in Chapter 1, if an opening humorous remark prompts laughter, you can be sure that the audience will be listening closely to whatever you say next.

The introduction

Once you have successfully engaged the audience with a pre-introduction, you can safely proceed to outlining the sequence of topics to be covered. And the key words here are 'sequence' and 'outline'. The idea of sequence is important because the structure of a presentation refers to the order in which topics are dealt with and developed over a period of time. And the idea of an outline is important for the obvious reason that it's no use putting up a slide and announcing, as I have seen speakers do, that the presentation will deal with the list of 10 or 15 topics displayed on the screen. Audiences will simply recoil at the prospect of the massive overload of information about to be inflicted on them, and are likely to switch off even before the talk has got properly under way. For them to be able to grasp an overall sense of structure, you have to outline it as simply as possible, and describe it as clearly as possible. There is no hard and fast rule as to how many sections there should be, but experience suggests that many more than three or four will start to put a strain on the audience's ability to retain the overview for the duration of the talk.

🔍 The main body

You will already have put the topics into sections and the sections into a sequence during the Brainstorming phase. Most of the time spent on preparation will be devoted to getting the main body together, and it's useful to bear in mind that the various sections themselves, and especially the longer and more important ones, can benefit from having beginnings, middles and endings. Given that audiences cannot always be relied on to remember the overall structure for the entire duration of a presentation, they will welcome occasional reminders of 'where we've got so far', and the ground still to be covered. The use of signposts that point backwards to where we have been, and forwards to where we are going, not only helps the audience to keep on track, but also reminds the speaker to stick to the structure announced at the start.

🔍 The summary and conclusion

Just as it's important for a presentation to get off to a good start, so too can the way it ends have a critical impact on the audience. The trouble is that speakers often find it difficult to draw things to a close. Even though most people on our courses dread being asked to speak for five minutes, the fact is that very few actually stop speaking after five minutes. Even the repetition of promising indicators that the end is nigh, such as 'in conclusion ...', 'finally ...' and 'just before I finish ...', is no guarantee that they are about to stop. In one extreme case, the first 'finally' occurred more than 1,000 words before the end actually came.

This highlights a difficulty that relates to the earlier discussion of how speaking in public differs from speaking in the much more familiar world of everyday conversation, where silences tend to be embarrassing and signals of impending trouble (see Chapter 2). In some situations, as with political or after-dinner speeches, there's a good chance that the silence at the end will be immediately filled by applause. But on most other occasions, you know that, as soon as you stop speaking, you'll be confronted by an uncomfortable and seemingly endless silence. However tempting it may be to try and keep that awful moment at bay by adding just a few more words (and a few more after that), the fact has to be faced that sooner or later you will have to stop speaking.

One step towards overcoming this problem is simply to be aware of it. Another is to have a clear strategy for bringing the talk to a decisive close. This is why it's useful to treat the end of a presentation as consisting of two distinct tasks. The first is the traditional 'tell them what you told them', or, in other words, a brief summary of the main point(s). The second is to draw out from that a concluding statement that encapsulates the key message that you had decided on much earlier when analysing the audience. Given that this is the last thing the audience will hear, every attempt should be made to package it in as punchy and memorable a way as possible – which can often be done by using the rhetorical toolkit described earlier (see Chapters 6–7).

🔍 Returning to base

One way of embarking on a closing sequence that can be very effective is to refer back to something you said during the introduction or pre-introduction. Doing this is a way of letting the audience know that the end is near in a less overt way than with lines that explicitly refer to structural elements, such as 'in summary …' or 'to summarise…'. At the same time, the link back to the opening theme or idea makes it appear that the presentation had an impressively rounded structure and had been well planned right from the start.

An example of this came in a speech by a company director at an annual conference for senior managers. He had started by saying that he was going to talk about the 'landscape of opportunity that lies ahead'. Towards the end, he began the summary by referring back to the same image, and developed it with a series of related metaphors:

Summary→
> That's why I began by referring to what lies ahead as a landscape of opportunity.
> We've seen the main roads to success.
> We know the pitfalls to be avoided
> and we know the destination we want to reach.

Conclusion→ All that remains now is to make sure we get there.

4. Saying it creatively

None of the above stages needs to take more than a few minutes, but will already have taken you a long way towards solving the problem of structure: what to say, the main headings under which to say it and the sequence in which they will be presented have all been decided on. In fact, if all you wanted to do were to give a slide-dependent presentation, the preparation process would be more or less complete at this point. Your only remaining task would be to load the main headings and subsidiary bullet points on to slides for use as prompts during the presentation itself.

But there is another very important step for anyone who wants to have a more positive impact on the audience than presenters who follow the industry standard model. As was seen in the previous chapter, this involves going beyond deciding *what* to say, to work out *how* to say it in as effective a way as possible. It means looking for interesting ways to get the contents of each section across and making use of the tools of rhetoric and imagery whenever you can. Some topics may lend themselves to being illustrated by an anecdote; for others there may be an appropriate metaphor or analogy that can be brought into play; while yet other points may be expressed in terms of a contrast or three-part list (see also Chapter 8).

A commonly asked question is whether there are any guidelines as to how frequently to use these creative tools within a presentation, or any limit on how much they can or should be used. Experience suggests that there are no hard and fast rules, and that there is considerable variation between individuals in the extent to which they use rhetoric and imagery to package their messages. In general, however, the more such techniques feature in a presentation, the better the response from the audience. And, as was suggested earlier, they are particularly adaptable for use as pre-introductions, conclusions and for summarising the gist of one section before moving on to another.

Notes or script?

In Chapter 4, I pointed out that you shouldn't think that there is anything shameful or inadequate about being seen to use notes or a script. But, whichever you choose, it's very important that the writing and layout should make it as easy as possible for you to lift the words from the text. Many people will have already experienced what can happen if you look down at print that's too small, handwriting that's barely legible or a mass of words that can't be read at a glance. It either results in panic and an *impromptu* decision to give up on using the notes altogether, or you become so preoccupied with getting safely to the next full stop that you come across as flat, monotonous and completely lacking in expression. As was touched on in the reference to the way Winston Churchill used to lay out his speeches (see Chapter 2), it's easy enough to avoid such problems. However, before looking at the solutions in a little more detail, we need to consider the question of whether a speaker should use a full script or rely on notes.

This issue has already been referred to in the earlier suggestion (page 283) about taking the number that will be present into account (Stage 1 of the process), where it was suggested that fully scripted presentations are usually more appropriate if the audience is going to be very large, or where timing is absolutely critical. Given that most speeches and presentations are to fairly small audiences, notes will usually be the most suitable *aide-mémoire* for the speaker. Some people, however, find it useful to write the whole thing out first, and then reduce it to shorthand headings for use when actually making the presentation. Others worry that, if they rely on notes, they won't be able to make much use of carefully phrased rhetorical lines, imagery or anecdotes.

The solution is to combine shorthand headings with fully scripted lines where they are needed. Luckily, however, people find that they don't have to do as much scripting as they expect when first setting out to incorporate rhetoric and imagery. For example, in the case of anecdotes, metaphors and other forms of imagery, it isn't always necessary to write the whole thing out. A single written word or phrase is all you need to trigger the story or the image. Similarly, if a three-part list involves the repetition of phrases or clauses, ditto signs are more than enough for you to be able to deliver the lines with the originally intended level of accuracy.

🔊 Cards or paper?

Deciding whether to write notes on paper or cards can help to make things more convenient for the speaker. Paper is fine if there's going to be a lectern, or if you are sitting at a table and can glance down at the sheets laid out in front of you. But when there's no such support, sheets of paper tend to flap about, which risks distracting both audience and speaker. This is where the extra stiffness of cards comes into its own. For speakers who worry about what to do with their hands (see Chapter 11), the added advantage of cards is that having to hold on to them more or less solves the problem. As for what size of card to use, 10 centimetres by 15 seems to work best. Anything smaller and you'll find that you can't write very much on them, and the pack becomes so thick that it is cumbersome and difficult to handle. And, obvious though it may seem, clear numbering of the pages or cards is a crucial defence against disasters like dropping them on the floor.

🔊 Turning pages

When reading from loose sheets of paper, we naturally turn each page right over so that it ends up facing downwards. The only useful purpose this serves is to make sure that the pages of the document end up in the same order as they were at the start.

However, as we never have to repeat a speech or presentation as soon as it is finished, it doesn't really matter if they end up in the reverse order, as happens when each page is moved sideways on to a growing pile, rather than turned over. Doing this draws less attention to the fact that you're turning a page, and removes another potential source of distraction – which can become quite serious if a microphone picks up the noise of rustling paper and amplifies it around the conference hall.

It can also be unnecessarily distracting if you make a habit of dropping each card to the table as you finish with it. This is not only distracting in itself, but is also likely to encourage members of the audience to start monitoring the ever-diminishing number of cards in your hand. And once they get interested in working out how much longer you are going to take, their attention on the talk itself will be significantly diminished.

From the point of view of both speaker and audience, there is something to be said for starting each new topic on a new card or page. Television newsreaders routinely do this, even though everyone knows that they are actually reading from a teleprompter. For speakers, the practice makes it more likely that they will conclude the last topic and start the next one with different intonation. This, combined with the association of topic changes with page changes, provides an implicit signal to the audience that the talk is moving on to another section, making it easier for them to keep track of the structure as it unfolds.

Writing speeches

If you plan to write out the full text of a speech, it's extremely important to take into account the differences between the written and spoken word examined in Chapter 3, and especially to make sure that you keep the sentences short. One reason why our written sentences tend to be longer than spoken ones probably comes from the convention of writing in paragraphs. This means that, apart from the first sentence which is indented, most of them start somewhere in the middle of a line. While writing or typing out the next words, it's therefore very easy to lose track of how long any current sentence is.

The solution is to stop arranging sentences in paragraphs, and to start each new sentence on a new line like this.

You'll then find it very easy to keep a continual check on the length of every sentence while you are writing it.

A useful guide is that the warning lights should go on whenever a sentence gets longer than about 16 words.

This is because the average length of sentences in speeches is around eight seconds.

At about 120 words per minute this comes to 16 words.

The important word here is *average*, as there will be some sentences made up of fewer than 16 words, and some of more.

If the continuous monitoring of sentence length is to become a matter of routine, it's a good idea to get into the habit of using the same-sized font.

Once you know where the words on the screen will be after 16 words, you will have a visual reminder of the point at which the sentence is in danger of becoming too long.

Starting each sentence on a new line not only enables you to monitor its length, but also makes its structure more visible than when the words are contained within a paragraph.

A particular word or phrase *might stand out as* being worth repeating.

It *might stand out as* a possible first part of a contrast.

Or it *might stand out as* a way of starting each item in a list of three.

Abandoning the paragraph is therefore one small step away from writing for the eyes of a reader, and a giant leap towards writing for the ears of an audience.

Speaker-friendly layout

Giving up writing in paragraphs is also important when it comes to laying out a script in a form that will make it as easy as possible for you to read a speech effectively from a text. Seeing a line at a time makes it easier to look down, pick up the whole or part of a sentence, look up and deliver it. This becomes even easier when the print is much larger than is usual in most written material –

though it's a mistake to think that typing the whole thing out in capital letters will help. Reading long sequences of words written in capitals is not something that we do very often, and there is evidence that people find them more difficult to read than words in lower-case letters. So the text of a speech, like that on road signs, will be much easier to read at a glance when printed in big lower-case letters.

The number of words on a line also has an effect on how easy it is to read from a text: the wider the line, the more difficult it becomes to scan it quickly. Just as the narrow columns of newspapers are easy to read, so too do narrow columns help to make life easier when reading a speech from a text. Like the choice of font size, the decision on column width will be very much a matter of personal preference, and it's a good idea to try out different options to discover which feels most comfortable. The following famous extract from a speech by Winston Churchill is a fairly typical example of a speaker-friendly script:

We shall not fail or falter,
we shall not weaken or tire.
Neither the sudden shock of battle,
nor the long-drawn trials of
vigilance and exertion will
wear us down.
Give us the tools and
we will finish the job.

As was mentioned in the earlier discussion of pausing and intonation (see Chapter 2), you can make things even easier for yourself by marking up the text in advance. Single vertical slashes can be pencilled in to indicate a short pause, or double slashes for a longer one. Alternatively, the text can be laid out with the end of each line being a place to pause. Words to be given extra stress can be underlined or highlighted with a marker pen. Entering simple mood descriptions in the margins, such as 'seriously', 'ironically', 'assertively', etc., can also provide effective reminders of changes in intonation and emphasis. Deciding on how to mark up a script depends, of course, on reading it aloud in order to try out what different alternatives sound like.

5. Creating the visual aids

The search for creative ways of getting points across is not confined to looking for opportunities to use rhetoric and imagery, but should also include thinking about what visual aids (if any) you are likely to need. Leaving the decision about these until this fairly late stage in the preparation process has two major advantages. The first is that you are likely to use far fewer visual aids than if you had opted for the traditional 'slides first' approach to preparation. The second is that the ones you do decide to use will be there to illustrate a particular point, rather than merely to remind you what to say next. Speakers who defer the decision about what visual aids to use until after they have got the basic structure together are therefore much less likely to make their audiences suffer from slide fatigue than those for whom the process of preparing a presentation stops as soon as a collection of slides has been filled with bullet points. Decisions about the selection and design of visual aids should also be guided by the more detailed discussion of the subject in Chapters 4 and 5.

6. Rehearsal

Although no professional actor would dream of going on stage without extensive rehearsal, the remarkable fact is that most amateur speakers hardly ever take the trouble to rehearse their talks beforehand. And rehearsal doesn't simply mean reading silently through the notes or script to yourself, because this won't help you to discover how it works when spoken aloud. The importance of rehearsal is that it not only helps in estimating the timing of a speech or presentation, but also provides an opportunity to discover if any of it needs revising, something that's obviously better done in advance rather than finding out that you have to make changes during the actual presentation itself.

The more you go though something aloud, the more firmly fixed in your mind will the words become. It is not so much a matter of learning a speech off by heart as becoming so familiar with what comes next in the overall structure that you become confident speaking from the notes or script. And, if you can recruit other people to listen to you rehearsing, you can get the benefit of useful feedback on how the audience is likely to react. Failing that,

> Reading silently through the notes or script won't help you to discover how it sounds when spoken aloud. The importance of rehearsal is that it helps to fix the sequence in your mind, to estimate the timing and to find out if any of it needs revising.

audio and video recording makes it possible to watch and evaluate your own performances. I know of a number of people who, having discovered just how much their performance improves with rehearsal, will listen to themselves on a car cassette player on the way to work, make a mental note of things to be improved, record it again, and then listen to the revised version on the way home.

7. Preparing for question time

One of the reasons why Margaret Thatcher was not very keen on the idea of televising the proceedings of the House of Commons is said to have been that she didn't want the public to see that she used briefing notes during Prime Minister's Question Time – presumably on the grounds that they might be less impressed if they thought that answers to anticipated questions had been prepared in advance. Some years ago, an applicant for a place at an Oxford College dried up and went white in response to one of the questions he was asked during an interview. When pressed as to what the problem was, he blurted out that he'd never heard that particular one before. It transpired that successive generations of applicants from his school had been briefed to make a note of all the questions they could remember having been asked during their admissions interviews. These had accumulated into a huge database of questions that were most likely to be put to candidates for a place at that particular college, and equipped their teachers with a solid basis for coaching and rehearsing pupils before they went to Oxford for their interviews. Not surprisingly, applicants from the school in question had a higher than average acceptance rate at the college.

These two examples highlight the fact that it's not only perfectly possible to prepare yourself for answering questions, but can also be very much to your advantage. And many speeches and presentations are, of course, routinely followed by a period of questioning. Quite often, as when a company is pitching for new business or you are applying for a job, the way you handle the questions can be at least as important as the presentation itself. Yet the curious fact is that most speakers spend far more time preparing what to say than preparing how to deal with the questions they will have to face at the end.

Anticipating and preparing for questions is a fairly straightforward business, and the following three-stage process has proved effective on numerous occasions. If possible, it's best to do it in a group: a few minds are always better than one, and are likely to generate more possibilities than when you try to do it on your own.

❑ Brainstorm to produce a list of all the possible questions that you think might be raised by this particular audience.

❑ Go through all the questions and work out the best possible way of answering each one.

❑ Having decided what to say, go one step further and think about *how* to get each point across in the most effective ways (using, wherever possible, all the techniques described in earlier chapters).

There is no rehearsal stage in this list, because it's not always as helpful as it is when preparing the presentation itself. Audiences tend not to be very impressed by answers that come across as too rehearsed. This means that, if you practise at all, the main challenge is to make your replies sound as though they are completely spontaneous and off the cuff.

This method of preparation consists of a seven-step process:

1. Analysing the audience

❏ Who's in the audience?

❏ How big is it going to be?

❏ What message is for this audience?

2. Brainstorming

❏ *Subjects:* Make a list of all the possible topics that could be included.

❏ *Sectionalising:* Put the topics into sections.

❏ *Sequencing:* Reorder the sections into a logical sequence.

3. Creating a structure

Aim for a structure consisting of five main parts:

❏ Pre-introduction

❏ Introduction

❏ Main body

❏ Summary

❏ Conclusion

4. Saying it creatively

Having decided what to say, go on to work out how to put your points across in the most effective way (see Chapters 6–8).

5. Creating the visual aids

Decide on whether you need any visual aids, and if so what would be most suitable (see Chapters 4 and 5).

6. Rehearsal

Go through the whole thing, saying it out aloud. If possible, record it, and/or get others to listen to it and give you feedback.

7. Preparing for question time (optional)

Take some time to anticipate possible questions and work out how best to answer them should they arise.

Unaccustomed
As You May Be

Making Social and Duty Speeches

I once went to a wedding, at which the groom made the following speech:

> I'd just like to thank everyone for coming. And thanks also to (the bride's) mum and dad for arranging everything, and to my mum and dad for all their help and support. So if you'd just raise your glasses I'd like to propose a toast to the bridesmaids.

After proposing the toast, he sat down and handed over to the best man, who had flown in from abroad especially for the occasion. His speech, also reproduced here in full, went as follows:

> I'd just like to say thank you on behalf of the bridesmaids. And – er – I've got some cards here to read out ... [reads out greetings cards].

The speech ended when he finished reading out the last word on the last card. To say that the audience felt a slight sense of anticlimax would be a serious understatement. On such occasions, they expect a little bit more than this, even allowing for the fact that the key players may have little or no experience of speech-making.

Weddings, of course, are only one of a wide range of social occasions at which almost anyone might find themselves having to speak, whether to propose a vote of thanks, to present a retirement present to a departing colleague or to introduce an after-dinner speaker. If we are the father of a bride, the groom or the best man at a wedding, we have no choice but to stand up and say at least a few words. Tens of thousands of such speeches are taking place every week, and they probably provoke more fear and dread than any other type of speech-making. A major reason for this is that, in a very high proportion of cases, it is the first speech the speaker has ever had to make.

1. Reasons for reassurance

In a book of this length, it's obviously impossible to include detailed advice on every conceivable type of speech that anyone might ever have to make. So this chapter looks at how the techniques described so far can help to ease the pain of being called upon to make a social or duty speech. The first and most important thing to be said is that all the basic principles covered in this book can be used just as effectively on these social occasions as at political rallies or business presentations. And there are some added bonuses for social and duty speakers that can reassure them and help to boost confidence in the face of so daunting a task.

In the first place, the challenge of keeping the audience awake is much less of a problem than in many other situations. One reason for this is that these are speeches that audiences positively look forward to as the focal point of an occasion: everyone can concentrate for a few moments on the reason why they are all there. You can therefore take heart from the fact that you are doing something that everybody expects and wants to be done, but no one actually wants to do. Another reason why audience attentiveness is likely to be less of a problem than on many other occasions is because social and duty speeches are, or should be, fairly short, ideally lasting only a few minutes rather than a few tens of minutes. Finally, you don't have to worry about how to simplify complex material into a form that audiences will be able to understand. The subject matter is much more straightforward and clearly defined, as the central topic of the vast majority of social and duty speeches is one particular person or, in the case of weddings, two people.

2. In praise of persons

When it comes to speaking about particular individuals, rhetorical techniques and imagery are no less adaptable for packaging messages about a person than they are when talking about any other subject matter. For example, the opening lines of the most famous funeral oration in English literature included a three-part list and two consecutive contrasts:

Friends, Romans and Countrymen.
Lend me your ears.
I come to bury Caesar, not to praise him.

The evil that men do lives after them;
the good is oft interred with their bones.
So let it be with Caesar. **Shakespeare** (*Julius Caesar*)

Lord Spencer began his speech at the funeral of his sister, Diana, Princess of Wales, with a three-part list:

I stand before you today the representative of a family in grief, in a country in mourning, before a world in shock. **Lord Spencer**

Ronald Reagan's address after the Challenger shuttle disaster in 1986 featured a puzzle about why there was a coincidence that day. He solved this by contrasting the astronauts with a famous explorer of the past, inserting a three-part quotation along the way:

There's a coincidence today.
On this day 390 years ago, the great explorer Sir Francis Drake died aboard ship off the coast of Panama. In his lifetime the great frontiers were the oceans, and a historian later said, 'He lived by the sea, died on it, and was buried in it.' Well, today, we can say of the Challenger crew: Their dedication was, like Drake's, complete. **Ronald Reagan**

The speech ended with some powerful imagery taken from the first and last lines of *High Flight*, a poem by John Gillespie Magee, Jr., a Royal Canadian Air Force officer who died in a Spitfire crash in 1941:

We will never forget them, nor the last time we saw them, this morning, as they prepared for their journey and waved goodbye and 'slipped the surly bonds of earth' to 'touch the face of God'. **Ronald Reagan**

And, as was seen in Chapter 7, effective imagery also featured at the funeral of the Queen Mother:

Like the sun, she bathed us in her warm glow. Now that the sun has set and the cool of the evening has come, some of the warmth we absorbed is flowing back towards her. **Archbishop George Carey**

These are, of course, well-known examples from the public domain, but a central message of this book is that exactly the same techniques that work so well for the famous can be used just as easily and effectively by anyone else. As in the earlier discussion of business presentations, none of the following examples are invented, but are taken from real speeches made at various types of social occasion.

Three virtues

Whether the speech is a funeral address, or any other type of speech about a particular person, it is very easy to divide points up into lists of three:

As a child, he was cheeky, naughty and the loudest kid in school.

So many of the letters we've had refer to his warmth, his sociability and his great big smile.

As far as he was concerned, obstacles were merely there to be overcome.
Red tape was there to be cut through.
And visions were there to be turned into reality.
He is one of the friendliest, funniest and most generous people I've ever met.

Inserting a third item that contrasts with the first two introduces an element of surprise and humour into the sequence, as in the following comments by the best man at a wedding:

He was well known throughout the college for his companionship, good humour and unswerving faith in the fortunes of Oxford United.

The same format can be used to deliver the solution to a puzzle that projects a three-part solution:

When it came to his job, he had three unstoppable qualities: professionalism, determination and downright obstinacy.

Contrasting qualities

Contrasts are also useful for summing up a person's essential qualities:

We're sad to see you go.
But glad to have had the privilege of working with you.

In her life she taught me the meaning of friendship.
Her death has taught me the meaning of courage.

At a dinner for the old boys of an all-male school, one of the speakers proposed a toast to the girls from the local school for girls – with whom many of those present had had their first dates. A woman guest who had been at the girls' school in question replied on their behalf with a single sentence consisting of a contrast that rearranged the words in the first part. It went down so well with the audience that they responded with a spontaneous standing ovation:

The girls you all remember [PAUSE] all remember you.

🗨 *Imagery and anecdotes*

The various kinds of imagery discussed in Chapter 7 are often used to highlight a feature of someone's character:

For him, new technology was always a servant, never the master.

She has the determination of a terrier that won't let go of a bone.

He was like a corporate gardener, sowing seeds today so that the company could reap the harvest tomorrow.

However, of all the techniques described in earlier chapters, the one that really comes into its own in social and duty speeches is the anecdote. A well-chosen story that represents some key characteristic of a person can be so effective that it is often the only thing that anyone ever remembers about such speeches.

Sometimes, anecdotes are as short as a single sentence, as in the following example, which was introduced to illustrate what the speaker meant by describing the person in question as 'a great romantic':

> When I was ill in hospital, he managed to smuggle in smoked salmon and a bottle of wine, physical tokens of the love and support that helped me through, and speeded my recovery.

More usually, anecdotes extend over several sentences, as in this illustration of someone's relationship with his personal assistant:

> When he recruited Brenda as his PA, he told her that what he really needed was 'a mother hen'. On occasions she took him literally, especially when supervising his frantic last-minute dashing about from meeting to meeting. Did he know where he was going? Who was he meeting? Had he got his papers, keys, briefcase? Once she was heard to shout down the corridor after him: 'And have you got your dinner money?' It was just as well she asked – he hadn't any cash for parking, and could she lend him a tenner?

At the funeral of a man in his twenties, who had died suddenly from an undiagnosed heart condition, the centrepiece of the eulogy by one of his best friends was widely commended afterwards by the mourners as a brilliant summing up of the essence of his character. The story was set at a beach bar in the Far East:

Having partied the night away, the rest of us were faltering. But Johnny was determined to squeeze the last drop of fun from his holiday. As we sloped off, Johnny, as only he could do, managed to get chatting to two Canadian circus performers and an Irish girl, who instantly took a shine to him. As they got chatting, a rather large man at the bar took umbrage to it, as he was under the impression he was with the girl. He proceeded to charge at Johnny in a drunken attempt to attack him. However, on his way, he stumbled in the sand and fell at Johnny's feet. But Johnny was completely oblivious and, thinking he had fallen over, helped him up, dusted him off and asked if he was all right – to which his assailant replied with a head butt. Johnny, definitely a lover not a fighter, turned tail and made a run for it – at which point, his new circus performer pals saw his predicament and chased his attacker into the sea … Although funny, the story also shows to me Johnny's natural tendency to see the good in people. In every way, he was a predominantly good person, and it was one of the things I now realise I admired and also relied on the most.

It struck a chord with the congregation because it highlighted characteristics that everyone could recognise as typical of the deceased. And what made it all the more impressive was the fact that it was the first speech that the speaker had ever made in his life.

3. Lines for any occasion

In quite a number of the above examples, I deliberately made no reference to whether the lines were taken from a wedding, funeral

> Preparing speeches for social occasions is much the same as preparing any other kind of speech. The main difference between different types of social and duty speech lies in mood, emphasis and striking the right balance between humour and seriousness.

or a party to celebrate a birthday or the achievements of a departing colleague. This was to show that a common feature of many of them was that they could have been used on any of these occasions where the central focus of the speech was a particular person. Even in the case of the anecdote from the young man's funeral, it's easy to imagine the same story being told (apart from the last sentence) at his wedding, or at a party celebrating his promotion or move from one job to another. This demonstrates the general applicability of the techniques and approach described in this book, and the fact that the preparation and delivery of social and duty speeches is very similar to that of preparing and delivering any other kind of speech.

The main difference between the various types of social and duty speech lies in mood, emphasis and striking a suitable balance between humour and seriousness. At the two extremes are funeral addresses and the best man's speech at weddings. But a eulogy that is completely serious is unlikely to be as effective as one that includes some humorous lines or anecdotes about the deceased. These are not only an effective way of recalling affectionate memories about someone's life and character, but can also help to relieve some of the overbearing sadness that permeates the atmosphere at funerals and memorial services. At the other extreme, the balance shifts towards more humour than seriousness in best man's speeches at weddings. However, as will be seen later, this is not without its dangers, and doesn't mean that a best man's speech should be entirely devoid of serious content.

4. Analysing the audience

When preparing a social and duty speech, knowledge of who is going to be in the audience is so critical that it's worth doing some research beforehand. At family occasions such as weddings and funerals, there are likely to be people from widely differing age groups; there may be a complicated collection of ex-spouses and stepchildren to take into account; or there may be people of different nationalities, religions or ethnic backgrounds. An example of how to make audiences cringe with embarrassment was the memorable scene in the film *Four Weddings and a Funeral,* in which a best man goes through a catalogue of the groom's misdemeanours with previous girlfriends.

In speeches marking a colleague's retirement, you need to be aware of any special tensions there may have been between the person who is leaving and others who might be present, as well as any other office politics that might complicate matters. Knowing about the audience mix not only helps to minimise the chances of

Anecdotes play such an important part in social and duty speeches that a major part of the preparation process will involve a search for suitable stories, both serious and humorous, to illustrate essential features of the person's character, work or lifestyle.

giving needless offence, but may also guide the precise wording of a particular section of a speech. As was mentioned earlier (see Chapter 3), the safest way to avoid giving offence to some or all of those present is to exclude humour that might come across as sexist, racist or blue. Sexual innuendo and smutty jokes may go down well enough with some audiences that are young and male, but are unlikely to win many friends at family gatherings that span all age groups from the very young to the very old.

5. The search for stories

Anecdotes play such an important part in social and duty speeches that, whatever the occasion, a major part of the preparation process should involve a search for suitable stories, both serious and humorous, to illustrate some essential feature of the person's character, work or lifestyle. By far the best place to start is by asking other people who know or knew the individual concerned. This is because their response to such a request will invariably go beyond merely producing a list of descriptive adjectives ('kind', 'loyal', 'witty', 'generous', etc.), to give examples that back up these evaluations. Such examples invariably consist of stories that illustrate the particular characteristics mentioned, which makes this a fairly quick and easy way to get together a collection from which to choose the most appropriate ones.

Consulting with others is not only important as a means of gathering raw material, but also has another important advantage. Those who make social and duty speeches are rarely expected to confine themselves to their own personal feelings, but have a wider responsibility to represent and speak on behalf of everyone else. If we are members of the person's family, there may be details of their work or leisure pursuits that we know nothing about, while work colleagues may be just as ignorant of their family life. But one of the reassuring things about the search for stories that sum up a person's character is that they typically reveal a high level of agreement about what the person in question was really like. This no doubt reflects a basic fact of life, which is that whatever it is that we mean by an individual's personality, different people tend to come to the same conclusions about any particular person's essential character. The stories we collect will therefore almost invariably reflect and confirm our own views, and give us the confidence to develop them. The similarity of such anecdotes also means that there are unlikely to be many widely differing themes, which makes it much easier to narrow down and simplify the subject matter to be covered.

6. Avoiding overlap

As there tends to be a convergence of opinion about any particular individual, the first question to be asked by anyone invited to speak about someone is whether or not there are going be any other speakers. If there are, it's extremely important to have a word with them in advance about what points they are planning to make, and which anecdotes they will be using by way of illustration. Otherwise, there is a very high probability of overlap and repetitiveness. On one occasion, for example, a speaker at a funeral told me how relieved he had been to have spoken first, as all those who followed him did little more than go over the themes that he'd already mentioned.

7. Wedding speeches

Tradition decrees that three main categories of people – bride's father (or close relation or family friend), groom and best man – should speak at a wedding, and so these are speeches that are often impossible to avoid. For the first two, there is a fairly standard blueprint that makes it reasonably straightforward to decide what to say. Bridegrooms and fathers of the bride can also draw comfort from the fact that members of the audience are perfectly well aware that weddings are very emotional occasions for the main participants and their parents, and don't really expect either of these first two speeches to be the entertaining high spot of the proceedings. By contrast, the best man is in the unenviable position of being expected to go beyond his official duty of responding on behalf of the bridesmaids and reading out greetings cards, to supply the entertainment and release from formality that everyone has been waiting for. As such, it is perhaps the most challenging social and duty speech that anyone is ever likely to have to make.

Minimally, the points to be dealt with by the father of the bride are as follows:

- ❏ Thank people for coming.
- ❏ Refer to friends and relations who could not be present.
- ❏ Tell stories about his daughter's life so far.
- ❏ Welcome the groom into the family.
- ❏ Propose a toast to the bride and groom.

Replying to the toast is the main job of the groom's speech, which is likely to include some or all of the following:

- ❑ Thanks to bride's parents, his parents, everyone else involved in organising and helping at the wedding, guests for coming, wedding presents.
- ❑ Present gifts to bridesmaids, pageboys, ushers, etc.
- ❑ Comment on how the day is going so far.
- ❑ Story of how the romance developed.
- ❑ Express delight at having married his bride.
- ❑ Compliment, thank and then propose a toast to the bridesmaids.

🗨 *The best man's speech*

At various points in this book I have stressed the importance of speakers avoiding forms of language and styles of delivery that are likely to make them sound as if they are trying to play the part of someone other than their natural, normal selves. The trouble with the best man's speech is that people's perception of what the audience expects often leads them to try playing a part that doesn't come naturally to the vast majority of us. In fact it's such a difficult role to pull off successfully that the few who are able to do it can command huge fees as stand-up comedians and after-dinner speakers. As a result, many best man's speeches consist of an endless succession of jokes and supposedly funny stories about the groom, often poorly delivered and usually giving the impression that the groom is an idle layabout and serial philanderer, whose main interest in life is getting drunk.

This is a trend that is being actively encouraged by the hundreds of best man's speeches that are to be found on the internet, many of which use the same jokes, and assume that the main objective is character assassination of the groom. This may amuse a minority of those present – the groom's friends perhaps – but reflects an insensitive analysis of the wider audience as a whole, many of whom are likely to find such material at best inappropriate, and at worst downright embarrassing or offensive. This is not to say that all humour directed towards the groom should be eliminated, but there is a world of difference between outright character assassination and poking gentle fun at someone. There is also much to be said for softening the mockery of his foibles and eccentricities by contrasting these with some of his positive assets. A nice example of this was directed at a groom who was widely known to have excelled academically at school and university, and who could therefore hardly be made out to be a shiftless good-for-nothing. The best man read out extracts from early school reports that highlighted the contrast between the glowing comments about his academic performance and his complete hopelessness in practical subjects like woodwork. He then rounded the sequence off by noting that this explained the absence of DIY equipment on the wedding present list, and warned the bride not to expect him to be much use as a handyman around the house.

Apart from school reports, various other sources of material can sometimes provide themes that you can develop in a light-hearted way. There may be a topical event in the news that relates in some way to the groom's job, hobbies or interests. Dictionaries of dates occasionally reveal that some famous occurrence happened on the day the groom was born, and provide a basis for amusing comparisons to be made. It is also worth remembering that many first names originally had a meaning that might reflect or be at odds with the known characteristics of the groom. The astrological star signs of the bride and groom can also sometimes be mined for humorous purposes, as too can the predictions of newspaper horoscopes published on the wedding day itself (even if these are actually your own inventions).

Although the best man's speech will include a greater proportion of humorous material than most other types of social and duty speech, there is still a need for a certain amount of serious content, and even the minimalist example at the start of this chapter managed to include thanks for the toast to the bridesmaids and the reading out of cards. The more serious aspects of the best man's job will normally include some or all of the following:

❑ Thanks on behalf of the bridesmaids for the groom's toast to them.

❑ Reading out the cards from people unable to attend the wedding.

❑ Comments on the attractiveness of the bride and bridesmaids, on the wedding ceremony itself and the atmosphere of the proceedings so far.

❑ As the best man is the only one in the wedding line-up whose role includes speaking on behalf of all the guests, he may also wish to propose a collective vote of thanks to the parents of the bride and groom and everyone else involved in providing the hospitality.

❑ Act as master of ceremonies (if there is no official one), including:

- bringing the gathering to order;
- introducing the other speakers;
- making any announcements that may be necessary.

When it comes to being master of ceremonies, techniques that are useful to a best man, and anyone else who has to perform the role on other types of occasion, are described in the remaining sections of this chapter.

8. Using names to prompt applause

Whether introducing a guest, proposing a vote of thanks, commending or congratulating someone or awarding a prize or a gift to a colleague who is leaving or retiring, the speaker will want at some stage to set things up so that the audience shows their collective approval for the person in question. A common formula for doing this is the overworked cliché, 'Let us all now show our appreciation in the usual manner.' Effective enough though this may be, it is such a blunt and direct instruction that it's rather like using a sledgehammer to bludgeon the audience into applauding on demand. A rather more subtle and indirect way of orchestrating applause is to exploit the fact that audiences are very used to the idea of applauding when they hear someone's name – provided it occurs right at the end of a sequence.

The convention of clapping on hearing a name is so firmly established that it can even be used as a basis for humour, as was the case in a sketch depicting a spoof award ceremony on the 1980s satirical television show *Not the Nine O'Clock News*. The comic host, like so many of those who preside over such ceremonies in the real world, was a serial name dropper, with lines like 'when I was playing golf with Bob Hope', and 'as I said to Frank Sinatra', coming thick and fast. Every time the name of a celebrity was mentioned, there followed a loud burst of canned applause. The humour of the piece depended on the assumption that the mass television audience is familiar with the idea that naming a person is a standardised way of triggering applause – otherwise they would have been unable to recognise this as an example of things going slightly wrong, let alone that there was anything funny about it.

For a naming to work smoothly, the name has to come last in a sequence involving four distinct phases:

1   Identify the person being introduced/thanked/congratulated.
2   Say something about them.
3   PAUSE
4   Name him or her.

This is clearly illustrated by the following example from a speech by Margaret Thatcher:

1   I am very fortunate in having a marvellous deputy,
2   who's wonderful in all places, at all times, in all things.
3   PAUSE
4   Willie ⌈ Whitelaw.
            ⌊ [Applause]

The first stage informs the audience that the speaker is about to praise someone and who that person is. The second says something about his virtues. The pause between that and the name gives them time to get ready to applaud, so that they are poised to start as soon as, or, as in this case, just before the speaker finishes saying the name.

This basic formula can be adapted in various ways to meet the particular needs of an occasion. For example, when introducing speakers or giving a vote of thanks, you can extend the second stage to include more details about the person in question. In other situations, such as when reading out the nominations for prizes before naming the winners, you may want to keep the audience guessing about the identity of the person right up to the last second. The identity of the person to be named tends to be withheld in a similar way when hosts of television talk shows introduce their guests. To create this air of suspense, all you have to do is leave out the first step in the sequence:

2   My next guest is someone who made his name as the Saint, became even better known as James Bond and is now heavily involved as a roving ambassador for UNICEF.

3   PAUSE

4   Ladies and Gentlemen, Roger Moore. [Applause]

When using this technique, it's important to get everything in the right order, otherwise things can go badly wrong and cause confusion or embarrassment. For example, at a dinner marking the end of a company's sales conference, the managing director rose to hand out prizes to staff who had excelled in different fields. When announcing the first award, he made the mistake of naming the winner before saying anything about his achievements. But the mention of the name was enough to prompt an immediate outburst of cheering and applause that prevented the speaker from saying anything else until it had subsided. He then listed the winner's accomplishments before inviting him up to receive his award, at which point the ensuing burst of applause was considerably more subdued than at the first mention of his name. When it came to presenting awards to all the subsequent winners, the managing director started by describing what each had done, leaving it right to the end before revealing their name. In every case the result was an immediate burst of applause that provided a suitable backdrop to the winner's journey from seat to stage.

But not everyone is so quick on their feet as to be able to identify and rectify their mistakes as they go along. At a gathering of members of a college, the principal spent part of his speech thanking various people with lines like 'I'd like to thank Joe Bloggs and his team of gardeners for creating such an attractive backdrop to our daily life and work.' After a second or two of silence, one or two isolated claps were followed by what could only be described as a hesitant round of applause. The same thing happened several times in a row as the speaker went on to thank others for their contribution to the life of the college. Afterwards, members of the audience were to be heard complaining that they had found it all rather embarrassing because it had been so difficult to know exactly when to applaud – a problem that would certainly not have arisen if the speaker had followed the simple formula described above.

9. Mastering the ceremonies

The technique of orchestrating things so that an audience starts to applaud at the mention of a name is a useful part of the toolkit for anyone who has to take the chair, or act as the master of ceremonies, at functions where social and duty speeches play a part. And having someone in charge of making sure that everything runs smoothly is a key part in the organisation of such events. The importance of the role is underlined by the fact that, for very formal occasions, professional toastmasters or masters of ceremonies are often employed to preside over the proceedings. But in the vast majority of situations, the role of MC falls to an amateur, such as the best man at a wedding.

Whether professional or amateur, the MC's first job is to find out who will be speaking, and the order in which the speeches will take place. This includes not only being sure about what their names are, but also about the names by which they prefer to be known. There may, for example, be a question about whether to use titles and, if so, whether to refer to people as 'Mr', 'Mrs', 'Ms', 'Dr', 'Professor', etc. It's also as well to know which form of name to use: 'William Shakespeare', 'Will', 'Bill' or 'Billy'. Otherwise, embarrassing situations can arise, such as at the wedding of a man who had always been called by his second Christian name. This crucial piece of information had apparently not reached the vicar, who, much to everyone's surprise (groom and bride included), referred to him throughout the service by his first name.

At some stage, the MC will have to decide exactly when to start the formal proceedings. This usually means checking with the speakers that they're ready to start, or having a word with the caterers to keep the clattering of crockery to a minimum. Where people are eating, or milling about with drinks in their hands, your next problem is how to quell the noise so that everyone can concentrate on the speeches. This calls for decisiveness on the part of an MC. And doing something invariably works better than trying to say something, as it will be difficult for anyone to hear your voice above the general hubbub created by all the other voices. In the absence of a gavel or a gong, the best plan is to stand up and bang a spoon on the table or against a glass – and to keep it up until the noise shows signs of subsiding. Even then, there's no guarantee of instant success, and initial attempts to impose silence on an audience, especially when people are in high spirits, often fail. This may be one reason why the British tradition of preparing the way for after-dinner speeches with the loyal toast to the monarch has survived so long, as it works as an extremely efficient device for securing a smooth transition from noise to silent attentiveness. Once an audience has been called upon to stand up, raise their glasses and has said the words 'the Queen', all in unison, they are well on their way towards acting together as members of an audience, rather than as individual participants in numerous simultaneous conversations around the table. If there is no loyal toast, you may have to carry on tapping the spoon for quite some time before the audience settles down to a point at which they will be able to hear and listen to what you have to say.

10. Introductions

As the MC's main responsibility is to orchestrate the smooth running of the proceedings, it is generally not appropriate for him to speak for very long, or to do anything else that might divert the limelight away from the main speaker(s). It usually falls to him to welcome the guests and thank them for coming, before going on to introduce the speaker(s). As was seen earlier, this is one of the places where getting the audience to applaud at the mention of a name really comes into its own. The only preparation the MC has to do is to decide what and how much to say about the person who is about to speak (stage 2 in the technique), as a preamble to pausing (stage 3) and naming them (stage 4). At weddings, this is very straightforward, as the main players all occupy the familiar standardised roles of bride, groom, best man, etc. This means that there is no need for the MC to say anything more than 'Our first speaker is the bride's father: [pause] Mr Albert Smith.'

In other situations, such as introductions to a guest speaker or visiting lecturer, it is usual to provide rather more background information. It may, for example, be appropriate to say something about the speaker's job, interests, qualifications or achievements, and to mention the reason why they have been invited to speak to this particular audience on this particular occasion. However, in reaching a decision, the main point to remember is that the audience is there to listen to the visiting speaker, not to the MC, which means that brevity is the safest route to a successful introduction.

11. Off the cuff

There are some situations, such as public meetings or at the end of a lecture, where we find ourselves with an opportunity to speak, or may be called upon to say something without any prior warning. These are occasions about which Mark Twain had some rather worrying advice when he said, 'It usually takes me three weeks to prepare a good impromptu speech.' The serious point here is that you will usually have some idea in advance that you might have to speak, which means that it's well worth making the effort to have some lines ready just in case. It was said that Aneurin Bevan, a renowned orator and Labour cabinet minister in the post-war government, used to anticipate the most likely Tory heckles in parliamentary debates, and have witty put-downs ready in advance. And the earlier-mentioned case of the successful one-sentence reply to a toast to the girls of her school had also been prepared in advance – as a result of the speaker having been caught out and being at a loss for words at a previous year's dinner.

On the fairly rare occasions when there is no advance warning whatsoever, the most important thing is to have been listening to the proceedings before the dreaded moment when you're called upon to speak. This gives you a fair chance of rising to the occasion and saying something that actually relates to what has gone before. And, if you can think of three things, produce a suitable contrast or come up with a relevant anecdote, the chances are that you will have succeeded beyond most people's expectations. In other words, much the same criteria apply as for any other speech, the main difference being the need for some extremely quick thinking.

12. Conclusion

Social and duty speeches are a major source of anxiety because so many of those who have to give them have little or no experience of public speaking. But for them, as for anyone else, the basic principles outlined in the rest of this book will see them through. And, as was mentioned at the start of this chapter, they have some important advantages that are not always enjoyed by other speakers, lecturers or presenters. The subject matter is typically simple and straightforward, so you aren't faced with the problem of having to simplify detailed or complex material; you are hardly ever expected to speak for more than a few minutes; and the audience is usually in a very receptive mood.

1. Reasons for reassurance

Most people dread having to speak at a social occasion, but you can take heart from a number of encouraging facts:

❏ The audience is likely to be grateful that you are doing something that they all expect and want to be done, but no one actually wants to do.

❏ You aren't expected to speak for much more than a few minutes.

❏ The subject matter is more straightforward and clearly defined than in most other types of speech, so you don't have to worry as much about having to simplify complex material.

2. Approach and subject matter

❏ All the techniques described earlier work just as well in these as they do in any other type of speech.

❏ As most such speeches are directed towards particular individuals, anecdotes about them are an extremely important ingredient.

❏ In analysing the audience, it is important to take into account age differences, the relationship between people and any delicate issues that might arise from this. Above all, it's essential to avoid giving offence to any of them.

❑ If others are speaking on the same occasion, consult with them beforehand to make sure you don't all say the same things.

3. The master of ceremonies

❑ Your main job is to ensure that everything runs as smoothly as possible.

❑ Your first challenge will be to quieten down the audience, which can sometimes take more time and effort than you expect.

❑ Find out beforehand who's going to be speaking and the order in which the speeches will take place.

❑ Be sure to get their names right – and use the forms by which they prefer to be known.

4. Using names to prompt applause

A simple and effective way of getting an audience to applaud someone is to say a few words about them, and then say their name.

Part IV Exercises

Exercise 1 – *Translating messages*

☐ Take some political issue on which you have a strong opinion. Then translate it into a more persuasive form by using each of the following:

- A contrast.
- A puzzle–solution format or rhetorical question.
- A list of three.
- A position-taker.
- Any combination of the above.

☐ See if you can come up with any similes, metaphors or analogies that could be used to get the same message across.

☐ Select (or invent) a short anecdote that would provide a vivid illustration of the issue.

Exercise 2 – *Dividing things up*

☐ Select some organisation that you are involved in (e.g. work, college, sports club, church, charity, etc.) and make a list of the three things you would most like to see changed.

☐ For each of these three things:

- Make a contrast between the present situation and what it would be like after the change.

- Try to think of any similes, metaphors, analogies or anec-dotes that would illustrate the situation before and after each of the three changes.

- For each of the three things you would like to see changed, give three reasons why it should be changed.

Exercise 3 – Praising a person

□ Think of someone you know, and brainstorm a list of as many aspects of his or her character as possible.

□ Select the three most positive attributes, and decide the best order in which to list them.

□ Select one negative attribute that can be used to introduce a humorous contrast with the three virtues. For each of these:

- Select an anecdote about him or her to illustrate the point.

- Try to think of any similes, metaphors or analogies that would help to sum up what kind of a person he or she really is.

□ Go through your results, and decide which of them might be appropriate to deliver at the person's twenty-first birthday party, silver wedding anniversary, retirement presentation or funeral.

Exercise 4 – Preparing speeches and presentations

In learning to use the approach to preparation described in Chapter 9, one of the most useful exercises is to allow people an hour or so to prepare a five-minute speech on a subject that requires little or no research. This means that you can concentrate on the creative processes without having to waste time worrying about getting the facts right. Some possibilities are listed below, and your aim should be to prepare a well-structured speech of no more than five minutes, putting into practice as many as possible of the techniques described so far.

- ❑ Your favourite hobby or pastime, dealing with:
  - ● What it involves.
  - ● Why it appeals to you.
  - ● Why others should take it up.
- ❑ A best man's speech at the wedding of Henry VIII and Anne Boleyn, John F. Kennedy and Jacqueline Bouvier or Homer and Marge Simpson.
- ❑ Speech on the retirement of Judas Iscariot, Macbeth or James Bond.
- ❑ Vote of thanks by William Shakespeare on receiving the Nobel Prize for Literature.
- ❑ Eulogy at the funeral of Cleopatra, Scrooge or Sherlock Holmes.
- ❑ Imagine that you are a public relations consultant, who has been commissioned by International Tobacco Inc. to come up with some ways of improving their image. Prepare a presentation to them on (a) the problems they face and (b) your proposals on how to solve them.

PART V
BODY LANGUAGE AND SPEECH

Physical Facts and Fiction

Body Language, Movement and Tension

A number of topics that are often grouped together under headings like 'body language' and 'non-verbal communication' have already been discussed in earlier chapters: the role of eye contact in holding the attention of audiences (see Chapter 1), and the importance of intonation, stress and pausing (see Chapter 2). But there are various other claims about non-verbal communication that are heard so often that it is important to consider just how seriously they should be taken.

I. FICTION?

1. Comfort, cold or confrontation

Looking out on the audience in a crowded lecture theatre, I often notice that some people are sitting with their arms folded. If I believed all the modern myths about body language I would start worrying about what I'd said or done to prompt such a mass display of defensiveness. This is because it is widely claimed in the folklore of management training that people with their arms folded are on the defensive.

Luckily, I have two good reasons for not becoming too paranoid when I see people with folded arms sitting in an audience. One is that I have, on many occasions, taken the trouble to *ask* them if they are on the defensive. Usually, they say that they are feeling comfortable. Occasionally, they complain about the lack of armrests on the chairs, or about the inadequacies of the heating system. But never once has anyone said that they are feeling defensive. A second reason for not worrying about it is that there are invariably several people sitting with their arms folded. This is exactly what one would expect from observing how people behave in groups. It is a manifestation of what researchers have dubbed 'postural echo', which refers to our tendency to copy or reflect, albeit subconsciously, similar postures to those around us. The fact that there are a number of people with folded arms is therefore more likely to mean that they are responding to each other than mounting a collective display of defensiveness against me.

If, on the other hand, we fold our arms when confronted with an awkward question or some other kind of threat, it may well then be a sign of going on the defensive. This gives us a fourth possible meaning to add to comfort, missing armrests and feeling cold. So, just like words in a language, elements of body language can have different meanings in different contexts. The trouble is that many trainers seem all too ready to accept and propagate a more rigid doctrine, in which things like folded arms are assigned a single, unambiguous and unvarying meaning in all situations. Indeed, so widely entrenched has this particular view become that

I now advise people not to fold their arms when speaking, whether in a presentation, job interview or anywhere else where they are keen to make a good impression. This is not because I believe that folded arms are a sign of defensiveness, but because I know that there's a high probability that there will be someone in the audience who believes that it is.

2. Non-verbal sense and nonsense

The overstated claims about the meaning of folded arms are part of a much more general trend that has gathered pace over the past two or three decades. This is the rise of various modern myths about the overwhelming importance of body language and other non-verbal factors in human communication. It is a view that has been fuelled by a mass of books aimed at distilling the findings from research by social psychologists and others for the benefit of a mass readership. Some have become best sellers, and much of their appeal no doubt lies in the fact that, although people are vaguely aware of body language, there is an air of mystery about what it is, how it works and what it conveys. Such books therefore hold out the hope that, if only we knew how to crack the code, our social lives would be transformed for the better.

The trouble is that the process of popularisation almost inevitably results in research findings being diluted and simplified to such an extent that, by the time they reach a wider audience, they are presented as being far more definite and unambiguous than the original researchers ever intended. What started out as preliminary observations or hypotheses become hard facts, and few of the original author's words of caution about the methodological limitations of a particular experiment ever find their way into the popularised versions. One of the most spectacular examples of this is the claim that the words we use are by far the least important part of the communication process.

3. Is 93 per cent of communication non-verbal?

Type 'non-verbal communication', or something similar, into almost any search engine, and up will come a reference to a widely repeated claim about the relative importance of verbal and non-verbal factors in communication. The following version (from www.selectassesstrain.com/hint6.asp) is typical:

> Studies show that during interpersonal communication:
> ❏ 7% of the message is verbally communicated
> ❏ while 93% is non-verbally transmitted.
>
> Of the 93% non-verbal communication:
> ❏ 38% is through vocal tones
> ❏ 55% is through facial expressions.

Like almost all the other citations of these statistics, whether on websites or in books and courses on presentation skills, mention of 'studies' is not accompanied by any reference to what the original research actually consisted of, let alone who did it or when it was done. Nor, on the several occasions when I have asked lecturers or trainers who have presented it unquestioningly as 'fact', has any of them ever been able to cite the source, or to provide any further details about the original study.

None of this would matter were it not for the fact that the claim flies so flagrantly in the face of our common-sense experience. If true, for example, it would mean that anyone who is unable

> If only 7 per cent is communicated by the words we use, there would be no need for anyone ever to learn foreign languages, as we would already be able to understand 93 per cent of any particular one of them without any formal instruction at all.

to see a speaker's facial expressions, whether because they are blind, in the dark, listening to a radio or talking to someone on the telephone, would only be able to understand 45 per cent of what was said to them. It would have made more sense for Shakespeare to have had Mark Antony say, 'Lend me your eyes', and for the same correction to be made to the title of this book. Most absurd of all is the fact that, if only 7 per cent is verbally communicated, there would be no need for anyone ever to learn foreign languages, as we would already be able to understand 93 per cent of any particular one of them without any formal instruction at all.

Perhaps the most disturbing feature of claims like this is that they help to spread and consolidate the myth that non-verbal behaviour is so overwhelmingly dominant that the words we use to convey our messages are of little or no importance. This is not only grossly misleading, but also increases the normal anxieties of speech-making with a catalogue of extra things to worry about, like stance, gesture, movement and even what colour clothes to wear.

In some cases, there is a huge gulf between the originators of the research and their disciples, both in the amount of confidence shown in such 'facts', and in the extent to which they hold them to be generally applicable. This is certainly true of the 93 per cent claim, which first reached a wider public with the publication of the book *Silent messages: Implicit communication of emotions and attitudes* by Dr Albert Mehrabian, a social psychologist at the University of California, in 1981. But, as he pointed out to me in an e-mail, the research on which it was based dates from more than a decade before that, and was actually concerned with feelings and attitudes:

> This work of mine has received considerable attention in the literature. It was reported originally by Mehrabian & Weiner (1967) and Mehrabian & Ferris (1967). *Silent Messages* contains a detailed discussion of my findings on inconsistent and consistent messages of feelings and attitudes.
> Total Liking = 7% Verbal Liking + 38% Vocal Liking + 55% Facial Liking.
> (Albert Mehrabian, personal communication, e-mail, 16 October 2002.)

A key point to note here is that Dr Mehrabian's original percentages refer to different types of 'liking', and *not* to communication in all its forms. And, as one of the originators of these numbers, he writes with far more caution about their general applicability than is ever shown by the popularisers of his work:

> Please note that this and other equations regarding differential importance of verbal and non-verbal messages were derived from experiments dealing with communications of feelings and attitudes (i.e. like–dislike). Unless a communicator is talking about their feelings or attitudes, these equations are not applicable. (Albert Mehrabian, personal communication, e-mail, 16 October 2002.)

Unlike Dr Mehrabian, those who recycle these percentages with such confidence have few qualms about generalising way beyond anything he ever intended. Their cavalier disregard for the details of his research is also a matter of some concern to him, as he indicated in the reply to an e-mail in which I asked him what he thought about his findings being so widely used to mislead people about the relative importance of verbal and non-verbal communication:

> I am obviously uncomfortable about misquotes of my work. From the very beginning, I have tried to give people the correct limitations of my findings. Unfortunately, the field of self-styled 'corporate image consultants' or 'leadership consultants' has numerous practitioners with very little psychological expertise. (Albert Mehrabian, personal communication, e-mail, 31 October 2002.)

If this biggest of all claims about the dominance of the non-verbal over the verbal has been so exaggerated and distorted in its translation from the original to the training rooms of the world, the question arises as to the reliability of other 'facts' that make up the received wisdom about body language and non-verbal communication.

4. Does it matter what you wear?

A few years ago, a delegate on one of my courses reported that, after failing to get promoted, he was told that one of the main reasons for being passed over was that he had worn a green suit at the interview. Unfortunately for him, there were members of the panel who had been informed by an image consultant to be wary of men who wear green suits to business meetings.

Albert Mehrabian may be uncomfortable about self-styled image consultants with very little psychological expertise, but the situation may be even worse than he thinks: some image consultants are quite willing to make definitive-sounding claims without being constrained at all by facts or research. The seriousness of the situation first came to my notice when I was invited to speak on a conference panel with an image consultant, whose company specialises in advising people what they should wear, and what colours suit them best. At a briefing meeting some weeks beforehand, it seemed a wise precaution to check on whether the clothes I was wearing would contradict any of the advice she was planning to present to the audience. My suit was apparently fine, but my tie was 'the tie of a man going nowhere'. Fearing that there might be some hidden reasons for concern about my career prospects, I asked what kind of tie I should be wearing. The answer was that it ought to be bright red with prominent patterns on it. By now, I was beginning to wonder if there were whole new reservoirs of scientific data that I ought to know about, so I inquired about the knowledge base on which such claims were made. After a few moments' hesitation, she answered, 'It's loosely based on the Bauhaus movement in German art in the 1920s.'

When it came to the conference, I followed her professional advice by wearing a bright red tie with yellow arrows running up and down each side of it. On seeing it, the image consultant greeted me with the words, 'That's the tie of a man going somewhere – but that belt you're wearing should be buried.' Ties, it turned out, were at the heart of her presentation, the gist of which was that patterns smaller than a five pence piece were 'yesterday's ties and should be binned'. However, if the pattern was bigger than a 50 pence piece, it was apparently 'over the top' and should also not be worn. The key to success was therefore to wear a tie with a pattern somewhere in between the size of the two coins. What fascinated me most about all this was that, at the end of the session, members of the audience (all of whom were highly qualified professionals) formed long queues to buy her publications on the subject. Some even started to make enquiries about bringing her into their various companies to advise colleagues.

In effect, what consultants like this have done is to identify and tap into a market that seems to be based mainly on fear and anxiety. There are a lot of men who are so uninterested in fashion and so uncertain about what style of clothes to wear that they are prepared to pay for professional advice and reassurance. It's a market that has probably also been stimulated by an increase in the number of professional women, who unlike men, have no obvious uniform to wear at work.

5. Appropriate attire

This is not to say that how we dress doesn't matter at all. For example, after losing a legal dispute with Virgin Atlantic, Lord King, former chairman of British Airways, is reputed to have said that he would have taken Virgin boss Richard Branson more seriously if he had worn a suit and tie rather than his customary sweater and open-necked shirt. Many years ago, while I was being video-taped doing a lecture on a course for new university lecturers, the studio lights were so hot that I took my jacket off. At the feedback session, it became a matter for discussion: the tutor stopped the tape with the words, 'Here's a speaker who really means business.' Though nothing could have been further from the truth, the realisation that some people might see it that way has made jacket removal a routine prelude to almost every lecture I have ever given since then.

The point here is not that clothes don't matter at all, but that we should not be drawn into thinking that there is some scientifically based recipe that is guaranteed to enable us to convey a favourable impression to every member of every audience, regardless of the particular circumstances of the occasion. In my experience, most people get away with it through a combination of common sense and trial and error. There will obviously be times when advice and reassurance will be needed, in which case family and colleagues are likely to be just as helpful as professional image consultants, and certainly a great deal cheaper.

6. Are lecterns and tables barriers to communication?

The claim that folded arms are 'defensive' is partly based on the idea that putting your forearms in front of your chest places a barrier between you and your audience. As such, it's part of a more general theory to the effect that anything that can be construed as a barrier between speaker and audience is a bad thing.

I spent five of my teenage years at a school where daily attendance at a church service was compulsory. A lectern stood between the person reading the lesson and the congregation, but it never once occurred to me during all those years that it was a barrier, or that it was somehow reducing the effectiveness of the reader's impact. As far as I know, I was not alone, as I never heard anyone else worrying about it either. Nor do I remember any of us ever complaining about our teachers' desks being barriers that made it more difficult for them to communicate with us.

Many years later, more and more of those who read lessons in church have taken to standing next to the lectern in full view of the congregation. They then struggle to read the tiny print in the Bible they have brought with them. Often, this is made even more difficult by the fact that they are so nervous that they can't hold it without it shaking in their hands. A similar trend is evident in more secular settings, where more and more presenters are reluctant to stand behind tables and lecterns, preferring to move to one side or in front of them. Like readers in church, some of them also have trouble holding their notes in trembling hands, while those who leave them behind on the table have to keep turning awkwardly around to see what comes next, sometimes even losing their place altogether.

Whether or not audiences regard the lectern as a barrier, church architects have known for hundreds of years that it's an extremely efficient device for making it as easy as possible to read from a text. It positions a Bible with large easy-to-read print at a height and an angle that suits most adults. Readers can glance up at the congregation and down to the text without even having to move their heads, and without fear of losing their place. By comparison, tables are not such efficient resting places for notes or scripts, as they require speakers to glance up and down through an arc of nearly 90 degrees. But they are nonetheless extremely useful places for resting briefcases, computers, projectors and other paraphernalia associated with making a presentation.

All this raises the question of whether anyone would ever be in the least bit concerned about lecterns and tables if, like my generation of school children, they had never heard anyone describe them as 'barriers'. The way delegates on courses raise the topic suggests that it's not a particularly burning issue for them either. They are much more likely to ask generalised questions based on what they've heard – are they really barriers, is it a serious problem? – than to complain that they personally experience lecterns as terrible obstacles to effective rapport between speaker and audience.

This suggests that lecterns and tables are much less of a problem for audiences than is suggested by much of the received wisdom on the subject. The most sensible approach is therefore not to avoid them altogether, but to balance their undoubted practical advantages against the possible risk of giving the audience a negative impression. For example, when speaking without notes, or from notes on cards that are stiff enough not to flap about in trembling hands, speakers have nothing to lose by deserting the lectern or table. At other times, however, the advantage of not losing one's place while retaining eye contact with the audience will almost always outweigh any disadvantages that might arise from being seen to be standing behind the lectern or table.

If you do decide to use a lectern, it is important to be aware of an ever-present temptation that's best avoided. Sometimes known as 'white knuckle syndrome', it involves speakers gripping on to the sides of the lectern so tightly that the rigidity of their posture, and the nervousness that lies behind it, become visible for all to see. And, once you are locked into this stiff and static stance, there's almost certain to be a build-up of tension that will reduce the effectiveness of your delivery. This suggestion that immobility may have a negative impact on speakers and audiences runs counter to another modern myth about non-verbal communication, namely that you shouldn't move about while speaking because it distracts the audience.

7. Does movement distract?

I once worked with a presentation skills trainer who taught that speakers should not only stand still, but that there was a correct stance for presentation that involved placing one foot slightly in front of the other. After the lecture that included this advice, delegates regularly came to me pointing out a glaring inconsistency between what they had just heard and what they had just seen. While recommending them not to move about when they were speaking, he had spent most of the lecture wandering about the conference room. When asked if this worried or distracted them, delegates invariably said 'no'. Most went further, adding that it helped to hold their interest and came across as lively and enthusiastic. This positive reaction to movement is in fact typical of how members of audiences tend to react when commenting on each other's presentations. Movement features in their plus columns much more frequently than in their minus columns, which suggests that the best advice for the vast majority of people is that, if they feel like moving about, they should do so.

There is, however, a small minority of cases where speakers' movements do get a negative rating from audience members, such as when someone continually sways from side to side, or takes a few steps forwards and a few steps back, over and over again. What these negatively rated movements have in common is a relentless repetitiveness that is at best a distraction, and at worst a source of irritation to audiences. It may well be an awareness of this that leads some trainers to recommend that no one should ever move around at all while speaking. But the trouble with adopting such a blanket solution to what is a relatively rare problem is that it is likely to deter the vast majority of people from doing something that will have a positive impact on their audiences. Movement also has positive benefits for speakers themselves, as it helps to disperse adrenalin and reduce tension.

As for how to find out if you are one of the minority whose movements are likely to distract, the best way is through a simple practical experiment. The next time you make a speech or presentation, forget about standing still and move around in any way that comes naturally to you: then check on people's reactions afterwards. This is much more reliable than watching yourself on video, as we tend to be far too critical of our own individual performances. Many are the times that I have heard people denounce the way they move when they see themselves on tape, only to be contradicted by those who had been in the audience at the time. If one accepts that the audience is always right, the safest bet is to listen to what they have to say.

8. Do gestures distract?

The news from audiences about gestures is very similar to that on movement more generally. On almost every presentation skills course I have ever run, someone will say that they have been on another one where the trainer told them that gestures are distracting, and that speakers should keep their hands motionless during presentations. Meanwhile, it is just as rare for audiences to give negative ratings when they see speakers gesticulating as when they see them moving about. In fact they are much more likely to rate the use of gestures as a definite plus, often referring to it as evidence of expressiveness, individuality and liveliness.

As with the blanket prohibition on moving about while speaking, it may be that some trainers recommend the total suppression of gestures as an insurance policy against the risk that we might belong to the small minority whose hand movements are a source of distraction or irritation to audiences. These tend to be the ones that bear no discernable connection to what the speaker is saying. For example, a video-tape that I often use in training programmes shows a speaker continuously flapping his hand up and down. Everyone who has seen the tape not only notices it, but is also highly critical of it. Other uses of the hands that attract negative ratings include continuous hair tugging, hand wringing, or fidgeting with some other object (most usually the cap of a felt-tipped pen) or part of the anatomy. Like the randomly flapping hand, what makes these distracting and irritating to audiences is that they do not relate in any obvious way to what the speaker is saying.

The opponents of gestural freedom seem to have missed a number of key points about the use of gestures. One is that, as already mentioned, only a small minority of people, perhaps as few as 10 per cent, exhibit any such problems at all. Another is that as skilled an orator as Hitler would hardly have practised his gestures in front of a mirror if they were such a waste of time. And if it really is a distraction to use gestures, there must be tens of millions of people distracting each other every second of every day. This is for the very obvious reason that gesticulating while speaking is a thoroughly natural and normal part of the way humans communicate with each other. As such, any deliberate or conscious effort to suppress gestures may well impede a speaker's fluency, and restrict their ability to express themselves. At the same time, completely motionless hands look distinctly odd to those who are listening, whether they are in conversation or sitting in an audience.

One of the uses of gestures is as visual aids to illustrate or emphasise what we are talking about. For example, when Winston Churchill spoke of an 'iron curtain' descending across Europe, he moved his left hand downwards at the same time. When Bill Clinton said that there was nothing wrong with America that couldn't be solved by what is right with America, he stabbed the air just before the words 'wrong' and 'right'. Sometimes speakers move their left hand during one part of a contrast, following it with a similar movement of the right hand during the second part. When listing three items, it's quite normal for people to count them out on their fingers, or to make three hand movements at the same time. Even very young children have no problem in pointing at the thing they are asking for, or in holding their hands a certain distance apart to show how big something is.

We don't have to be explicitly taught to do any of these things, and are more or less completely unaware that we are doing them. Nor do we give much thought to the fine degree of precision timing that it takes to get it right, even though words and gestures have to be closely coordinated if they are to come across as natural rather than clumsy or awkward. So the advice on gestures is to do whatever comes naturally, because the chances are that it will make a presentation more expressive and animated than would otherwise be the case. In fact, different people gesticulate in slightly different ways, which makes it one of those behavioural details that plays a part in conveying a person's individuality. As such, using gestures is much more likely to help you to get your own personality across to an audience than adopting a stance that makes you look like a stuffed dummy whose hands have been firmly glued to its sides or behind its back.

Finally, there is a close parallel between the use of gesture and one of the points made about intonation in Chapter 2. This was the observation that the bigger the distance between speaker and audience, the more will changes in tone and emphasis tend to flatten out. In the same way, slight gestures that are perfectly visible at close quarters in a conversation become progressively more difficult for the audience to see as their distance from the speaker increases. If, as was suggested earlier, you can avoid the problem of monotone by exaggerating your normal conversational patterns of intonation, so too can you make your gestures more visible by exaggerating your normal conversational hand movements. And the bigger the audience, the more expansive and flamboyant you can afford to be.

II. PHYSICAL FACTS

1. Physical tension and the problem of nerves

Feelings ranging from nervousness to sheer terror are common reactions for many people when faced with the prospect of having to make a speech or presentation. Being well prepared and well rehearsed takes speakers a long way towards defeating the problem (see Chapter 9). But this is a battle that will never be won completely, and perhaps never should be, as overconfidence almost inevitably results in a poor performance. There are even reports of some very experienced speakers taking deliberate steps to preserve an element of tension while speaking. For example, the late Enoch Powell, a former Conservative and Ulster Unionist MP, used to refrain from visiting the toilet before making a speech, because he believed the added tension from speaking with a full bladder gave his delivery an edge that it might otherwise not have had. This is not to suggest that everyone should follow his example, but it does draw attention to the fact that, when it comes to dealing with nerves and tension, the objective should be minimisation, rather than total elimination.

2. Causes and consequences of nerves

Before looking at some techniques that can help to reduce the negative impact of nerves, we need to be clear about the main causes and consequences. And the first thing to be aware of is that speaking, whether in conversation or in front of an audience, is a much more stressful physical activity than most people realise. Quite apart from the obvious physical factors, such as breathing and moving the mouth and tongue to produce sounds recognisable as words, speaking is associated with a rise in blood pressure, irregular heartbeat and, in extreme cases, profuse sweating. But potentially the most debilitating factor is that the tension directly affects the very parts of the body that produce the voice, causing muscles in the chest and neck to tighten up. This not only restricts our ability to vary our tone and emphasis, but can also result in a quavering or more highly pitched the voice than usual. Underlying all this is the rush of adrenalin that comes from the primeval urge to fight or flee when we find ourselves in a difficult situation. Running away or assaulting the audience are obviously not serious options, which is why walking about and gesticulating help to

> Speaking is associated with a rise in blood pressure, irregular heartbeat and, in extreme cases, profuse sweating. But potentially the most debilitating factor is that the tension directly affects the very parts of the body that produce the voice.

dissipate some of the adrenalin, and why physical exercises of the kind described later can be a useful precaution to take just before making a speech.

Pitch

It was to counteract the problem of pitch that Margaret Thatcher underwent voice coaching with the National Theatre. As women's voices are naturally more highly pitched than those of men, any raising of the pitch is more likely to reach a point where it will be heard as 'shrill' or 'screeching'. With the election of their first female leader, Conservative Party managers were concerned that this might create a negative impression in the rough and tumble of parliamentary debate. Tapes of Thatcher speeches before and after voice coaching show that she achieved a reduction in pitch of about half the average difference between male and female voices. While this was no doubt a sensible precaution to take in the case of such a prominent public figure, experience of listening to presentations by hundreds of speakers suggests that it isn't something most people should worry about. In only a tiny minority of cases, certainly less than five per cent, have I ever found it necessary to refer anyone, male or female, to a voice coach.

✦ *Fear of the audience*

As well as the physical causes of tension, various psychological factors also come into play. At the heart of these is the fact that speaking to audiences is such an extremely rare event in most people's talking lives that they are not sure how to go about it, or how best to get their messages across in such an unfamiliar medium. Half the battle is therefore to understand the nature of the problem and the available solutions to it, which is why earlier chapters have focused on how speaking in public differs from the familiar comfortable world of everyday conversation, and on how to express ourselves in ways that will appeal to audiences.

One of the most widely cited causes of nervousness is the feeling of being threatened or exposed by being looked at by so many people all at once. This is obviously a very different experience from that of interacting with a handful of other people in a conversation, and most people certainly feel safer sitting in an audience than standing in front of it. A commonly heard remedy is that you should imagine that members of the audience are sitting there wearing nothing but their underwear. Although this may work for some people, the trouble is that it implies that the relationship between speaker and audience is an essentially hostile one, and that you are therefore right to feel intimidated whenever you become the focus of so many people's attention. But such a view is contradicted by two important facts, an awareness of which can also help to reduce the nervousness that is an almost inevitable consequence of adopting this confrontational 'us and them' attitude towards audiences.

The first comes from people's responses when asked whether, when they are in an audience, they sit there feeling hostile towards speakers, hoping to see them fall flat on their face and make a fool of themselves. The answer is invariably 'no', at which point it dawns on them that, except in very rare cases, such as public meetings about controversial issues, audiences are much more amicably inclined towards speakers than is commonly thought. A second fact is that members of an audience are not, as many people seem to assume, wired up to each other in such a way as to constitute a collective mind that somehow enables them to conspire together against the speaker. A more realistic view is to think of yourself as one individual who is communicating with a number of other single individuals. Once you start viewing your relationship with the audience as consisting of a number of one-to-one encounters that happen to be taking place at the same time, it starts to feel more like a conversation and therefore less intimidating

3. Techniques for tackling tension

While movement can help to release some of the adrenalin while actually making a speech or presentation, it is also usual to experience a major build-up of tension beforehand. And, as mentioned earlier, this can affect our vocal apparatus in such a way as to cause trembling, quavering or uncertain pitch. The best way to deal with this is to tackle the main physical causes of the problem, namely tension in the neck, chest and ribcage, with a series of simple exercises aimed at freeing up and relaxing them before taking to the floor.

Most obvious, perhaps, is the fact that deep breathing and more or less any other standard relaxation exercises will help to reduce the negative effects of tension on the voice. Other simple routines are the following:

❏ Move the neck and head to one side as far as you can (i.e. until it starts to feel a strain to move it any further), then relax. Do the same thing in the other direction and repeat a few times.

❏ Move the head downwards until the chin presses against the lower neck. Relax, and then move the head backwards as far as you can. Relax again before repeating the routine a few times.

❏ Rotate the head in circular motions a few times.

❏ Tense the shoulders upwards as far as they'll go, then relax them. Repeat a few times.

❏ Chew gum, or tense and relax the jaw a few times.

❤ Breathing is the foundation of good delivery

Taking deep breaths before a performance is not only good news for the calming sensation it creates. It is also essential to control the shallow breathing which inevitably accompanies the 'fight or flight' response provoked by feelings of nervousness. Shallow breathing is designed to boost athletic activity – but is the enemy of the speaker. Otherwise it would not be necessary for actors, singers and wind instrument players to learn so early on in their careers that, to make a great sound, they need to breathe deeply.

The first step towards understanding how to breathe effectively when speaking is to learn how to control the diaphragm. This is a dome-shaped sheet of muscle located at the bottom of our lungs, which works to regulate our breathing without any conscious effort. All day and all night long it works like bellows, taking air down, and then pushing it out. But it's possible to consciously interrupt the process by pulling in enough air through our lungs to inflate the diaphragm fully. To do this, imagine there is a balloon sitting at the bottom of your lungs, and you are trying to fill it with air. Once you feel your diaphragm is inflated – you will notice your abdomen swelling outwards – release the breath slowly while speaking or humming. You will find an instant increase in the volume of sound you create, but without the hardening of sound associated with overstraining the vocal chords (which is how most people attempt to increase the sounds they make). This deep-breathing technique has three main benefits:

1 It has a calming effect on most people.
2 It allows you to speak as loudly as you need to for the audience to hear you clearly.
3 Pausing to take a breath enables you as a speaker to formulate the next sentence, while at the same time allowing the audience to take in your information at a steady rate (see discussion in Chapter 2).

If your mouth is not fully open you will sound dull

An easy way to discover just how much intonation is governed by how widely we open our mouths is to try reading a speech while deliberately opening your mouth more than usual. When people on courses do this, they routinely complain that it feels a crazy and embarrassing exercise to perform. But they hardly ever continue to complain once they have seen and heard themselves on video-tape. More often than not, they admit that, although it feels odd at first, opening their mouths more widely than usual goes a long way towards eliminating the problem of monotonous delivery.

Further examples of this can be seen by watching television presenters in action. They may look perfectly natural, but they do in fact tend to open their mouths more widely than most people typically do. The opposite can be seen by looking at speakers with reputations for speaking in a rather flat tone of voice. Three famous examples are the Queen, Prince Charles and former Prime Minister John Major, none of whose mouths open very widely while they are speaking. So if you feel your performance is hampered by a tendency to sound monotonous, making a conscious effort to open your mouth more widely will give an instant brightening effect, and increase the tonal variation in the sounds that come out of your mouth.

🗨 *Most people speak too fast*

One of the important differences between public speaking and conversation discussed in Chapter 2 is the need for more pauses and a slower pace when addressing an audience. The suggested reduction was to bring the conversational rate down from around 170–180 words per minute to 120–130 words per minute in a speech or presentation. The trouble is that, to most people, this feels uncomfortably slow, especially in a situation where they are desperate to get their talk over with as soon as possible. The problem is further complicated by the fact that it's obviously very difficult to gauge just how fast we are speaking when in full flow. It is therefore something that repays practice, and there's a useful rule that works for the vast majority of speakers: if what you are saying sounds to you to be too slow, and if the pauses sound too long, then you have probably got the pace about right.

🗨 Alcohol is never the answer

Because drinking alcohol is associated with relaxing social occasions, many people think that a drink or two will help to give them confidence before making a speech. This is one of the biggest mistakes any speaker can ever make, for the simple reason that alcohol directly affects the brain. In excess, it causes speech to become slurred and incoherent, but even a slight amount reduces our ability to keep a clear head and will have a negative impact on performance. So the rule is simple: *never drink anything alcoholic before making a speech*.

However, drinking water or a soft drink before or during a presentation is a perfectly acceptable and recommended solution to the more or less inevitable problem of a dry mouth and throat.

Summary

Various claims about the relative importance of verbal and non-verbal communication have become so widespread that it's important to know which ones are worth taking seriously.

1. Claims to be sceptical about

- ❑ What we actually say plays a minor role in communication.
- ❑ 93 per cent of communication is non-verbal.
- ❑ There is some scientifically based secret of what clothes will have most impact.
- ❑ People with folded arms are always on the defensive.
- ❑ Lecterns and tables are barriers to effective communication.
- ❑ Moving about while speaking distracts the audience.
- ❑ Using gestures distracts the audience.

2. Claims worth taking seriously

- ❑ Speaking is a physically stressful experience that can cause a rise in blood pressure, irregular heartbeat and, in extreme cases, profuse sweating.
- ❑ Physical tension both increases nervousness, and directly affects the parts of the body that produce the voice.
- ❑ Breathing is the foundation of good delivery.

❑ If your mouth is not fully open you are likely to sound dull and monotonous.

❑ Most people speak too fast.

❑ Alcohol is never the answer.

❑ When it comes to reducing tension and nervousness, the aim should be minimisation, rather than total elimination.

The Power of Speech

Restoring Confidence in the Spoken Word

We take it for granted that effective musical and sporting perform-ances depend on the players understanding exactly what they are doing and being equipped with the necessary technical skills to do it. Effective public speaking is no different, except that the virtual disappearance of rhetoric from the curriculum in schools and universities means that the necessary knowledge is much harder to come by. Add to this the rise of the slide-driven presentation, mix in a few modern myths about the overwhelming importance of non-verbal behaviour, and it's all too easy to get the impression that all you need to do is to make sure you have plenty of slides, and not to worry too much about the words you actually use in getting your messages across. In the face of such widespread misconceptions, it's hardly surprising that making an effective speech remains such an elusive aspiration for so many.

1. Time for a change

One of my main aims in writing this book has been to do some-thing about filling this gap in the knowledge available to speakers, and to equip them with the technical skills needed to produce an effective performance. However, as with music and sport, knowing what to do and how to do it are not enough on their own to guarantee success at public speaking. Like any other activity involving knowledge and technique, effectiveness depends on practice, and the more you practise, the better you get. This is why practical exercises have such an important part to play in training programmes. It is also the reason why, at the end of a course, I always say that I hope delegates will take their new-found skills back to the real world, and treat each speech or presentation they have to give as another chance to practise. I also urge them not to revert to the slide-dependent style of speaking from which they have just liberated themselves, and only to use visual aids for the benefit of audiences rather than themselves (see Chapters 4 and 5).

The trouble is, of course, that the industry standard model of presentation is so firmly entrenched in the culture of so many companies and organisations that people often see it as too radical a step to start doing things differently. However, as was mentioned in the discussion of flip charts (see Chapter 4), those who are 'daring' enough to abandon slides in favour of chalk and talk typically achieve better rapport with their audiences than they had ever experienced before. Shortly after attending one of my courses, a woman who had been summoned to give a presentation to the main board of her company decided to take what she saw as a major risk. She prepared a script along the lines described in Chapter 9, used a lot of rhetorical techniques and illustrative anecdotes (see Chapters 6 and 7) and rehearsed it several times beforehand. At the end of the presentation, the chairman rose to

> The climate is right for a wider cultural revolution aimed at replacing the current bias towards the overwhelming importance of non-verbal factors and slide-driven presentations with a renewed confidence in the power of the spoken word.

his feet, not as she initially feared to dismiss or demote her, but to congratulate her on what he described as 'the best presentation anyone has ever given in this boardroom'. Her reputation as a good communicator began to spread, and she found herself being asked to give more presentations on behalf of the company. This has not only given her more opportunities to practise, but has also significantly improved her career prospects.

This example is further evidence of a deep groundswell of dissatisfaction with the industry standard model of presentation, and a greater receptiveness to change than is commonly thought by those who worry about doing things differently. If this is so, then the climate is right for a wider cultural revolution aimed at replacing the current orthodoxy with a renewed confidence in the power of the spoken word. But this depends on many more people taking action than a few converts who happen to have attended a course. Another reason for writing this book is therefore to put the case for change to a wider audience of readers. My hope is that they will not only benefit personally from an improved technical understanding of effective public speaking, but will also become active campaigners for change.

2. The continuing demand for speeches

Not long before writing this, I appeared on a radio programme, in which I was asked the question, 'Do we live in an age in which public speaking is dead?' The assumption seemed to be that modern technologically based media are replacing, rather than merely supplementing, more traditional forms of communication. My reaction to this was and is that it seriously underestimates the extent to which there is still a tremendous demand for public speaking, and that the power of the spoken word remains undiminished. For example, when the Challenger shuttle exploded in 1986, the American people needed to have something said about it on their behalf, and Ronald Reagan rose to the occasion with a memorable and moving speech. Similar famous examples since then include Lord Spencer's eulogy at the funeral of his sister, the Princess of Wales, and some of Tony Blair's speeches in the aftermath of September 11th. What all these had in common was that they caught the mood of a nation at a time of tragedy. The impact of Blair's September 11th speeches even crossed national borders to have a major impact on American audiences. The power of his oratory was widely considered to have reflected the feelings of US citizens more effectively than anything said at the time by their own president. Such was his impact that, for a while at least, many Americans looked on Blair, rather than Bush, as the world's leading spokesman against global terrorism.

Away from the public stage, there are countless localised audiences waiting to be moved, inspired, informed or entertained by a speaker. If managers had no residual faith in the power of the spoken word, they would hardly go on spending the millions it costs for so many people to participate in so many business

> Like any other activity involving knowledge and technique, effectiveness depends on practice, and the more you practise, the better you get.

presentations. Meanwhile innumerable retirement parties, weddings, funerals, birthday celebrations and other social events are still indispensable parts of the fabric of everyday life. They are attended by people who want and need to hear someone speak, and by some who desperately want to speak, but are not quite sure what to say or how to go about saying it.

3. Becoming a gifted speaker

When it comes to mastering the power of the spoken word, the only thing that separates the hesitant majority from the gifted few is an understanding of the needs of audiences and the techniques that meet those needs. Where the gifted minority have the edge is in having had the good luck of being blessed with an intuitive grasp of how to do it. The rest of us need to work at it, but the good news is that everyone who is able to get messages across in a private conversation has the potential to do the same in public. Time and again, I have seen people who dreaded public speaking at the start of a course discovering after a day or two that there is a buzz to be had from achieving good rapport with an audience. And the great thing is that anyone can do it, once they know how.

Index